TO HIS EXCELLENCY
THOMAS JEFFERSON
Letters to a President

ALSO BY JACK McLAUGHLIN

The Housebuilding Experience

Jefferson and Monticello: The Biography of a Builder

To His Excellency

THOMAS JEFFERSON

Letters to a President

SELECTED AND EDITED BY

JACK McLAUGHLIN

W·W·NORTON & COMPANY

New York   London

Printed in the United States of America.

The text of this book is composed in 11.5/13.5 Fournier,
with the display set in Nicolas Cochin.
Composition and manufacturing by Maple Vail Manufacturing Group.
Book design by Margaret Wagner.

First Edition.
Library of Congress Cataloging-in-Publication Data

McLaughlin, Jack
To his excellency Thomas Jefferson : letters to a president /
selected and edited by Jack McLaughlin.
p. cm.
Includes bibliographical references and index.
1. Jefferson, Thomas, 1743–1826—Correspondence.   2. Working
class—United States—Correspondence.   3. Presidents—United States–
Correspondence.   I. Jefferson, Thomas, 1743–1826.   II. Title.
E332.86   1991
973.4'6'092—dc20   90-27824

ISBN 0-393-03016-4
W.W. Norton & Company, Inc., 500 Fifth Avenue, New York, N.Y. 10110
W.W. Norton & Company, Ltd., 10 Coptic Street, London WC1A 1PU

1 2 3 4 5 6 7 8 9 0

FACING THE TITLE PAGE. A presidential portrait by
Rembrandt Peale of Jefferson at the start of his second term,
at the age of 62.

Contents

THIS collection of letters written to Thomas Jefferson during his presidency is dedicated to the bicentennial celebration of the Massachusetts Historical Society (1791–1991). The Coolidge Collection of Jefferson papers in the society's archives is the most important trove of Jefferson's personal and family correspondence in existence. All who have written of the life and career of Thomas Jefferson are indebted to the Massachusetts Historical Society for preserving and managing this national treasure with close conservation and fluid accessibility.

Preface

THE idea for a collection of letters sent to Thomas Jefferson during his presidency came to me when I was reading through Jefferson's unpublished papers for a previous book, *Jefferson and Monticello: The Biography of a Builder.* I found myself stopping to read letters that had nothing to do with the topic I was researching, simply because they were fascinating. Some were funny; others were angry, threatening, adoring, passionately political, or begging. Although they seemed to have little in common, I soon discovered that many of them shared a single characteristic: they were sent unsolicited to the president from laboring-class Americans with little formal education. Here was a cross section of the constituency that had elected Jefferson president for two terms. It occurred to me that it might be of value to publish these letters, if some sort of an order could be imposed on them. This is the book that resulted from that initial chance discovery. It is the first time that a collection of Jefferson correspondence of this kind has ever been published.

The general reader will find in this work the voyeuristic pleasure of reading other people's mail, of looking over the shoulder of one of America's most admired figures as he opens his correspondence, and of sharing his sympathy, frustration, indifference, and at times anger at those who have written him. Everything that is known about most of the letter writers, for Jefferson and for us, is there on the page, written with an urgency and immediacy that has not been lost in nearly two hundred years.

What is remarkable about these letters is that they exist at all. No European farmer would have dared to write to his monarch as these letter writers did to their president. But American farmers, artisans, and shopkeepers found themselves in the extraordinary position of being permitted, even encouraged because they did not have to pay postage, to write directly to their chief of state. Jefferson was the first president elected by the less privileged classes, the kind of men whose place in history consists of the single piece of writing which appears here for the first time. How were they to write to him? What were the proper forms of address, and the acceptable codes of etiquette? Many of Jefferson's correspondents apologize profusely for fear that they have violated epistolary decorum. Of course they were insecure about addressing the nation's chief executive; how could they know how it was to be done when it had rarely been done before?

Because so many of those who wrote to Jefferson were poorly educated, these letters are often not easy to read. Some of these semi-literate writers handle language gingerly like a hot chestnut, others with the confidence of a child blowing up a balloon, oblivious of its bursting point. In preparing them for publication, I have followed modern editorial practice, but the printed page can never capture the obvious struggles with language that appear in the originals. The quill pen was not a comfortable instrument in the hands of most of these writers; it blotched their paper and confused their thoughts. I think the time given to a close reading of them, however, will be rewarded with a glimpse of a real human being, preserved in a moment of history. I have, in my introductions and notes, attempted to expand the historical context as widely as possible, and to offer interpretations and suggested readings.

I have clustered these letters into what I think will be useful or revealing patterns. They are, in effect, a mosaic of rough but colorful stones, each unique, each with lights, shadows, and flaws. Each can be turned in the hand and scrutinized closely, although such an examination may produce more questions than answers. The larger design is also at times indistinct and indeterminate, one that could easily have been shifted into another shape by a different editorial hand. Nevertheless, these patterns create, I believe, a Jeffersonian moment in American history.

My hope is that the selection and arrangement of these letters may allow readers to experience the same feelings of discovery and delight I felt when I first came across the lives of these obscure men and women.

I WISH to thank the staff at the Clemson University Cooper Library for its professional aid in my research for this collection. Julia Pennebaker and Cathy Sturkie of the Interlibrary Loan Office were particularly tenacious in tracking down miles of microfilm. The staff of the Clemson Computer Center was also uniformly helpful and cooperative. Research was aided by a Clemson University Provost's Research Grant.

Several readers examined all or portions of the manuscript and offered useful advice and suggestions. I want to thank: Joyce Appleby, John Catanzariti, Robert Lambert, John McGuigan, G. S. Rousseau, and Lucia C. Stanton.

Rob Roy McGregor was able to identify and correct many mangled quotations from the classics by unschooled writers; I am indebted to him for his translations.

I thank James Bear, Jr., and Lucia C. Stanton for allowing

me to read before publication *Jefferson's Memorandum Books, Accounts, with Legal Records and Miscellany, 1767–1826,* 2 vols. (Princeton, N.J.: Princeton University Press, forthcoming).

Henning Gutmann edited a difficult manuscript with intelligence, historical awareness, and a sensibility to the architectonics of structure and balance. I am indebted to him for numerous improvements in style and content.

Donald S. Lamm, president of W. W. Norton & Company, is something of a dying breed in publishing, a CEO who, as he puts it, reads not only annual reports but also manuscripts. His admiration for Thomas Jefferson is reflected in the enthusiasm he has shown for the publication of these letters.

My wife, Joan, was always willing to share this project with our family life, and to freely offer her knowledge of women's studies and her wisdom of women's ways. Her advice, criticism, and proofreading are silent enrichments to this collection.

Introduction

A COMMON lament of social historians is that history, in attempting to illuminate the past, is little more than a candle flickering on a few prominent objects while the greater landscape remains hidden in darkness. If this distressing view is truthful—that the eyes of historians are so myopic that they perceive only what is large and conspicuous—the reason is not difficult to find; it is the discipline's traditional enslavement to the written word. Men and women from times past who never wrote, whose writing was not valued, or whose lives were not considered important enough to be written about, have been missing from history. Unfortunately, this includes the vast majority of the human race, and in the history of the United States, most of the laboring-class people from the early years of the nation.

Social and cultural historians have in recent years attempted to recover the lives of these lost generations of Americans through oral histories, which capture the memories of unique individuals, and by a close analysis of the public records of such universal rites of passage as births, deaths, marriages, and that equally universal ritual, work. Demographic studies, some encompassing whole populations, others limited to a town or community, have given features to what were once mere shadows of past peoples. Still, it is the written word, in letters and diaries of men and women who were not public figures, that best captures a likeness of the lives of common folk.[1]

These are people who left no indelible mark on the political, legal, or aesthetic history of the nation. They were elected to no office, acquired no significant amounts of property, limned no pictures or wrote no books, but their lives were touched with tragedy, heightened with bliss, and intimately linked with the lives of family, friends, and co-workers, no less than the lives of the worthies of traditional history. Such writings are not plentiful—in the case of American slaves they are especially hard to come by—but in recent years, now that their value is recognized, personal letters, diaries, and journals of ordinary Americans have appeared with increasing frequency.

Reclaiming these lives suggests a neo-Wordsworthian romanticism that raises "incidents and situations from common life" to "the primary laws of our nature," as Wordsworth put it[2]—or Marxist proletarianism, with its insistence on the dignity of the working classes. Social history of the kind I am describing certainly has its roots in both ideologies, but there is also the much more simple and powerful moral imperative of Arthur Miller's *Death of a Salesman*. Miller's Everyman, Willy Loman, must not be allowed to die unrecognized, his wife Linda insists: "attention must be finally paid." Besides the larger historical value of these letters, therefore, another modest goal of this collection is to pay attention to the lives of some of the Willy Lomans and his women counterparts in the early years of our American democracy.

Recognizing these lives is made possible by the existence

of one of the great magnets of American history, an attraction so pervasive that it drew to its gravitational field all within its orbit. This force was Thomas Jefferson, a man who fixed his personality upon the imagination of the American public as have few figures of his era. He assumed the presidency of the United States in 1801 as a champion of republican ideals, dedicated to the removal of all vestiges of aristocracy, a plangent irony, since he was himself a vested member of the Virginia plantation aristocracy. Nevertheless, he was swept into office by farmers, mechanics, and small businessmen who saw him as their protector against the powerful Federalist interests of banking, land speculation, commerce, and a large and corrupt governmental bureaucracy.

As a custodian of the ideal of government by the many, Jefferson quickly disposed of all traces of aristocratic reserve. The rituals of formal etiquette, of dress and ceremony, which had marked the administrations of Washington and Adams, were eliminated. He traveled by horseback rather than coach, his clothing was simple, even careless at times, and most remarkable of all, he was accessible to virtually anyone who desired to see him. One visitor, for example, reported that he arrived unannounced at the President's House at 8:00 A.M. without letters of introduction, which his friends told him would be unnecessary because the president was a man of no ceremony. He was treated with great courtesy, and eventually left, "highly pleased with the affability, intelligence, and good sense, of the President of America."[3]

The conviction by Americans that their president was a man they could communicate with on a personal level is responsible for a written record of the lives of numerous individuals who represent the broad American public of the Jeffersonian era. Not only was Jefferson's office open to anyone who wanted to see him, but Americans could also write to him, postage free, paying only the cost of paper and ink,

and be certain that he would personally read their letters.*
Hundreds of men and women took advantage of this free-franking privilege and wrote to their chief executive, pouring out their needs, desires, miseries, joys, opinions, and accomplishments. And because Jefferson was temperamentally incapable of throwing anything away, he saved these letters, leaving us a treasury of insights into the lives of ordinary Americans of the early nineteenth century.

This is a collection of many of those letters. Most have never before been published; they are part of thousands of pieces of Jefferson's correspondence located at the Library of Congress, the Massachusetts Historical Society, the Missouri Historical Society, and the National Archives. Princeton University Press will eventually publish all of Jefferson's own writings in its Papers of Thomas Jefferson project, and will in another decade or two publish some of these letters chronologically. Many will be abstracted, however, because they are not directly related to Jefferson's career. (If everything written to Jefferson were published, the Papers project would go on for another half century or more.) This collection is unique, therefore, in that it gathers together letters written from 1801 to 1809 which seem to have only one thing in common, that most of them were written to the third president of the United States by total strangers. In reading these letters, however, I soon discovered that they had a great deal

---

*At this period in American postal history, postage could be prepaid as it is today, but letters were usually sent without postage, to be paid for by the addressee; therefore, Jefferson's free-franking privilege for letters sent and received allowed his correspondents to write to him postage free. The money saved was considerable. Depending on distance, postage cost from eight to thirty-five cents for a single sheet of paper; two sheets cost twice as much, three sheets three times, and so forth. This was at a time when laborers worked for a dollar a day. Many of Jefferson's correspondents wrote letters of a dozen pages or more. The fact that the postage was free no doubt encouraged prolixity, and is responsible for some of the repetitive, long-winded letters Jefferson received. Wesley Everett Rich, *The History of the United States Post Office to the Year 1829* (Cambridge: Harvard University Press, 1924), 137–39.

more in common, and this is their value, I believe, as social history.

Most of these writers are men and women who want something from their president—money, a job, release from debtors' prison, educational help. Some are professional people, but most are poor, often semi-literate, barely able to communicate the ache of penury or the lust for education. Many are young, and many are women. Some of the stories told in the letters are pathetic—widows with small children, unable to survive in a society with no institutionalized security other than family, friends, or neighbors; or young men bursting with ambition and energy ("a burning desire vibrates in my breast," one wrote), willing to give anything for a few books, but with scant opportunity to get them. There are the Yankee tinkerers and craftsmen, certain they have unlocked the secrets of perpetual motion, and religious zealots with the secrets of heaven. Madmen spill out the secrets of a disturbed mind, and informers have secret information about assassination plots. Some writers send gifts, pamphlets, or books; others offer honest advice about such issues as the settlement of western lands or the problem of slavery.

There are patriotic love notes to one of the most popular men in America, but there are also anonymous hate letters from Federalists, abusive and insulting. Political letters reflect the popularity of Jefferson's Louisiana Purchase, and the unpopularity of his 1807 embargo against foreign shipping—not because of abstract political theory, but because the Louisiana acquisition offered opportunities for moving a family to cheap western lands, and the embargo resulted in the loss of jobs and hungry children.

The letters also reveal something about the way Americans considered Jefferson to be a republican king, a benevolent father who could solve their problems with his wisdom and largess. In spite of his attempts to eliminate all traces of monarchy from the presidency by discouraging ceremonial salutations, many citizens continued to address him as "my lord," "excellency," "honored," or "revered"—showing that traditional attitudes toward authority were not easily dropped.

These letters elbowed their way into Jefferson's office with every mail delivery, swelling the volume of an already-onerous correspondence. During his presidency he received an average of one hundred thirty-seven pieces of mail a month. This may not seem excessive by our standards, but there was no junk mail then; every letter was written by an individual with the expectation of receiving a reply. Jefferson often fell weeks behind in opening these letters because of his twice-annual trips to Monticello, periodical migraine headaches that rendered him incapable of working, and the press of official business. At such times the steady stream of letters would pile up on his desk. Much of the mail was official correspondence from Jefferson's cabinet members or from Congress, but he also received unsolicited letters from every state and territory in the nation. In addition, Jefferson asked his cabinet members to send him every day "a packet of all their communications for a perusal of the President." This was modified to include only those letters for which *"judgment must be exercised,"* but it still added a heavy burden to Jefferson's work load.[4]

All this correspondence, some of it many pages long, was written in ink with a quill pen. There were letters with beautiful calligraphic penmanship and some written in a readable stenographic hand like Jefferson's. But an equal number of writers wrote with a hand that can only be described as challenging. It was not only the semi-literate writers with their phonetic spelling that required an imaginative reading to decipher the text; many of Jefferson's own cabinet members, including his Secretary of the Treasury Albert Gallatin, who wrote Jefferson daily, Secretary of State James Madison, and Secretary of War Henry Dearborn, wrote in a hand that was barely legible. Fortunately for Jefferson, some government officials used a clerk to write or copy correspondence. After a lifetime of reading poor handwriting, however, Jefferson was very good at it: at times, the only way to determine the spelling of a correspondent's name is to get the correct version from Jefferson's endorsement on the letter.

Jefferson read, answered when he chose to, and filed all his heavy correspondence himself. He was extremely secretive about his personal life, and this included his correspondence. Although he had a secretary throughout his two terms as president, he opened and read all his mail himself. He wrote his own letters and copied them himself, either on a letter press or later on his polygraph. (The letter press made a copy by pressing a damp piece of tissue paper against the letter. The tissue was affixed to a sheet of white paper, ink side down, so that the writing could be read through it. The polygraph was a device with two pens connected by a series of rods and springs; what was written with one pen was exactly duplicated by the second.)

He handled his incoming mail with characteristic efficiency. The letters that were delivered to him were an odd assortment of shapes. In an era before envelopes, a letter was folded neatly but in no standard size, addressed on either the back of the letter or on a cover sheet added for this purpose, and secured with either wax, or a moistened flour-and-gum wafer that sealed when it dried. In opening a letter, great care had to be taken not to tear the part of the letter where the wafer adhered. Many letters in Jefferson's files have a hole in the text where the wafer stuck to the paper as it was opened. (This was one reason for using a cover sheet; another was to prevent reading the letter by examining its print-through.)

After he opened and read a letter, Jefferson placed his endorsement on it, usually at the top right hand corner of the first or last page, but if the text did not provide a margin, on any available edge.[5] The endorsement consisted of the writer's last and first names, the place of origin, the date it was written or postmarked, and the date when it was received. Occasionally Jefferson also added a word or phrase identifying the contents. This was almost always done on anonymous letters. A job application might be endorsed "office"; a letter about an epidemic, "yellow fever"; depending on their content, others were labeled "madman," "insane," "abuse," "ribaldry," or "assassination." A typical endorsement on a letter detailing a scheme for a perpetual-motion machine reads: "Buchanan, George, Wadesbro' N.C. July 1. 07. recd. July 19. perpt. motion." The dates sent and received give an idea of how long it took for mail to travel during the first decade of the nineteenth century. From Wadesboro, North Carolina to Washington, a distance of four hundred miles, took eighteen days. Letters from the western territories often took months.

After reading and endorsing the letters, Jefferson placed them in a pile alphabetically by author and then copied each endorsement into his Summary Journal of Letters, a written account of every letter received and sent. This was kept on letter-size sheets divided into two columns, on the left "Written" and on the right "Received." The Received column was always two or three times the length of the Written column. Jefferson wrote an average of fifty-seven letters each month during his presidency; some were short notes, others lengthy messages to Congress or governmental officials. He was, however, an economical letter writer; he could explain the most complex idea or minute set of instructions in two pages. Nevertheless, the weight of his correspondence was oppressive, for it included not only governmental communications, but correspondence dealing with the operations of his plantations, the construction of Monticello, letters to family and friends, as well as unsolicited mail from strangers. He often complained of it. In the first year of his presidency, he found that "writing is now got to a steady and uniform course. It keeps me from 10. to 12 & 13 hours a day at my writing table, giving me an interval of 4. hours for riding, dining & a little unbending. . . ."[6]

Jefferson's filing system was as efficient as his Summary Journal of Letters; he boasted that he could locate a letter from his files in minutes. His method for filing his correspondence was explained to a writer who asked that several letters be returned to him. Jefferson replied that he had only a single letter. "My papers are arranged first according to states, & alphabetically under each state," he wrote. "I find at once & in its proper place your letter of Oct. 12, 1806 but no other paper."[7]

In addition to carefully processing and filing each letter, he indexed the Summary Journal of Letters. There are several indexes, the largest one covering the presidential years, done entirely by Jefferson. Two other indexes of earlier correspondence were apparently written after his presidency, possibly by his granddaughters. The monumental task of indexing this document and copying the index in pen and ink can only be explained as obsessive behavior. That Jefferson should invest this much time and energy in arranging his correspondence so that he could locate anything he ever wrote or was written to him in a matter of minutes says worlds about his compulsive need for order and efficiency. He filled Monticello with gadgetry he called "conveniences"—the dumb waiter to bring wine from the cellar, double doors that opened together when one was pushed, the lazy-susan dining room door for serving food, the double-faced cannonball clock that tells the days of the week. His Summary Journal of Letters index was just such a convenience. One can question whether the time saved in finding letters ever balanced the time it took to index them, but Jefferson's perception that he was being efficient more than repaid the effort. Undoubtedly he took pleasure not only in using his index, but also in writing it. Paging through the Summary Journal of Letters and its indexes also helps explain why Jefferson answered so few of the letters collected in this volume.

These unsolicited letters were a dilemma for Jefferson—not only could he never hope to respond to them personally, but he also could not offer charity to those who requested it. To do so would have beggared him of time and money. (Some asked that he send hundreds or even thousands of dollars to them in a letter.) He wrote to one correspondent that he was pressed perpetually by "an overflow of business," and adopted the rule "of never answering any letter, or part of a letter, which can do without an answer."[8] He therefore responded to only a small fraction of the unsolicited mail he received, although some requests for information were passed on to others for action. He also gave money indirectly at times to those who could be immediately helped with a small sum.

Because so many of his writers were needy, this collection appears at times to be a series of Dickensian etchings of want and distress, but poverty is only one of its many faces. It is more like a Monet landscape with shifting patterns of light and color, an impressionistic portrait of the Jeffersonian era. These letters portray men and women alive with energy, hope, and a belief in progress, but there are some whose hope has been shattered. They show how Americans idolized their president, and how this worship turned to hatred for many of them.

Jefferson's replies to the letters reveal his private reactions to them—he is civil, gracious, and generous, but occasionally irritated or impatient. His responses, or lack of them, also illustrate his personal, cultural, and political attitudes toward the presidency and the exercise of presidential power. And finally, this correspondence introduces us to a young republic, its legs still unsteady on the rough terrain of free speech, but already taking strides toward the ideal of complete independence of expression that was to be sought for in its maturity.

Editorial Method

LETTERS that have been previously published have been transcribed anew from the microfilmed originals for this edition. Most of the letters in this collection, however, have never before been published.

The editorial method followed in transcribing letters from Jefferson is essentially that of the Princeton University Press edition of the Jefferson Papers (John Catanzariti et al, eds., *The Papers of Thomas Jefferson* [Princeton, N.J.: Princeton University Press, 1950–　], 1:xxv–xxxviii).

The letters written to Jefferson present special problems because so many of them were written by poorly educated men and women. To make them accessible to the modern reader, more editing was necessary than in the case of Jefferson's letters. I have followed the following editorial principles:

DATING

The dateline will appear at the beginning of each letter, regardless of where it appears in the manuscript. Missing dates appear in brackets when they are obtained from Jefferson's endorsements. Jefferson regularly placed the name of the addressee at the end of the letter; here it will be placed above the dateline.

PUNCTUATION

Periods will be placed at the end of all sentences.

When the exact punctuation of a manuscript cannot be determined—distinguishing commas from periods or semicolons, for example—modern usage will be followed.

Passages that are obscure or unintelligible because of a lack of punctuation will be silently punctuated. The standard for adding punctuation will be readability. Where there is no punctuation at all, it will be added minimally. Dashes will be changed to periods where appropriate, or eliminated where they are placed at random, or where they duplicate other punctuation; otherwise they will be retained.

SPELLING

Jefferson misspelled certain words regularly, such as *knolege* for *knowledge,* *tho* for *though,* and *thro* for *through,* for the sake of orthographic economy. He regularly reversed the vowels *i* and *e* to produce such spellings as *recieve, concieve, yeild,* and *feild.* He also misspelled the possessive *its* as the contraction *it's.* He spelled names inconsistently, even of those persons he wrote to regularly. These misspellings are all retained.

Where semi-literate writers misspell names, locations, or words to the degree that they are unintelligible, the correct spelling is added in brackets immediately after the misspelled word.

Slips of the pen by literate writers are silently corrected, but misspellings that are characteristic of a writer are retained.

CAPITALIZATION

The first letter of all sentences is capitalized, a practice Jefferson did not follow.

Proper names, titles, geographical locations, days of the week, and months are capitalized, even if they are not capitalized in the manuscript.

Random capitalization, or capitalization for emphasis is retained.

In cases where capitalization cannot be determined in the manuscript, modern usage is followed.

ABBREVIATIONS AND CONTRACTIONS

Abbreviations are retained where the meaning is obvious, such as the ampersand, days of the week, months, and locations (N.Y., Phila.).

Where the abbreviation of a proper name is obscure, the name is expanded in brackets.

Contractions are retained where they are used to indicate dropped letters, such as wou'd or tho'.

Superscript and subscript letters are brought to the line and a period added to abbreviations, as in Mr., or Obdt. Servt.

MISSING PASSAGES

Where the manuscript has been torn or mutilated, conjectural readings are supplied in angled brackets (⟨ ⟩).

If no conjectural reading is possible, the missing portion is indicated by a bracketed ellipsis ([. . .]).

Ellipsis is also used in excising portions of letters that are irrelevant, unintelligible, or repetitive. (The complete manuscripts of all letters are available in microform editions at the Library of Congress and major research libraries. All are available through interlibrary loan.)

PARAGRAPHS

Few of the manuscript letters are broken into paragraphs according to modern usage; many have no paragraphs at all. Some writers space sentences at odd positions on the page, often by whim. The saluation and complimentary close, in particular, are often positioned at either the right or left margins, or sometimes centered.

Paragraphs are retained when the writer used them, but they have also been silently added, according to modern usage, where dictated by clarity or readability.

The lack of paragraphing has been retained, however, where it seemed an essential part of a writer's style.

The salutation and complimentary close have been placed at the left and right margins, respectively, except where the close is a part of a new paragraph, in which case the original paragraphing is retained.

ENDNOTES

The location symbols in the notes are those used in the National Union Catalog of the Library of Congress. They are:

DLC   The Library of Congress, Washington, D.C.
DNA   National Archives, Washington, D.C.
MHi   Massachusetts Historical Society, Boston
MoSHi   Missouri Historical Society, St. Louis

Annotations for individuals named in the letters are given when possible, but many are so obscure as to be unidentifiable.

Place names are also annotated where it is deemed helpful. Quotations are identified when possible.

Descriptive notes supply additional information on a person or topic, offer interpretations, or suggest historical contexts.

TO HIS EXCELLENCY
THOMAS JEFFERSON
Letters to a President

1

Politics

"Thomas Jefferson, you infernal villain"

THERE are three faces of Thomas Jefferson, only two of them well known. One is the public figure—author of the Declaration of Independence, governor, secretary of state, vice president, and president. The second is the Sage of Monticello, wrapped in the bosom of his family, engaged in science, philosophy, agriculture, architecture—America's Renaissance man.

In these pages we meet a third, less-familiar Jefferson. Here, he is a solitary figure, alone at his writing desk. We see him casting and retrieving, stretching lines of communication the length of the land, weaving the myth that was to become Jeffersonian America. This myth, at least partly the legacy of his voluminous correspondence, was shaped by the political controversies of his administration: the continuing conflicts with the Federalist party and Great Britain, the Louisiana Purchase, the Aaron Burr conspiracy, and the embargo. Many of the unsolicited letters he received were in response to these issues, and in them are captured dramatic, personal views of the main political events of the times.

It is not surprising that many of the critical letters sent to

Jefferson about political affairs were not signed. The republic was still in its infancy, and even though freedom of expression was guaranteed by the Constitution, citizens had seen men sent to prison during the previous administration for defaming President John Adams in print. The right of the lowliest citizen to castigate elected figures with impunity had not yet achieved its present protected status.

Jefferson did not ignore letters simply because they were sent anonymously. "The motives which induce a writer of a letter to withhold his name are generally significant, but not however always blameable," he wrote. "I consider anonymous letters as sufficient foundation for enquiry into the facts they communicate."[1] Quite a few writers forwarded information they thought was useful to the president, but for personal reasons failed to reveal their identity. A woman, for example, wrote Jefferson anonymously to report a conversation she heard involving Arthur St. Clair, the former governor of the Northwest Territory. St. Clair, an ardent Federalist, had vigorously opposed the Republican attempt to gain statehood for Ohio. After the state was created in 1802, Jefferson removed St. Clair from office. The anonymous informant wrote that she was in a room in Washington next to where St. Clair and "a Number of Men form the N. Western Country" were staying and she overheard several conversations that convinced her "they ware treasonably inclined." "St Clare said that Thomas Jefferson, the presidant was damed Villon & Albert Gallaten, was no better. . . ." she wrote. Several of St. Clair's cohorts "had all sworn to do all in there power, to turn you out of offis, or sacrafise them selves in the attempt. The reason I did not right [write] before was I wanted to consult my husband, who said it ought to be maid known to you which I now do," because the president should be informed of this "deep la[i]d sceme." "You Honnored Sir," she ended, "will never know whom I am, but be asured your well wisher, & True friend, altho a woman."[2]

The first report Jefferson received about the Burr conspiracy was a note from an anonymous writer. It described Aaron Burr's alleged plan to sever the western states from the Union and set up a monarchy in Mexico, an act for which he was ultimately tried and exonerated.

[1 Dec. 1805]

SIR

Personal Friendship for you and the love my Country induce me to give you a warning about Cl. Burr's intrigues. You admit him at your table, and you held a long, and private conference with him a few days ago *after dinner* at the very moment he is meditating the overthrow of your Administration and what is more *conspiring against the State.* Yes Sir, his aberrations through the Western States *had no other object.* A foreing Agent now at Washington Knows since February last his plans and has second'd them beyond what you are aware of. Mistrust Burr's opinions, and advice: be thoroughly persuaded B. is a new Catilina.* Watch his conexions with Mr. M[err]y and you will find him a British Pensioner, and Agent with all the activity of ambition, and the wickedness of disapointement.**

altho anonimous
YOUR FRIEND.

How seriously Jefferson took this warning is unknown; it was not until nine months later that he indicated in writing that Burr was "unquestionably very actively engaged" in a conspiracy to separate the western states from the Union.[3]

Aaron Burr's attempt to gather a military force on the Ohio

---

*Catiline (108?–62 B.C.), the consul who conspired to overthrow the government of Rome.
**Anthony Merry, British minister to the United States.

River and descend with it to New Orleans had a devastating effect on commerce along the river. The following letter by a Pennsylvania merchant who was attempting to ship produce down the Ohio during the Burr conspiracy relates how the civil liberties of his crew members were severely abused by the militia forces guarding the river.

Greensburg [Pa.] 11 Feby 1807

His Ex. Thomas Jefferson

Sir

. . . [I pursue] a Merchantile Vocation, in which I have chiefly to depend on the purchase & transport of the Country Produce for my principal source of Remittance, for which the Navigation of the Western Waters, & the N. Orleans afford much the most effectual, economic & saving Market. For the purpose of executing engagements of some early spring Paym'ts, & invited by the hopes of profit, by being the first in Natches or N. Orleans market (which late news of a scarcity of provisions there, well justifies) prepared two Boats, whose value & outfit Expenses, when at Natches, would Amt. to nearly $3000, with James Fleming, my Clerk, as Supercargo, to descend the River by a winter freshet. They started, on the Allegany on 17 Decr. Ult. Before this time, the lively apprehensions of the Citizens of the western Country, had excited much alarm on the highly suspicious conduct of Col Burr, & your Excellency's Proclamation had caused Centries to be posted on the different parts of the Ohio.* Under these peculiar circumstances, I conceived it proper to take measures which should give to the Inspecting officers, the best possible Evidence of the property being solely my own, & the Boats to be sent on a fair Trading Voyage. . . .

---

*Jefferson issued a proclamation on 27 Nov. 1806 declaring that a military expedition had been launched against Spain, that it should be broken up by the militia, and that arrests should be made where warranted. Thomas P. Abernethy, *The Burr Conspiracy* (New York: Oxford University Press, 1954), 189–90.

[The boats were held up for investigation at Pittsburgh, and again at Marietta, Ohio.]

Released & got under way on 15 Ult. The still falling water, & increasing quantity of Ice gave them difficult passage untill it completely blocked them up on the 19th, 45 miles below Marietta, where after laying for 6 days, the *active & vigilent* Militia of Wood County [W. Va.] under Col. Phelps, hearing of them proceeded 10 miles down the River (& 3 miles over the County line into Mason County) where they lay, & took possession of the Boats. They declared *"the cargo to be public plunder & would do what they pleased with it,"* according broach'd the whiskey & Boat stores (the Boat guard of 15 men, consumed half bb. whiskey in 36 hours—i.e. 1 Gal. each).

The Supercargo & hands (the passengers having previously left the Boat) were now marched under guard back to Belville (10 miles up the River in Wood County) & brought before Justices Avery & Neal. Their proceedings were similar in the principles to those of Marietta, but they added the ignominy of a Military guard to their judicial investigation. They confined the arrested in a Chamber under Guard, & took them out singly like victim sheep for the stall, to go before the Court, as evidences, then conducted them to the Negroes Kitchen, & there put under Guard.

They told the Supercargo that it was his *misfortune* for having the papers which I had procured, & tortured trifling & accidental circumstances into strong presumptous evidence of guilt. After 24 hours detention, the Magistrates acquitted all the accused, & directed us to call on Col. Phelps for the Boats & Cargo.

The Col. refused to deliver them untill further orders from Government & advised them to go about their Business. The Conduct of the Militia here, was more abusive then that at Marietta. They proceeded to search person & papers after the acquital. . . .

Permit me to make a few reflections on the subject. The 6, 7 & 8 Articles of Amendment of the U.S. Constitution are invaluable Provisions for personal safety.[4] Seizures were made without warrant of arrest. Persons, Places, & Papers were searched without Oath of probable cause, or even a common warrant for the purpose. They were twice & thrice tried for the same cause, or rather same pretences of suspicions. They were not only prohibited from confronting evidences but were even to become their own accusing evidences themselves. These circumstances, certainly bear a like complexion to some of those complained of against Great Britain by our ever memorable Congress of 1776. . . .

While much of the value of the produce depends on the River Road to Market, the numerous, unjust & oppresive shackles of its navigation would disgust them with the Adminstration that conducted them. Indeed, as far as I am acquainted with them, from the censorious remarks which I have already heard uttered on my case, I know no means so readily to dispose them in favor of Mr. Burr's scheme of separating the Union. I will even venture to pledge my veracity (as far as you may please to value it) that such measures on the part of the Government are the only best possible [way] of producing such an hated event. . . .

With all due submission to your superior wisdom in the premises, I subscribe myself in behalf of Henry Weaver Jnr.

Your most obt. Servt.
HENRY WEAVER SR.

The problem of unlawful seizures by overdiligent militiamen was well known in Washington. Secretary of the Treasury Albert Gallatin wrote a memo to Jefferson on February 21, 1807, indicating that he, at least, was quite willing to bend the law in times of emergency.

Would it not be proper to attain an appropriation for making compensation in the case of provisions seized on the Ohio by militia? There is now an applicant in town. If the War Department has no appropriation applicable to the object, I apprehend vexatious suits may be brought against the officers, and supposing these to have somewhat exceeded their instructions, yet they should not be punished for their zeal.

When the Burr conspiracy was publicly revealed, the role in the plot played by General James Wilkinson, governor of the Louisiana Territory, became a subject of debate. For some time, Wilkinson, described by one scholar as "the most skilful and unscrupulous plotter this country has ever produced," had been accused of being in the pay of the Spanish government, a charge that recent scholarship has substantiated.[5] As the details of the Burr conspiracy were exposed, Wilkinson came increasingly under attack as a co-conspirator, although he was never convicted of being one.[6] The following letter, from a Revolutionary War veteran, demonstrates the heat of public opinion generated by the Wilkinson-Burr connection.

Baltimore February 24 1807—

Thomas Jefferson Esq

DEAR SIR

    I am all most to old to write but I think it my duty as a True American to give you my decided Oppinion considering all this noise about little Burr. I am now 79 years of age and have Served Seven long years in the late contest with Great Britain and hold my self still in readyness Should my Count[r]y be in danger which I think is not the case at present. I am also one of those that admire your administration. I dont like Burr nor never did but my dear Sir / I have it from good authority directly—from the State of Ohio and the western country that our great general Wilkison is as deep in the mud as little Burr is in the mire which will Soon be proved and my friend also writes me the people in general

disiprove very much of Wilkisons conduct and do realy Say
that of the two Wilkison is the greatest rouge and that he is
in Spanish pay; therefore my dear Friend as a gaurdian of
the people watch this impostor as well as the little divel and
I hope you will be rewarded in heaven.

Your Sincerely
CHARLES GEIRS.

Jefferson's political support came mainly from the South
and West. His home state, Virginia, was the anchor of
Republican party politics, but Kentucky, Tennessee, and the
new state of Ohio were equally bound to him. The political
leaders of these western states were mostly expatriate Virginians, many of them close Jefferson friends, and the new
residents who surged westward in ever-increasing numbers
were farmers and mechanics, the natural constituency of the
Republican party.

The following letter is from a Kentucky mill owner and
faithful Republican, who typifies the fears, concerns, and
aspirations of westerners during the Jefferson era. He has
been victimized by the lack of free navigation on the Mississippi, has suffered from hardships, dangers, and personal
tragedies, and is God-fearing, patriotic, and independent. But
he is also restless, ready to pull up stakes and move even
further westward, lured by the fabled, lush, free lands of the
Louisiana Territory.

Ogle's Mill Bourbon County, Kentucky
Apr. 28th 1805

His Excellency Thomas Jefferson Esq.
President of the U.S. of America
HONOURED SIR,
    With the most Sincere & highest Respect as Your Fellow
citizen & a Stranger, I hereby address You as my Fellow

Citizen, a Gentleman whom I have never had the pleasure to be personally acquainted with, but by Charactor, and as a Needy Man (I hope) on the most Excellent grounds I may with Propriety also Style You—my Friend, and therefore have used the freedom to trouble You with this Scrawl, in hopes that Your Excellency will have it in his Power and be Pleased to favour his petitioner some way, as in his Opinion may appear most proper—on hearing my Situation, a Sketch of my Life, my Sentiments ⟨and W⟩ishes.[7]

I have resided in this place about Nine Years & five months under considerable embarrassments, through various disappointments ⟨Losses⟩ & Afflictions by death, Sickness &c. Have been anxious, for eight years ⟨pas⟩t, to [go to] some other part of the new Country, but was prevented for want of Specie to purchase Lands and so detained here yet, tho' I still feel anxious to go hence and experience some other Climate. I am a Man of weak Constitution, have a Wife and five Children & a few Negroes, a small tract of Land and a Mill. I was born in New Castle County, S. Deleware the 25th of Decr. 1759. Moved with my Father and family to Monokesy Creek—seven miles above Frederick Town in the Spring [17]65, where I lived (his only Son) Thirty Years and a half at the Mills known by our name, and came to this State with my Family in the Fall [17]95, to the place where I now live. . . .

I had for a considerable length of time before I left Maryland contemplated coming to some part of the back Country, to get more Land for myself and family—than I was likely to own there. And tho' (I think) I can say in truth I have always been Sober, Industrious and Carefully engaged at my business, Yet I have not obtain'd as much as I sold there.

About three years ago I adventured to send three Boatloads of Flour to New Orleans. (I believe) of excellent quality as any that ever went out of this State, and what with it's being a little damaged by the difficult navagation of our small Rivers, the Glut of the Market then and the Caprice of the

Spaniards who were then in possession of that place, and lost thereby about two thousand dollars. And by the loss of three houses by fire and other damage by water together about three thousand dollars more, and having lost several of my Chil[dren] here too, my eldest Daughter in her third Year being drowned, my second and Darling Son at about seventeen Years of age—last Fall with the Nervous Fever, at which time myself and four other of my Sons & two black persons suffered much with the same Disease.

Having experienced that the Soil here (tho rich) ⟨an⟩d the Climate too—is neither well adapted to produce wheat of a ⟨good⟩ quality, and (I believe) will not in half or a whole Century to come, which Illy answers my occupation, being in the habit of Millering, the precariousness of sending our produce so great a distance to market, and in this rich soil the scarcity and meaness of the timber in many places, the innumerable disputes about the Titles of Land in this State, and what appears to be worst—as a general Vexation, is the Imperious carriage and the unjust & Wicked disposition of some of my Neighbouring fellow citizens, particularly—[a] Professor of Religion (somewhat like St. Paul['s] false brethern), all join'd together makes me Desire much to seek my Fortune in the Louisiana Country.*

I began house keeping in the year 1783, and tho' I never was so much attach'd to any place to be unwilling to exchange it for another, Yet, I have only moved once in the above space of about twenty-one years. I have seen Dr. John Sibley's report of said Country which to me appears reasonable and encouraging, have also seen Mr. John Fowler's circular Letter, in which I noticed the account of an allowance of some ⟨land⟩ to persons ("actual Settlers on the 20th of

*The reference to St. Paul's false brethren is possibly from 1 Corinthians 5.11: "But I now write to you not to associate with anyone named a brother, if he is immoral, greedy, an idolator, a slanderer, a drunkard, or a robber, not even to eat with such a person."

December 1805.")* Which as I am not able at present to purchase Land—with Cash—would well suit ⟨me⟩. I have a small Cargo in a boat now lying in Licking, waiting a rise of water, and intend (if I live), to go along and before I return, to explore some part of said Country, in hopes to find an Assyllum for the reception of myself and Family. Have for several Years past contemplated going to see the Louisiana Country even while held by the Spanish Government, and since [being acquired by the United States] with abundantly more pleasure, and had thoughts frequently about a year ago of writing to You on the Subject of my going there with my Family, and to purchase some Land soon as my Circumstance would admit, and under the Sanction of Your Excellency, to have Enjoyed the benefit of some Office. But that time has elapsed.

And now, Sir I crave the Favour of some one the smallest. If (from the experiment of inquiry and Just recommendation of any of my Friends & Acquaintances) You should think proper to bestow on me, at least, Sir, in case my Life is spared to go and see said Country, and there can be any Land obtain'd by me, and it's agreeable to You—Please to recommend me to some of your Friends there, and write me a Letter. Probabaly it might find me at the Natchees or on the Red River. I know none who live in that Country except Mr. James Brown (Atty.) of this State, ⟨and⟩ Mr. Sibley by Character only.** I wish, (Fearing the diseases prevalent in the ⟨warm⟩er Climate), particularly to see the Red River and three or four hundred Miles up it, where if I can get Land well suited for small grain, [. . .] and Navagating Water, will be willing to Build a Mill and occupy it there. . . .

*Dr. John Sibley wrote Jefferson an account of the Indian tribes of the Louisiana territory and was appointed an Indian agent by the president. John Fowler (1755–1850) served as a congressman from Kentucky from 1797–1807.
**Possibly James Brown (1776–1835), brother of John Brown of Kentucky, a schoolmate and friend of Jefferson. James Brown practiced law in Frankfort, Kentucky, served as Secretary of the Louisiana Territory, and as a Louisiana senator from 1813 to 1817.

I can (I think), with the greatest solemnity vouch for the truth of what I have wrote, tho' I fear the diction is Ill. I am Honoured Sir, with the Sincerest Respect as above Your Most Obt. Servant

ALEXANDER OGLE

The enactment of the Embargo Act in December 1807, at the end of Jefferson's second term, caused a marked decline in the popularity that had been steadily increasing during his presidency. The embargo against all shipping to and from foreign ports was passed into law as a last resort short of war to force Britain and France to lift restrictions on neutral American shipping. The embargo quickly became the most hated public act of Jefferson's presidency in the seacoast towns of the north and mid-Atlantic states where its economic effects were most painfully felt.* The shipping ban was repeatedly violated, prompting Jefferson to insist upon increasingly harsh enforcement, which in turn led to a further disintegration of his popularity.

By the end of the first year of the embargo Jefferson received some two hundred petitions against it, and numerous anonymous letters, many of them threats. The hostile anonymous letters chipped away at the president's fine-edged reserve. In response to a complaint by James Madison about a scurrilous unsigned letter he received, Jefferson wrote angrily:

> . . .This is one of the wretched, & dastardly productions, to which the cowards dare not put their names, of which I have received, & you will receive thousands. Of all the anonymous letters which have been constantly pouring in upon

---

*Some 30,000 seamen were unemployed, as well as workers in allied trades. Robert N. Johnstone, Jr., *Jefferson and the Presidency: Leadership in the Young Republic* (Ithaca: Cornell University Press, 1978), 253.

me, not more than half a dozen have been written with good views, & worthy of being read. They are almost universally the productions of the most ill-tempered & rascally part of our country, often evidently written from tavern scenes of drunkenness. They never merit one moment's attention.[8]

A month after the enactment of the Embargo Act, Jefferson received the following strange letter. The first part is an impassioned diatribe against Jefferson for being responsible for the writer's fall from "Glory." Jefferson was once his friend, he writes, but in some unnamed way has injured him, possibly by removing him from office ("He takes my life / who takes the means whereby I live"). He signs himself "Mortuus"—dead. The postscript is about the embargo; the writer asks Jefferson to continue it, and calls himself "a true Republican." The first part of the letter is angry, hostile, and depressed; the second part, possibly written after an alcoholic binge, is reconciliatory.

Jefferson endorsed the letter "bitter enough."

[26 Jan. 1808]

Sir

You must Know that there is a point of submission, beyond which no man Can pass without ceasing to be a man, and that there is a spirit in man and the inspiration of the almighty giveth him understanding. You must also Know that I have feelings as delicate as yours, and that any wounds inflicted requires as speedy a cure, as the wounds of any other man. Shakespeare spoke well and worthy of a man when he said

... He takes my life
who takes the means whereby I live[9]

I, a few years since, stood exalted in the public estimation. I was upon an eminence, where I scorned the breath of the slanderer. "Above the vulgar level of the great," I was conscious of my integrity, and was "glad of mine innocence."

No one could say—This man has wronged me in anything. My sails were filled with the "Aura Popularis" [popular favor] and I was sailing down the stream of time, which would have carried me to my destined port, loaded me with the honours of my country, and elated with the applauses of my fellow Citizens—had not the pestilential breath of your accursed mouth, blasted my expectations, and like the destructive mildew—ruined my situations. Now yours, nor any other human power cannot avail to raise me from the ground and reinstate me in my former Glory, yes I w⟨ill⟩ emphatically call it *glory*. And if you could, you are so filled with the insanity of Napoleon, that you would rather endeavour to remove mountains, ⟨and⟩ alter natures most perfect works, than assist, a fell⟨ow⟩ man. Such is the pride and naughtiness of your soul.

"The Evil that men do lives after them
The good is oft interred with their bones[10]
So let it be with Jefferson"

So let it be with Jefferson, did I say? No forbid it Justice. Let all his good be brought, that all may see his "good works," & wonder at the perfection of human nature. But this is too serious a place for irony. Life, precious life is concerned. We are treading upon the ashes of a ruined Character and touching the ashes of the dead. I say Let none of his good deeds be interred with his bones, but let them be shewn, and we shall then see what an infinitely little part of his motions, are marked with Good Intent.

Vita bene acta efficit senectutem jucundam.

[A life lived well makes for a pleasant old age.]

I wish with all my heart that it would apply to you. You once professed your friendship to me, but a life of experience has convinced me, yes, has placed it beyond all doubt, that,

"Friendship's a name to few confin'd
The offspring of a noble mind"

"That generous warmth which fills the Breast" has never approached yours. You are with all your experience and wis-

dom, still in the gall of Bitterness & Bonds of Iniquity. O
Hypocrisy, Like the treacherous Hyena you have wooed me
to your assistance, and then have glutted, your bloody Maw,
with the too credulous victim. Perhaps like the Crocodiles of
Egypt you have wept over the palpitating heart—But then
you have returned to your accursed repast with the fury of
the Blackest demon in the realms of Pluto. But I must put a
stop to these gloomy considerations. As I think upon the joys
of the past, they overwhelm me with grief. Perhaps, indeed
they "bear a just resemblance to my fortune, and suit the
gloomy habit of my soul." Yet for all this, I must turn my
mind to some thing else, which will relieve me. I hope you
will consider these things, and recur to your former actions.
You may perhaps hear from me again—I am miserable. Ver-
ily, I say unto you, you shall have your reward.

Yours
MORTUUS

Sat Eveng. 12 o Clock
January 26, 1808.

When your "Embargo" first appeared in the public prints,
many others as well as myself, were very much opposed to
it, supposing that it would have a very contrary effect to
which it has had. But I wish you most honoured Sir to continue it as long as seemeth good to you. It is the sincere wish
of many of my neighbours & as well as my own, that the
"Embargo" may continue at least four Months longer.

Grant me this request, since it is in your power, and I ask
no more, & your petitioner will ever pray—

Most honoured Sir
Your very humble Servt.
a true Republican—

Merchants were virtually unanimous in their opposition to the embargo. As it continued, with no signs of an end, ship owners became increasingly restless, as the following anonymous note indicates.

N York June 30 1808

Thomas Jefferson
Sir/
I have waited with greate Patience for Six Months, or More, thinking that your foolish Experiment at Embargo would Come to an end, But Can Discover no end to it. My Ships I wish to Send to Sea. By your recommending this embargo to Save My Property Perhaps your Intentions were motives pure and good—but to my Dissatisfaction, I dont thank you for [it]. I wish you as you have the power Vested in you—you would have the goodness to ⟨take⟩ it off. I am Sir a friend to Commerce & No friend to your administration.

your &c
A Merchant

The same anonymous writer sent another note two weeks later. The sarcasm directed at New York Republicans identifies the writer as a disgruntled Federalist.

N York, July 14 1808

Tommy Jefferson
Sir /
By this time you have Recd. all Communications from your Worthy Minnisters at foreign Courts & you must of Course be Convinced that your Experimental Embargo has Not that Intended Effect that you & your French & democratic renagodus Expected. How Wonderfull is the disap-

pointment to your advocates in N York. Many of your friends found out what an excelent thing was the Embargo. Greate wisdom in our Most worthy Congress; they Save all the American property &c. Let me tell you Sir the Merchant dont thank you or you[r] Collegues for Your prudent Measures. Take off the Embargo return to Carters Mountain and be ashamed of yourself, and never show your head in publick Company again.*

One of the worthless part
of Community—

The following anonymous note was written on both sides of a strip of paper one and one-half inches wide by ten inches long.

[4 July 1808]

Mr. President if you know what is good for your future welfar you will take off the embargo that is now such a check upon the American commerce and lay it upon something else or if you could lay it upon the hot weather it would add more to your credit. I say you are a friend to France but not to G Britain which I am sorry to inform you of. I am in hopes you will point our affairs in a good bairing. I bid you adue for the presint and trust you will see matters terminated properly by doing which you will gain the applause of your country men. Your friend as long as you act with propriety toward your country but when you depart from that I am your enehmy.

A lover of his Country

---

*Carter's Mountain: This is a reference to the place where Jefferson, then the war governor of Virginia, took refuge from Col. Banastre Tarleton's raiders in 1781 when they attempted to capture him at Monticello. The Federalists used the incident to accuse Jefferson of cowardice.

A shortage of money as a result of the embargo prompted a New Hampshire writer to suggest a law making farm products legal tender for debts.

Charlestown Newhamshire August 12, 1808

SIR

I have respected your laws and your government for the Younited States of Merrica and I wish to have you continue your laws and government and keep the embargo on til you see fit to take it off, though it is very trying to the people in this contry about thare debts and it is my wish that you would make some laws to pay our debts with out paing the money and if the[re] is a law to pay with perduce [produce] & cattle and horses I think that the[re] orter be a tender act so we can pay our debts with out money. I sopose that you think strange of my writing to you but the reson of my writing is becase I have a father and a mother and thay cant take care of them selves and as times are I cant pay for thare place so that we could live & respect your laws and I hope that you will take som notis of me and write to me as soon as you get my letter so I may know if your oner will do a little for me.

JONATHAN HALL CAPT.

As the embargo wore on, the anonymous letters became more aggressive. The following attack on Jefferson and the Republican party uses incidents and language commonly found in the Federalist press. Jefferson endorsed the letter "abusive."

August 29th. 1808

THOMAS JEFFERSON

I address my self to you and to you only because I consider you the mother of our distresses: you was the first founder of your party; you have ever ben determined to support it and gain the majority of the people and you have done it but how! by deceiveing and holding up false ideas to the people. You have dispised and annihilated those golden rules layed down and practised by the imortal Washington: you have fostered and supported those vile reches whose whole life has ben spent in ridiculeing the adminstration of Washington and his successor Adams: Look of the situation of our Country when you took the chair and look at it now. I should think it would make you sink with despair and hide your self in the Mountains.

You have not made the constitution your guide. You have sat aside and trampled on our most dearest rights bought by the blood of our ancesters. You have displased those worthy Sitizens from office who done honor to them selves and their Country and have put in their stead some of the most worthless beings of society. In fact you have sacrefised every honest and just principal for the support of your party. I find by your reply to the people of Newhampshire and by your private correspondance with them that you are determined to persist in your distructive measures. We see that you are determined on the total distruction of our Commerce especially the Northern states.[11] And you and your Cabinet are rejoiceing at our situation. It is too mutch for the people of a free nation to bear. They have allready bourn more than could have been expected. They have sent respectful petitions to you for the releaf of their distresses but you have turned a deaf ear to them and treated them with scorn. You and your party are fattening your selves on the spoils of our Country. You have rejected those peaceful offers of England and have payed all the attention posible to France.

We have too greate reason to believe that you are a bartering away this Countrys rights honor and Liberty to that infamous tirant of the world (Napolien). From you origionated all the calamities and evils this Country now suffers. You was the mother of the deathlike measure, the Embargo:

and by you it is Continued. You can not be considered any thing but a curse to this Nation and the whole wrath and indignation of an injured people is pointed at you! And you may rely upon it that if you persist in your distructive measures your Blood shall repay the abuse of injured people.

A sitizen suffering under the evils accasioned by you—

The most serious evasions of the embargo occurred along the Canadian border.[12] Smuggling there was easy and lucrative because British traders on the other side of the border were eager to purchase American goods, particularly lumber and potash, products of the vast tracts of forests in the Northeast.* The following informative letter, written skillfully by an observer with an eye for detail, captures vignettes of frontier life along the border, and suggests why Jefferson's embargo was doomed to failure.

New York, Sept. 29. 1808.

Sir,

Being the owner of certain lands in the Northern part of this state near the Canada Line, and hearing that there were people in the neighbourhood cutting down timber & making potash without permission, and having never explored the country, I embarked in a sloop the 7 ulto., arrived at Albany the 9th., proceeded to Lansingburgh the 10th., & finding no Stage, & unwilling to wait & lose time, I agreed with the driver of a waggon loaded with pork, to carry me to Skuns-

*Potash was obtained by leaching wood ashes and evaporating the solution in iron pots to a calcined residue; it was used as fertilizer, and for bleaching linen. Jefferson once considered manufacturing it. See Edwin M. Betts, ed., *Thomas Jefferson's Farm Book* (Princeton: Princeton University Press for the American Philosophical Society, 1953), 495–500.

borough, where I arrived the evening of the 10th.* This place is the head of the Champlain & is 240 miles distant from New York.

Here I had to wait several days for a wind. Skunsborough & this end of the Lake are shut up by high and inaccessible mountains so that a great part of the year the sun is not seen till mid-day. The north wind brings a fog tainted with the raw smell of mud & decayed vegetables from the lake, which at this season is from 4 to 6 feet lower than in Spring. Intermitting fevers very common. But for being the head of navigation this place had certainly never been the residence of human beings! The morning fog, opaque & white as new fallen snow, and almost as cold, filling the valley to a certain height, & the tops of barren & inaccessible mountains, emerging as it were out of a sea of cotton-wool, are phoenomena as singular to contemplate as they are baneful in effect.

Early on the 16th, the wind was south and fair for going down the lake. The sloop in which I embarked was loaded principally with pork: we arrived at Burlington [Vt.] at sunrise the next morning. Prosperity has here built palaces for aristocracy to reside in. The working class, if I may judge from the samples I fell in with, are the rudest men & the most prophane swearers that can exist. I landed to go the post-office. The Gaol is just opposite. A number of people were at the window. One of them was telling how he and his wife had assisted in taking one of the murderers—"that there villain," says he, pointing to him, "& if he is not hung, there's neither law nor justice in the country." The place was black & dirty, more like a den for wild-beasts, than a prison. A place more calculated to degrade unfortunate men & render them totally insensible of shame could scarcely be contrived! I hurried away from this disgusting scene.

In the afternoon we sailed for Peru [N.Y.], where next morning we got breakfast. Whilst at table the landlord told

*Skenesboro, now Whitehall, New York.

our Capt. of three men whom he (the Capt.) knew, that had a fortnight before returned from Canada; that they had with them in money the neat profits of their traping, which they divided at his house; that they had in one bag, which was wrapped in a Buffaloes hide, fifteen-hundred Guineas; that they had part sold their lumber at thrice the price it had heretofore obtained; and that, but for the embargo, they should not have carried home more half dollars than they now carried Guineas. They intended to reap their wheat, and as the market for it was very low, to stack it, set their fall-seed in the ground & to return into the woods as soon as possible to prepare lumber for the ensuing Spring market.

In the evening arrived at Plattsburgh [N.Y.]. The landlord here told me, that the Canada market had been so brisk for lumber and ashes, that there was not a poor man in debt in the country; that there was also a very profitable trade carried on in smuggling from the province English Goods, particularly articles of non-importation. From here I went on horseback to view the Lands. The 22nd. August retd. & embarked at Cumberland-Head in a sloop having on board 66 bbs. ashes & 9 Firkins Butter seized the day before by Gen. Woolsey for attempting to pass the line to Canada.* In the evening arrived again at Burlington.

At the Tavern, where I lodged, I found some intelligent & communicative travellers. One was direct from Quebec. He told me, that on the heights of Abraham the English were constructing a number of round stone Towers; that the Governor had expressed his opinion, that the province was & would be found to be, of greater value to England than it had ever yet been supposed. That provisions were scarce; that the pork of which I had seen so much, was principally for Quebec, from whence it was shipped to Halifax, the W. Indies, &c. That pot-ash had actually been worth $300—*three hundred dollars* per Ton, but was now lower; that bills on London

---

*Melancthon Lloyd Woolsey was Collector of the District of Champlain in New York.

were at a discount of 7 per Cent. & that he had met, at St. John's $50,000 going from Newyork to purchase bills.

He also mentioned the smuggling of English goods into Massachusetts from the province, with this observation, that it would destroy all political allegiance & morality, & that the present generation would learn a pernicious trade, which they would not soon forget, but very probably teach it to the next. It was wittily observed by one, that if the U.S. should declare war agst. England, the people, in the states joining the province, or benefitted by the Canada market, would call *town-meetings,* to consider *which side* it would be the most for their *interest* to take! Another said, "We have no means, at this time, of paying our debts, & supporting our credit, save the article of ashes. Wheat is not in demand. Ashes the same, at N York; but in Canada we can get a price for it more than double what it was ever before known. One barrell will bring as much almost as three barrells did but a few years since. Ashes are not contraband of war, there is no rebellion, no treason, no revolutionary principles in ashes surely. If I saw any evil in sending ashes to a good market I would not send them; the money we get in return is certainly a blessing, for it clears our lands, builds our houses & keeps our mechanics & labourers employed." Talking of a seisure it was observed, "that the loss (if condemnation followed) would be heavy, but the lake would be frozen, and a good sleighing season would enable them to baffle Gen. Woolsey, & to make it up again."

One, with whom I had been talking about the value of wild lands, said, mark what I say—your lands will have their value fixed & regulated by the Canada market; it is the proper market for their produce & of which the city of New York will, e'er long, feel the effect." The next day I, by chance, heard of an empty waggon, going to Troy for a punchion of rum: I took my passage in it, & thence proceeded, by way of Albany, to New York. . . .

With sincere respect, and with the single view of commisserating, for your information & amusement, these few facts & observations, I am,

Sir, Your most obt. Servt.

CHARLES CONNELL

Jefferson received a number of threats on his life and warnings of assassination plots throughout his presidency. They were a reflection of the intensity of party rivalry during this period and were seemingly sent to cause Jefferson anxiety, for there are no records of any real assassination conspiracies. Jefferson never reduced the number of his public appearances or changed his patterns of free personal access because of these written threats.[13] Typical of the assassination warnings was one received at the end of Jefferson's first term. His laconic endorsement was "assassination."

Philadelphia December 6th 1804

MOST HOURNOURD SIR

This Comes from A Stranger but A Friend. You Must [know] that there is a plot formed to Murder you. Before the Next Election a band of hardy fellows have Joind to do it. They are to have ten thousand Dollars if they Succeed in the attempt. They are to Carry dagger and pistols. I have been invited to Join them but would Rather Suffer death. I advise you to take Care and be cautious how you Walk about as some of the assasins are already in Washington.

A friend to the Constitution

NB You must excuse me not Mentioning the Men.

Most of the threats on his life came after the passage of the Embargo Act. The following threat apparently did not trouble Jefferson seriously, for he endorsed it "embargo ribaldry." The assassination warning may have been bluster, but the anger, need, and frustration seem serious and deeply felt.

Boston Sept 19 1808

PRESIDENT JEFFERSON

I have agreed to pay four of my friends $400 to shoat you if you dont take off the embargo by the 10th of Oct 1808 which I shall pay them, if I have to work on my hands & nees for it. Here I am in Boston in a starving Condition. I have by working at jurney wurk got me a small house but what shall I git to eat? I cant eat my house & it is the same with all the Coopers. I cant git no work by working about on the warves for you have destroy'd all our Commerce & all the ships lie rotting in our harbours & if you dont take off the embargo before the 10 of Oct. you will be shott before the 1st of Jany 1809. You are one of the greatest tirants in the whole world. You are wurs than Bonaparte a grate deel. I wish you could feal as bad as I feal with 6 Children round you crying for vittles & be half starved yours⟨elf &⟩ then you woud no how good it felt.

The following writer attempted to extort from Jefferson permission to sail two ships to London, in violation of the embargo, in exchange for overlooking a debt the president supposedly owed him. Jefferson's response, merely hinting that an attempt to bribe the president of the United States was a criminal act, brought forth a plea of innocence from an eighteen-year-old boy.

Norfolk October 4th. 1808

THOMAS JEFFERSON ESQR.
President of the United States of America

I beg you Excellency will permit me to call your attention to the contents of this letter which the Embargo ocasions me to write as I got my bread by going to sea and am now deprived of it and am beholden to my relations who feel the effects of it nearly as bad as myself. I am persuaded to address you and make known to you I am the son of William Hunter who is the surviving partner of Joseph Royle & Co. who held your Bond for 75 £ St[erling] bearing interest from date. When last I saw my Father he told me the Bond was lost. But necessity compells me to seek all the aid I can; therefore take the libberty of making known to you this bond which appears unpaid and upon receiving payment the principal only I will give the following Firms as security that the bond never shall appear, v[i]z: Donaldson Thosburn & Co of this place, Gallego Richards & Co of Richmond. Either or both can I give. If you can recollect this I have no doubt but your Honor will pay without any more trouble but that of my getting the security.

Or if your Honor will grant permission for the American Ships Charles Carter of Planter to go to London with a load of Lumber consisting of Masts, Yards, topmast Oak pieces &c. Either or both of the ships have got licences from his Majesty assuring them to go and return to the United States untroubled by any of his ships of War. If you will grant either or both these ships the liberty of sailing destined as above mentioned it will enable me to live with[out] asking the afore said Claim which otherwise I must beseech your honor to grant me some assistance in this my state of starvation. I both beg, pray and beseech your honor to take in to consideration the contents of this letter and grant me some aid for which God Almighty can only reward you. Please let me here from your Honor as soon after the receipt of this as convenient and I reamain

Your Obdt. Sert.
GEORGE HUNTER

Mr. George Hunter, Norfolk
Washington Oct. 14. 08.

Sir

Your letter of the 4th. inst. was recieved a few days ago.
You have been greatly decieved by the information that I had
never paid the debt to William Hunter & that the bond is
lost. I paid it to Joseph Royle's executor & have a perfect
recollection of the fact, and I have no doubt that at Monticello I can produce satisfactory evidence of it; probably the
bond itself.

I am not willing to believe that the proposition not to ask
this claim, on my granting permission of two ships to go to
London, was seen by you in the light of which it is susceptible and in which you will certainly see it on having your
attention recalled to it. I add my salutations.

Th: Jefferson

Norfolk October 20th. 1808

Thos. Jefferson Esqr.

Sir

I am honor'd with your letter of the 14th. Inst. and from
its contents am satisfied with respect to the bond. And on
recalling my attention to the proposition have found my self
in error. Allude it to my inexperience and want of age, being
now only in my eighteenth year. I hope you will forgive me
of the error for which I am indebted to your Honor for pointing out to me as it will be a guard to me in the future.

I remain Your very Humble and Obdt. Sevt.
Geo. Hunter

If not troubling you should like to know if your Honor receives
this.

In contrast to the many hostile letters of complaint Jefferson received on the embargo issue, a Massachusetts resident, reputedly speaking for the citizens of several towns, is obsequious in his request that the embargo be lifted.

(Plymouth County, Mass.)
Hanover Octr. 12. 1808

Thomas Jefferson, Esqr. President of the United States.

MAY IT PLEASE YOUR EXCELLENCY,

With that respectfull awe and reverence due to the first magistrate of a free people, I would approach the footstool of your excellency with the hope that you will deign to notice the language of a private citizen. Selected from among many resputable citizens of the towns of Hanover, Pembroke, Marshfield and Situate [Scituate], to request your excellency if consistent, with the duties of your office, to inform them, through me, whether, in your opinion, the conduct of the beligerents, towards this country, will warrant e'er long the removal of the Embargo.

Living in the vicinity of the ocean our interest and prosperity are intimately connected with commerce. That ship building, with all its consequent and various employments have heithertofor yeilded an abundant reward for our labours. We pursued our several callings with pleasure, and gladness smilled in our dwellings. But for nine months past these sources of wealth have vanished; instead of cheerfull industry, our work shops and ship-yards are dressed in gloom and melancholly, the stimulus to industry is weakened and our joy turned into apprehension. We would assure your excellency that we venerate the laws of our country, we respect its constituted authorities, we will submit to every privation necessary to preserve our just right and Independence as a nation. We bow, in submession to your superior wisdom and patriotism, and with the most sincere confidence in your integrity and good conduct, we pledge ourselves to support the measures of the present administration of our national government. With every sentiment of esteem I have the honour to be, your excellencys most obedient, and very humble Sevt.

ELIJAH HAYWARD

In the following letter a Philadelphia seaman struggles valiantly to express his personal anguish at being left unemployed by the embargo. A number of workers felt the government should compensate them for lost wages.

Philadelphia Dat[e] Novamber 14th. 1808

We Destrsat Seamen of Philadelphia
Petitioners to you Honour
Thomas Jeffarison President of the Unitad States

We Humble Bag your Honur to Sum weekly allowance. Sir at as Hard times [u]pon us Seamen your Hounr Nos [knows] 50 or 60 Coasting vissels will not Carry 4 or 5000 Seamen Out of this Port. Sir we Humble bag your Honur to Grant us destras Seamen Sum relaf for God nos what we will do. Your Petitioners is at Present utterly destitute of all Employmant. We Humble Bag Honur to grant us Som Employamat. 200 of us mat in the State Hous yard on Friday Last. We Have all mises & famlys. Sir we Humble bags your Honur Pardon of at mis [if amiss].

THOMAS FREEMAN

The silent victims of the embargo, as many of Jefferson's correspondents observed, were the wives and children of men thrown out of work. The following writer, the youthful wife of a sea captain, perhaps still in her teens, refused to sign her name, for fear of having her plight discovered by those who consider "Poverty as a crime instead of A misfortune." The name she gave as a forwarding address for the charity she hoped to receive from the president was probably that of a friend or relative.

Like most of the letters Jefferson received from women asking for help, the writer relates her story as a way of eliciting pathos. She came from a good family, was married to an honest, hardworking man, and has been reduced, by no fault of her own, to helpless indigence.

Her hope was that virtue would be rewarded in life as it was in the sentimental fiction her letter imitates, but Jefferson dismissed her appeal with the terse endorsement "begging." The comment seems heartless, but the appeal came at a time when Jefferson was increasingly frustrated with the unpopular and ineffective embargo. He had also discovered that his own finances were in shambles, and that he was in no position to be granting charity to anyone.*

Alexandria January the 3 1809

WORTHY AND MUTCH ESTEEM'D SIR

I Flatter myself you will pardon The very great liberty I take in addressing A few Lines to you; as nothing but dire Necessity, and the Renown generosity of your Charactor should ever have compelled me to Sutch A Step. The very Idea of Applying to you for pecuniary asistance harrows my Soul. I am at A loss for words to express my Feelings on the occation; my hand trembles my pulce throbs and I am almost tempted to throw by my pen; but as Some excuse for my troubling you Suffer me (if you will condesend to read it) to give you the outlines of my past life.

---

*Two weeks after receiving this letter, Jefferson wrote Thomas Mann Randolph: "Nobody was ever more determined than I was to leave this place [Washington] clear of debt. But trusting to estimates made by my head and confident that I had the thing quite within my power, I omitted till too late the taking an accurate view of my calls for money. The consequence is that I shall fall short 8. or 10,000 D[ollars]." (17 January 1809, DLC)

To be brief I was born in Virginia of respectable parents And Nursed in the lap of affluence. I lost my Father at A very early age; in consequence of which my Education was very inferior to that of my Elder Sisters, daughters of my Mother By A former Husband; but however as I grew up if I was not accustomed to all the Superfluityes, at least I was to all the Comforts of life. At the age of fourteen it pleased the divine disposer of all Events to rob me of my other Sir-viveing parent; then Behold me an Orphan, dependent on A vast Number of relations; and never was an Orphan Blessed with kinder, but Still my proud heart Sighed to be Independ-ent, which caused me to Marry very young to A Sea Capt. and came with him to live in Alexandria. True I did not live In the Stile I had been accustomed to but Still I was content. I wanted for nothing. . . .

For three or four years my husband Continued constantly to go to Sea; I was grieved to part with him but knew he was compeled to go for A livelihood. I was Situated in that man-ner when the Embargo took place and of course he was thrown out of imployment. The Butcher Supplyed us with meat, the Flower Merchants with Flower, in Short every one knew the honest upright heart of my husband; and feared not to trust him; Saying at the time pay me when you get imployment.

About Six months ago he had an offer of running A Vessel on Shares from this to Norfolk and gladly excepted it, but alass As Soon as he could Step his foot on the Shore he was Sorounded, all crying, you have got Imployment, pay me A little and pay me a little. Great god it was but a little he could possible make. I found we must want. I wrote Notes and Sent to Beg for Needle work and when I could get it I would not be content with working all day; but many A night have not lain my head in the pillow untill I have thought it would Burst with pain. But Oh Sir how true I have found the words I have Somewhere read of, Alas! how Small A portion of the worlds wealth falls to the lot of the humble Industrous Female who by continued Labour can Scarce gain Sufficient to Supply, with the coarcest food the wants of nature or to Shield with decent Cloathing her limbs from the inclemency of the weather.

About four weeks ago my husband return'd home with A high fever. Those that he owed had procured A load for him to take away; he was ill; I begged, I entreated him not to go but Stay and have the avise of A Doctor. But all in vain; I saw him depart, the picture of death. And Still I retain my Senses; if he returns Alive tho Sertain he will be ill the balance of the winter. Those that formerly gave me work now say the times is So hard they must do their work themselves and I am reduced to want the common Nesasarys of life.

Will what I have Said cause your generous heart to give me any Asistance? Their is not that person in Existance; except your Self that I would aply to; but their is one thing I have to Say I fear you will disapprove of; that is I do not intend to put my name to this letter. Consider dear Sir Should It fall into less worthy hands than yours; it is not from you; but the Cruel misjudgeing world; that considers Poverty as A crime instead of A misfortune; that I wish to hide it. Could I bear to be pointed ⟨at⟩ A petitioner of Charity; no I feel that I could ⟨not.⟩

No Sir I Beg I intreat, as you value the peace of A fellow mortal that you will let what I have Said find A Safte repository in your Bosom. I feel Convinced it will; for I never can be deceived in that Charactor that I always considered as the Model of perfection. Should you favour me with one line and express the Most distant hint I will Amediately inform you of My Father and Husbands Name but untill then I Shall keep it A Secret. . . .

Should you Sir think propper to favour me with A line please to direct to Eliza Ann Pollard and it will come Safe to my hands.

Another appeal for money from a widow with children brought the same endorsement: "beggery."

Janury 21. 1809

To the Right Honourabel Mr. Jefferson
President of the United States

Bagg pardon for so bold a tempt to ofer to ask releaf from your Bounty full hand, But nesity oblidges me. I have for abou[t] 3 years past suported my selfe & two Children By working in mens Clothing from the Taylors. But sense your honours have Been pleased to Lay on the imbargo theyr has Been noo work too doo which has destrest mee & Brought mee too want Bread after seling what Littele I had Round mee hopeing it wod Bee taken of[f]. But I Cannot Subsist no Longer theirfore I sincerely pray your hiness will hear the prayers of a widow & Helpless orphans & beestow what ever your honour will Beestow. Shall ever have the prayers of your destrest Sarvant

MARY UNDERWOOD

In short succession, Jefferson received the following two notes: a threat, and a prophecy.

Balam [Baltimore?] Jan. 17 1809

MR. PRESIDENT

Take of[f] your Embargo & restore us to freedom, or 300 Yankees Youths between 18 & 29. & 150 of City Washington are resolved on your destruction.

Look to it.

One of the three hundred—
by the order of the Sectary
FILO LIBURTUS

[18 Jan. 1809]

O Thomas thy Deceit & Wickedness is great upon the Earth and when thou retirest from Office, Thou will be asshamed to look an honest Man in the Face, and I am sure, no honest Man can look upon Thee with Complacency. Thy Society in this Wo[r]ld, will be composed of the most Wicked, & Worthless part of Creation, and in the other World, of Devels & infernal Spirits.

PROPHESY

Two of the most hostile denunciations of the embargo Jefferson received were from men who did not fear to sign their names. The first is from a Philadelphia seaman, the second from a Boston laborer who confesses to stealing food, and who vows vehemently to "take to highway robbing" to feed his children. These are desperate letters.

Philadelphia June 4th. 1808—

DEAR SIR,

I wish you would take this embargo off as soon as you possibly can, for damn my eyes if I can live as it is. I shall certainly cut my throat, and if I do you will lose one of the best seaman that ever sailed. I have a wife and four young one's to support and it goes damn'd hard with me now. If I dont cut my *throat* I will go join the English and fight against you. I hope, honored Sir, you will forgive the abrupt manner in which this is wrote as I'm damn'd mad. But still if ever I catch you over there, take care of your honored neck.

your
T. SELBY

No. 9 Pine St. If you want to see him, you damn'd rascal.

Boston, August 8, 1808

THOMAS JEFFERSON,

You infernal villain. How much longer are you going to keep this damned Embargo on to starve us poor people. One of my children has already starved to death of which I [am] ashamed and declared that it died of an apoplexy. I have three more children which I expect will starve soon if I dont get something for them to eat which can not be had. You must either take this Embargo off & save all us poor people from starving or afford us some kind of relief. If you dont God knows what I shall do. I certainly must & will take to highway robbing. Every day we hear of Houses more or less being broken open in the night & rather than see the rest of my children starve I'll be damn'd if I dont do the same.

I'll commit murder for the sake of money. I can get nothing by begging. Every body says why don't you go to work but where is the work to be had. None under Heavens. There is a set of you damned Jacobin rascals have got together to see how much mischief you can do & how many poor people you can starve. You are the greatest villain on earth. Suppose you fetch me a tax bill; how am I going to pay it. I cannot get money to buy victuals with & I have to go barefooted all the time & there is hundreds in this town as bad off as I am & some worse, if it's possible for them to be so. I dread the winter that is to come; rent to pay & nothing to pay it with; fire wood must be had & no way to get it but to steal it. If I try to catch fish it is most an impossible thing here when there is so many catching fish all the time. If I get any I have nothing to cook them with. The alms house is so full that I cant get my children into it. The way that I get the paper I write on is to beg for it & borrow ink.

A few mornings since I saw some salt fish lying spread about on the ground. I asked a gentleman to give me one but he told me I was a lazy son of a bitch and said if I wanted anything [to] eat to go and work for it but afterwards I was drove by hunger to steal four of them which I told my wife was given to me. Afterwards I saw a Baker going by my house. I took a basket in my hand and told my wife I was going begging. I went to the baker and asked him to give me a biscuit but he refused. I followed him & saw him stop to go into [a] house & saw nobody in the street. I took this opportunity to steal 4 Biscuit & 3 Loaves which I told my wife I worked for & this is the way a great many poor people in this town have to do. They cant get anything to eat any other way.

I could once get a living by day labour but now I cant get anything to do. I rove from wharf to wharf from Street to Street all day till at night I feel more fatigued than I should by hard work. I wish you could feel as bad as I do, in debt Expecting every day to be put into Jail & then what will become of my wife and children? My wife is a weakly & Sickly woman and cannot do any hard work & my children all too small to earn their own living.

> I am a Federalist
> JOHN LANE JONES.

On March 4, 1809, the date of the inauguration of James Madison as new president, the Embargo Act was finally repealed, commending to the political grave Jefferson's unsuccessful experiment in economic coercion as a foreign-policy measure. Although his popularity plummeted in New England because of the embargo—as the hate mail he received makes clear—"the fundamental strength of his popular prestige," as one historian concluded, "was largely unshaken." He returned to his home at Monticello to widespread acclaim.[14]

2

Patronage

"For god's sake get us relieved"

WHEN Thomas Jefferson stood before Chief Justice John Marshall to take the presidential oath of office on March 4, 1801, his predecessor John Adams was conspicuously absent; he had departed from the new capital of Washington only hours before and was on his way home to Quincy, Massachusetts. Adams had left his successor a little gift, however, one that angered the controlled and even-tempered Jefferson so much that the mere thought of it could raise his ire years later. In a final flurry of so-called "midnight appointments," before he stepped down from the presidency, Adams had packed the judiciary with Federalists, denying Jefferson the prerogative of placing members of his own party in those offices.

Three years later, in an attempt to reconcile with Abigail Adams, whose former close friendship had been shattered by the partisan rift between her husband and the new president, Jefferson found himself unable to refrain from telling her that Adam's appointments had been "personally unkind." Those appointed "were from among my most ardent political enemies," he wrote, "from whom no faithful cooperation could ever be expected." He felt that it was "common justice" on the part of Adams "to leave a successor free to act by instruments of his own choice." Although he used the expression "common justice," he meant "common decency," for he had privately referred to "Mr. A's indecent conduct."[1]

Jefferson subsequently removed the men Adams had appointed and filled the posts with staunch Republicans, but the problems with patronage, which the "midnight appointments" had dramatized in the opening days of Jefferson's presidency, were never resolved. On the contrary, patronage became an ever-growing, devouring insect, gnawing constantly at the president's time. Washington and Adams had faced the same problem and it was to grow with each succeeding presidency, but Jefferson had to deal with it virtually single-handedly with only intermittent aid from cabinet members.[2] Filling federal jobs, striking a balance between party loyalty, competence, and the pressures of friendship, was one of his most wearisome presidential duties. He was constantly under siege by candidates for office, high and low. It was a battle never to be won, for every man chosen for office left dozens of unsuccessful candidates and friends disgruntled and unhappy. Once in exasperation he wrote to his Secretary of the Treasury Albert Gallatin, "for god's sake get us relieved from this horrible drudgery of refusal."[3] Once an appointment was made, however, he assumed a stoic reserve toward any recriminations that followed. "My usage is to make the best appointment my information and judgment enable me to do," he wrote, "and then fold myself up in the mantle of conscience and abide, unmoved, the peltings of the storm."[4]

THE most persistent office seeker in Jefferson's eight years as president was the Reverend David Austin, who badgered Jefferson relentlessly with appeals for virtually every appointive office in the federal government. His correspondence with the president is the record of the dogged persistence of one man in conflict with the equally willful resistance of another.

Austin was a forty-one-year-old Presbyterian minister from New Haven, Connecticut, who, by his own account, had fought the British in his native land during the Revolutionary War, and had then gone to Europe where he met John Adams in London and Benjamin Franklin at Passy, France.[5] He came to Washington from New England to recoup his fortunes after a series of devastating professional and personal setbacks that would have crushed a less resolute man. He had been minister of the Presbyterian church in Elizabethtown, New Jersey, when he became convinced that the second coming of Christ would occur on "the fourth Sabbath of May, 1796." Hundreds of excited believers converged on the church from neighboring communities, but when the appointed day passed and nothing extraordinary happened his congregation turned on him, accused him of suffering from delusions, and fired him.

He returned to New Haven and spent his patrimony, and the fortunes of his friends and family, on building expensive houses, stores, and a wharf to be used for the embarkation of the Jews, who, he was convinced, would be using New Haven for their return to the Holy Land. When this misguided scheme predictably failed, he went bankrupt and landed in debtor's jail. While a prisoner, Austin escaped, was pursued and finally captured, but escaped once again on horseback. He was in a tavern refreshing himself with a drink, when he learned that the sheriff of New Haven had offered a fifty-dollar reward for his capture, whereupon he returned to New Haven, presented himself to the sheriff, and demanded the reward.

So antic and unpredictable was his behavior that many considered him insane. One friend, who had known him as a boy and young man, was asked if he was mad. "No more than he was from infancy," was the reply. "He never was like other folks." If men who talk with God are insane, William Blake was a lunatic, and perhaps the Rev. Austin was too, but both were also poets, one considerably more talented than the other. Like Blake, Austin's imagination ran consistently to metaphor. A friend told of crossing the Connecticut River on a ferry with him. Austin commented:

> "A noble river, Sir." "Yes," I replied, "a very long river for the size of it." "Yes," said he—"suppose it to be a tree;" and stepping one foot forward, as though he were grasping the trunk, he added, "raise it up here—what a tree it would be! two hundred miles high! the towns on the branches would be leaves; the meeting houses would be the birds' nests; and (hitting me a rap) we ministers should be the birds' eggs."[6]

This was the man who swept into Washington with a master plan for a Republican millennium. He claimed to have received visionary messages and prophecies; in particular, after five years of consultation with God, he had devised a "chart of proceedings," a master plan for world harmony and peace. He was willing to part with his chart for a position in Jefferson's cabinet or $12,000—a proposal that was not designed to win the sympathy of a president who edited his own version of the New Testament with all supernatural references removed, who believed passionately in the separation of church and state, and who thought it the duty of citizens of a republic to offer their services freely to their country. Jefferson also had no particular fondness for Presbyterians. In later years he wrote that they were "the loudest; the most intolerant of all sects, the most tyrannical and ambitious. . . ."[7]

Austin began his epistolary campaign for a governmental office on March 9, 1801, five days after the inauguration. He wrote to Jefferson from Philadelphia, introduced himself, and

forwarded a paper outlining his plan for "universal pacifica-
tion." On the same day he wrote a second letter, recommending himself as an appointee to a peace commission to
France, and two days later he amplified these remarks in yet
another letter. When he received no response, he wrote again
on March 15, his tone now ugly and threatening:

> I therefore, Sir without the least hesitation state to you, in
> the name and by the authority of the most High God, that
> you are a dead man, in case you refuse Obedience to the
> voice of Heaven. . . . I again demand that you shut not the
> door of this American sanctuary against the legitimate
> knockings of the voice of the Almighty.[8]

On March 21, after hearing that Jefferson needed a private
secretary, Austin applied for the job and listed his qualifications—long on generalizations and short on particulars.

> I submit the matter to the consideration of the President;
> & as it is probable little may be known of the abilities of the
> applicant for the discharge of the duties of this office; he may
> be pardoned for suggesting that so far as a Liberal education;
> a tour through several parts of Europe; a general acquain-
> tance with men & things, & a close attention to the affairs
> of our Revolution may be plead as qualifications, so far, the
> President might rely on the accuracy of the appointment should
> it be thought necessary or proper.

He was also available for any other vacancies that might
occur.

On March 30, he asked to be made Revenue Collector for
New Haven, a position that his father had held. In fact, when
Jefferson was secretary of state under Washington, he had
signed the senior Austin's appointment papers.[9]

During the month of April Jefferson received not a word

from Austin, and he may have believed that his silence had finally worked its desired effect. But on May 15, shortly after some violent weather had swept through Washington, Austin sent the following letter. Its pulpit oratory, reverberating with the organ tones of Cotton Mather, is rich with portents and prophesies, threats and warnings. It is typical of his correspondence with Jefferson; only he can read the palm of God's providential hand, so it is essential that he be given a governmental post where he can advise the president on matters of state.

Philadelphia May 15th. 1801—

MR. PRESIDENT—

Seeing in the paper of this City, some sketches of a Tornado, said to have fallen out at Washington on the 7th. inst. & thinking, perhaps the purport of this tempest might not be rightly understood; you will have the goodness to excuse this intrusion, in view of offering a ray of light on this subject. . . .

This *Tempest* hath relation to things under the hand of the present executive; and the arrangement of Providence exemplifying the hidden instruction will be opened in its order— but I now tell you Sir, that moving, solely by the counsels in your presence, you have this tempest to meet. It is more than you can do to meet it, or to avert it. The God of our Nation is of one mind, & none can turn him. There is an order laid down by the Supreme Architect; & whatsoever now fails to work by that order will finely fall into the tempest. The designs of the Almighty are sketched out upon a Chart, not visible to all; & the operations of his providence comment upon that hidden design.

Suffer me Sir, to suggest once more, that your own honor & the safety of the administration, not to say of the Nation depends upon your being so far in possession of the invisible design, as to have the rays of its power, to fall upon the Chart of your proceedings.

As it is understood that the Office of Secre'y of the Treasury is, in a sense, vacant, it will be easy for the President to supply that Office with an able Manager, & his own counsels with no contemptible aid.

This done, a chart shall be laid before the President, by which sailing, success will be ensured.

As there is no little uneasiness upon the public mind, in relation to the appointment of Mr. Gallatin to this Vacant Office the President may calculate, that providence opens the door for the execution of things I state.*

I am at present, in the presence of Crouded Audiences, laying a foundation for a General Union among all administrations of Professing Christians, in the United States, & am gladly heard by the Clergy & people, almost without discrimination.

And I shall only add, that if the matter now stated, prove not acceptable to the President, the time will come when the federal ship will be found so far stranded; that advice from this City will be necessary, in order to heave her off, or to deliver her from the surchargings of the tumultuous sea, with which, as things now go, she has soon to engage.

With all due esteem
DAVID AUSTIN

No. 352 S. Front Street

By June 9, Austin had traveled from Philadelphia to Washington, still continuing his epistolary assault on the president. During the month of June, he wrote a total of thirteen letters, with no response.

---

*Because of fierce opposition by Federalists to the appointment of Albert Gallatin as Secretary of the Treasury, Jefferson withheld his nomination until after the Senate adjourned; the incoming Senate would be Republican controlled. This is the "vacancy" Austin refers to. Noble E. Cunningham, Jr., *The Process of Government under Jefferson* (Princeton, N.J.: Princeton University Press, 1978), 13.

From his letters to Jefferson, Austin appears to be the megalomaniac that many members of his former congregation believed him to be, but his religious and political support in Washington was powerful enough to win him an invitation to preach a Fourth of July sermon before the House of Representatives. Austin was reportedly an impressive pulpit orator. He was dignified and polished in manners, a Yale graduate with a classical education and an inventive mind that was alive with spiritual metaphor. His sermons, though, were elliptical prose poems spun from his visionary imagination and made no rational sense at all. He was able to attract listeners, however, who enjoyed the music of his preaching with little concern for its meaning.

Austin's oration at the Hall of Representatives was to launch an ambitious ecumenical project, seemingly a harbinger of the "Second Great Awakening," the nineteenth-century religious revival movement just beginning to sweep southward from New England. His goal was "to bring the different denominations of professing Christians in the City, to a more united concurrence in the general principles of Christian unity. . . ."[10]

Jefferson could not have been happy to discover that Austin, in the meantime, had infiltrated his own household. He had agreed to officiate at the marriage of two of Jefferson's servants, but first insisted that they get the president's permission.[11] This finally forced Jefferson to write to Austin, telling him there was no impediment to the marriage.

[14 July 1801]

SIR

Understanding that Joseph Dougherty and Maria Margery, servants in my family propose to intermarry, and that on application to yourself to perform the ceremony, you expressed a wish to know whether it was with my knowlege

& approbation, I with satisfaction declare they have conducted themselves within their several departments so as to merit & obtain my approbation, and that I know of no impediment why they should not be joined together in marriage, both of them being free in their condition & of an age which requires [no more] than their own consent to the ceremony. I pray you to accept assurances of my respectful commisseration.

TH: JEFFERSON

Austin was back campaigning for a position on July 17; this time he wanted to be secretary of the navy. His appointment would quiet complaints of irreligion on the part of Jefferson by having a chaplain in his cabinet.

During the months of August and September, he wrote four letters giving political advice to the president, and on September 14, he once more gave reasons why he should be Jefferson's secretary. On November 28, he again requested a job in the secretary of state's office.

He began the new year on January 11, 1802, with a new solicitation; Congress had just passed a Library of Congress bill, giving the president the power to appoint a librarian. Not surprisingly, he wanted the position.

At long last, Jefferson lost his patience with Austin and sent the following letter. It is a masterpiece of the literary art of severing the head from the body with deftness, polish, and efficiency.

The revd. David Austin
Washington Jan. 21. 1802.

SIR
    Having daily to read voluminous letters & documents for the dispatch of the public affairs, your letters have con-

demned a portion of my time which duty forbids me any longer to devote to them. Your talents as a divine I hold in due respect, but of their employment in a political line I must be allowed to judge for myself, bound as I am to select those which I suppose best suited to the public service. Of the special communications to you of his will by the supreme being, I can have no evidence, and therefore must ascribe ⟨all of⟩ them to the false perceptions of your mind. It is with real pain that I find myself at length obliged to say in ⟨common⟩ terms what I had hoped you would have inferred from my silence. Accept my respects & best wishes.

TH: JEFFERSON

This gloved insult would have crushed most men, but it did not silence Austin; on March 20 he sent another letter offering political advice and appealed once more for Jefferson to allow him to help the United States. He ended by thanking the president for "the polite note with which you was pleased to honor me." In the meantime, Austin had turned his writing to the publication of tracts. In January 1802, he published in Washington "The national 'Barley Cake,' or, the 'Rock of Offence' into a 'Glorious Holy Mountain:' in Discourses and Letters," a ninety-page pamphlet.[12]

After the spring of 1802, Austin's letters became increasingly pathetic. His grandiose plans for an ecumenical revival in Washington met with failure; on April 26, 1802, he was in Baltimore, writing the president to report, "my thoughts are for Phila. or farther eastward." He had remained in Washington "as long as finances would serve" and now he regretfully was forced to abandon his quest for "national harmony." He was enroute to a meeting of the General Assembly of the Presbyterian Church in Philadelphia. "They expect something from me: but I am without strength, until the Presi[den]t pour a little national oil upon my head."

On May 4, 1802, however, he was back in Washington requesting the job of collector for the port of New London, Connecticut.[13] For the first time, Austin revealed something of his personal life. He wanted the New London post because it was

> such a very short distance from the residence of my father in Law & of Mrs. Austin who is at present, with her father. The family is opulent & distinguished for their probity and punctuality. Mrs. A. is a Candidate for perhaps 30,000 dols. at her father's decease, who is a man of 80 years of age, & she is unwilling to leave the neighborhood of her parentage & patrimony. On this account my residence at any distance from her is rendered inconvenient.

While he was in Washington Austin presented Congress with a petition "signed by 170 subscribers," proposing that instead of a memorial statue, a national cathedral be built to honor George Washington. Washington's remains would be interred at the cathedral "in token that the glory of Mount Vernon yields to the advancing splendor of the city of Washington." The Clerk of the House tabled the petition.[14]

He next returned to Connecticut where he must have been considered a hopeless failure by his wife and in-laws. His father had been a successful merchant who held an important government post in New Haven, but Austin, after petitioning for two years for a federal job, was forced to return home once more with nothing to show but an empty purse. He had also failed to get an ecclesiastical appointment in Philadelphia.

Jefferson heard no more from Austin for more than a year. Then, in a letter from his wife's home at Norwich, Connecticut, written January 24, 1804, Jefferson read a familiar refrain: "I have a mind to clothe the pacific operations of your administration, with a glade of prophetic lights, such as I perceive the nation is entitled to receive, from the medium of providencial atmosphere in which it moves." He also wished "a station at Washington of easy employment."

The president received one last appeal from Austin, on October 5, 1804: "Should there be any place near your dwelling that might afford me employment & support, I should be happy to lend my aid in the discharge of such duties as might be assigned to me." He was willing to go anywhere, a comment that did not bode well for his family life. This too went unanswered, and as each month passed with no further word from the Rev. Austin, Jefferson's silence seemed finally to have accomplished its intended end.*

JEFFERSON'S procedure for dealing with the hundreds of requests for federal jobs, demonstrated repeatedly in the case of Rev. Austin, was a refusal to reply to them. He considered the message implied by his silence to be perfectly clear: no letter, no job. In an age when the mail system was notoriously undependable, however, no response might mean the letter never got there. This often led to repeated mailings of the same job request. In the case of close political allies, silence could be an affront.

On November 26, 1804, for example, Jefferson sat down at his desk at the President's House and picked up a letter from Larkin Smith, a Virginia Republican who had supported his presidential bid.

---

*Austin returned to Elizabethtown, New Jersey, in 1804, then moved on to New England, where he preached for a number of years in various Connecticut churches. With the death of his father-in-law, he was able to live comfortably on his wife's inheritance. In 1815 he became minister of a Congregational church, where he presided until his death at seventy-two in 1831.

King & Queen [County, Va.] Nov. 10th. 1804

DEAR SIR

I have heretofore taken the liberty of addressing two letters to you, and confess that I feel myself mortified that neither of them have received from you the smallest attention. I did think myself entitled at least to your notice. To this communication I neither expect, or wish an answer; my last letter which was founded in the strictest truth, wore some appearance of humiliation. This I did not feel, because it contained a statement of facts. Since writing that letter I have married the daughter of your acquaintance the late Mr. Henry Tazewell, his patrimony has in a great degree relieved me from my pecuniary embarrasments.* I therefore Sir am no longer an applicant for office, nor should I ever have been, but for the forcible reasons offered heretofore.

When I reflect on the toils attendant on a seven years war, with the ravages which have been made on my constitution; and that my best services throughout my life have been devoted to my country; added to which that I am one of the very few revolutionary characters who opposed their chief in politicks (believing that he had departed from sound principles) and when I view the circumstances which have produced this letter, there surely is some cause for the chagrin which I have expressed in the early part of it.

Being placed on the republican electoral list, I shall probably be chosen an elector for this state; in which case I shall certainly vote for you as President of the U. States for two reasons, first because I disdain to suffer anything of a private nature to affect me in the discharge of my public duties, & secon[d]ly because I think your conduct as the Presiding

---

* Henry Tazewell (1753–99) served in the Virginia General Assembly and state judiciary, and as U.S. Senator from Virginia from 1794 until his death. Jefferson attacked Tazewell in the General Assembly in 1775, but the two men later became friends.

member of our government has been eminently calculated to give prosperity & happiness to your country.

I am with great respect
Your Excellencies Obt. Servt.
LARKIN SMITH

After reading the letter, the president laid it aside, and slipped two sheets of paper in his polygraph, the recently acquired precision writing instrument that made a perfect copy of each of his letters. He grasped a pen suspended in a writing position on the device and dipped it into the inkwell. Simultaneously, a duplicate pen, attached by rods and fine springs to the pen in his hand, dipped into a duplicate ink well. Both pens were lowered to their respective sheets of paper as he wrote:

Larkin Smith, esquire
Washington Nov. 26. 04.

SIR

Your letter of the 10th came to hand yesterday evening. It is written with frankness and independance, and will be answered in the same way. You complain that I did not answer your letters applying for office. But if you will reflect a moment you may judge whether this ought to be expected. To the successful applicant for an office the commission is the answer. To the unsuccessful multitude, am I to go with every one into the reasons for not appointing him? Besides that this correspondence would literally engross my whole time, into what controversies would it lead me? Sensible of this dilemma, from the moment of coming into office, I laid it down as a rule to leave the applicants to collect their answer from the fact.[15] To entitle myself to the benefit of the rule in any case it must be observed in every one: and I never have departed from it in a single case, not even for my bosom friends. You observe that you are, or probably will be, appointed an elector. I have no doubt you will do your duty with a conscientious regard to the public good & to that only. Your decision in favor of another would not excite in my mind the slightest dissatisfaction towards you. On the contrary I should honor the integrity of your choice. In the nominations I have to make do the same justice to my motives. Had you hundreds to nominate, instead of one, be assured they would not compose for you a bed of roses. You would find yourself in most cases with one loaf & ten wanting bread. Nine must be disappointed, perhaps become secret, if not open enemies. The transaction of the great interests of our country costs us little trouble or difficulty. There the line is plain to men of some experience, but the task of appointment is a heavy one indeed. He on whom it falls may envy the lot of Sisyphus or Ixion. Their agonies were of the body: this of the mind. Yet, like the office of hangman, it must be executed by some one. It has been assigned to me & made my duty. I make up my mind to it therefore, & abandon all regard to consequences. Accept my salutations & assurances of respect.

Th: Jefferson

Jefferson's response was direct and sharp, an expression of his exasperation at being placed in the impossible position of either answering every patronage request sent him or suffering the resentment produced by his silence. If he had been willing to allow his secretary to write form letters in response to job requests, he might have resolved the dilemma he describes, but he was unwilling to surrender autonomy over his personal correspondence.

At any rate, Jefferson's explanation satisfied Smith completely; on his return from a visit to the springs of western Virginia for his health in 1805, he wrote a note from Charlottesville apologizing for not paying a courtesy call at Monticello. "In justification to my own feelings," he wrote, "I cannot pass through your neighbourhood without paying to you that tribute for respect which you are so justly entitled to, from your preeminent services to your country." He ultimately received the appointment he had earlier been denied. On September 24, 1807, Jefferson offered the post of Collector of Norfolk, Virginia, to "Col. Larkin Smith," and Smith's name was subsequently sent to the Senate and confirmed.[16]

IN spite of his insistence that he never sent explanations for why he failed to make appointments, Jefferson did send a letter of explanation for dismissing a Federalist office holder. He received the following letter from the wife of Dr. James Mease, physician, agriculturist, and one of Jefferson's fellow members of the American Philosophical Society.[17] Mrs. Mease and her husband undoubtedly knew Jefferson socially when he had been vice president in Philadelphia.

The letter reveals gender priorities that have not changed a great deal in two hundred years. Mrs. Mease had heard that, with the election of Jefferson, the Federalist marshal of the Eastern District of Pennsylvania, John Hall, was about to be replaced by a Republican. Her concern was for Hall's large family, which would suffer from his loss of a job, rather than for the political issues involved. She was also willing to broach the subject with the president when several men were not.

Philadelphia March 20 1801

SIR,

... An opinion is generally entertained here that Mr. Hall, the Marshall, will be dismissed from his office. He is under that apprehension himself, and is made, I have been told, very unhappy by it. I have little knowledge of Mr. Hall, nor have I enquired what was his conduct under the late Administration. Of this, I doubt not, you are well informed, and must be the best judge, but I have learned that he has a very large family, eight children, who depend entirely upon his salary for support; and, should that cease, he has no other probable means of screening them from distress. Several gentlemen were requested to communicate to you the circumstances: they declined interfering. I can not view it in that light; but only as stating a fact, probably unknown to you, which may, perhaps, outweigh circumstances that would otherwise have determined you.

Mr. Hall, I have understood, is not personally violent; on the contrary, a man of mild manners, and private worth. The unfortunate state of dependance on an illiberal and intollerant party, which left not its agents always at liberty to act with moderation, or according to their own inclination may palliate his official conduct if as represented to you, it was improper. And I have no doubt of his subscribing to, and acting in conformity with the most just and equitable principles which now predominate. . . .

I pray you Sir, to accept of my best wishes and highest respect.

SARAH MEASE

Jefferson respectfully acknowledged this letter, but ruled that the political importance of the case exceeded personal consideration. It was a shame the family had to suffer, but this man had done irreparable damage to the rights of others by packing juries, and had to be replaced. And he was replaced.[18]

Mrs. Sarah Mease.
Washington Mar. 26. 1801.

DEAR MADAM,

I am honored with your favor of the 20th inst. on the subject of Mr. Hall, and I readily ascribe honor to the motives from which it proceeds. The probable sufferings of a wife & numerous family are considerations which may lawfully weigh in the minds of the good, and ought to prevail when unopposed by others more weighty. It has not been the custom, nor would it be expedient for the executive to enter into the details of justifications for the rejection of candidates for offices or removal of those who possess them. Your good sense will readily perceive to what such conducts would lead.

Yet my respect for your understanding & the value I set on your esteem, induce me, for your own *private and personal* satisfaction *confidentially* to say that an officer who is entrusted by the law with the sacred duty of naming judges [jurors] of life & death for his fellow citizens, and who selects them exclusively from among his [their] political and party enemies, ought never to have in his power a second abuse of that tremendous magnitude. How many widows and orphans would have been this day weeping in the bitterness of their losses, had not a milder sense of duty in another stayed the hand of the executioner. I mean no reflection on the conduct of the jurors. They acted according to their conscientious principles. I only condemn an officer, important in the administration of justice, who selects judges for principles which lead necessarily to condemnation. He might as well lead his subjects to the scaffold at once without the mockery of trial. The sword of the law should never fall but on those whose guilt is so apparent as to be pronounced by their friends as well as foes.

Pardon, my dear Madam, these rigorous justifications of a duty which has been a painful one to me, and which has yet to be respected in some cases of greater feeling. You will see in them proofs of my desire to preserve your esteem and accept assurances of my highest consideration & respect.

TH: JEFFERSON

Jefferson received many requests for military appointments, but none more colorful—or difficult to read—than the following letter from an Arkansas backwoodsman. His story is a reminder that in the late eighteenth century, European civilization was still confined to a narrow foothold on the American continent.

Arkansas
March The 20th—1807

Th: Jefferson Presedent of the United States

MAY IT PLEAS YOUR EXCELENCE SIR—

After My Redresses to you I shall indeavour to Put you in To The knolige of My Respectlibility and A Circumstance of Dificulaty. I was Born in Virginia. At Ten years old I strayed Away from My Parrents, wandred through The states Till I Came To The Frunttears of Georgia. There was Taken By some Muscac Indians and moved To There Town where I Be Came Naturl To Them and after I got To Be A Man I wondred From Town To Town and From nation To nation on Both the East and the West Sides of The Mississippi Till I got Among the Osag[e]s And from There with The Cyetans and Paunies Till Goverment Pirchisd This Contry.* I

---

* The author refers to Indian nations. The Osages were western Sioux Indians who lived in Kansas, Missouri, and Illinois. The Pawnees were part of the Caddoan family who lived along the Red River and its tributaries in Arkansas and Louisiana. The "Muscacs" were probably the Muskogees of Georgia, part of the Creek confederacy. "Cutans— A name used by [the naturalist Constantine] Rafinesque to describe a fictitious group of prehistoric people who lived in North America." John L. Stoutenburgh, Jr., *Dictionary of the American Indian* (New York: Philosophical Library, 1960), 85. It is doubtful that Howard learned this name from Rafinesque's writings. These are people he reputedly lived with.

Came In and Had A grate wish To Become As one of My Natives. With instruction I Lernt Severl Things But Nothing of importance. Her is whear I Find My difcilty. As I Am Not Like The Rest of My Natives, some to There stores some To There Farms and others To There Branch of Mecanicke. But Me Like Orsan From the Forrist, But First A Litle Better with My Armor For I had a Boe and Arrow and he had No weapon But his own Claus.*

And I had Rather hear the yeals and shouts of My inamee then To under Take any Thing That I Could not Doe. Where In I shall ask The Liberty and honnour of Baring A Commshian in the United States survis, As I May For git Those idle Toys Cald Boe and Arrows and Take up A sord in The Behalf of My Cuntry. An I May say once I Lived By My Boe and Arroes But Now I Live By My sord ind The Behalf of My Contry.

For Recommendations I have None But some smal ones For The use of My Travling and with out Relations or Frends Except The Common sorce of The Cuntry. If you would wish to see Me Personly I will Take The Troble To Come To The Sitty By having My Requist granted and sent To me As A Pointment For The same.

I am your humble servant
W A HOWARD

My Bodly Apearance will Be Recommendation But smal. In stature, it will Be thought that I am weak and Feable But [I am] Able to Bare a Comision If A Land the Liberty.

---

* The children's story, *Valentine and Orson,* is a medieval romance that became a popular sixteenth-century English chapbook. It was among the favorite adventure stories of eighteenth-century children. Twin boys are abandoned by their mother, one to be raised as a prince, the other, Orson, adopted and raised by a bear—hence, his only weapons are his claws. The brothers eventually meet, fight, and Orson is tamed by Valentine's kindness. The similarity of the writer's being reared by Indians and Orson by a bear, and the eventual return to civilized life by both, explains the obvious appeal this story had for Howard. Humphrey Carpenter and Mari Prichard, eds., *The Oxford Companion to Children's Literature* (New York: Oxford University Press, 1984), 557.

John O'Neill, an itinerant Irishman and self-styled "Citizen of the World," also wanted a military appointment. He wrote several long, chatty letters to Jefferson, and apparently also visited the President's House—one of many instances of the accessibility of the nation's chief executive to virtually anyone who wanted to see him. O'Neill was typical of many firebrands who emigrated to the United States as fugitives from an unsuccessful Irish rebellion against England in 1798. They invariably allied themselves to the Republican party and were considered dangerous "Jacobins" by the Federalists. This explains O'Neill's political difficulties in South Carolina. His letter also demonstrates the kind of adventurer drawn to the new Louisiana Territory, a man who in de Crevecoeur's words, "no sooner breathes our air than he forms schemes and embarks in designs he never would have thought of in his own country."[19]

Washington 30th. Oct 1805

His Excellency Ths. Jefferson

SIR,

I have not the honor to be personally known to your Excellency therefore you will no doubt think it strange to receive this letter from a person of whom you have not the smallest knowledge. But in order to state to your Excellency in as few words as possible the purport of this address, I am a young man, a Roman Catholic who had been born and partly educated in Ireland but finding like many others who had been compelled to Migrate from that Kingdom in consequence of the late troubles which had almost overwhelmed that unhappy Nation That it was impossible for me to do anything in my Native Country. I came into this Country a few years since as an adventurer but having had the [m]isfortune not to be bred to any particular profession which [I] can attribute to no other cause except that [I] had from a very early period cherished a design of entering into either the Land or Naval Service of this or some other Country whose Government would be congeneal to my wishes.

On coming into Boston in the State of Massachusetts which happened to be the first place that I had arrived at in America [I] had applyed to some of the principal Characters in that City in the view if possible to obtain a Commission to go out in a Frigate which had then been about to sail for the Mediterranean. But my efforts at that time proved unsuccessful. I however proceeded to Southwards particularly to the State of South Carolina where [I] had resided for some years; but during my residence in that State had the disagreeable misfortune to be known to a Host of Scotchmen and their offspring who had emigrated some of them since the Revolution in this Country and others of them still later.

They finding that my design was to get into the service of America and differing in political principles with them, for in a word they are all Monarchyts and they are all Tyrants, they were resolved to frustrate my design if possible by fabricating erroneaus Stories of me to those whom they knew were disposed to befriend me, which they Maliciously did and thereby my efforts in the State of South Carolina became as inefficient as those which I had made in the State of Massachusetts. I have ever indulged in the hope that this last effort will prove more successful than those which [I] have hitherto made. But should it happen to be otherwise I shall be fully contented to relinquish every claim to America and her service and either go to Europe and apply to some of those powers now at war or retire to the Territory of Louisiana. . . .

Looking upon myself at present as a Citizen of the World and as yet Isolated from the great mass of mankind and consequently not having much experience in the mode of addressing by letter highly respectable Characters I had thought it the least presumptuous plan to be the bearer of this Epistle myself that thereby you may have an opportunity of seeing the person who has had the boldness to address your Excellency this very prolix letter which should it please your Excellency to give me some little Office or appointment in that extensive Country of Louisiana It should be my constant endeavour to merit the same by fidelity and an indefatigable attention to whatever business I should be assigned. May I have the satisfaction in whatsoever Country or situation [I] may be in to hear of your Excellencies long continuence of your Natural powers unempaired to conduct the Helm of this Extensive Country which are the sincere wishes of your Excellencies Mo. Obt. Hum. Servt.

JOHN O'NEILL

The author of the following letter does not specify what kind of military appointment he is after, but he leaves no doubt that he wants to serve his country, or as he puts it, he "pants to shed his blood." Jefferson received a number of letters such as this from young men with no particular talent but their patriotism.

Balt[imore] April 12th 1801

Thomas Jefferson Esqr.
MOST HOND. SIR

I presumtively address your fealing soul; although elivated in lifes highest perogative. I daime to request what in my Country's cause, and for my Country's glory, and for the perminant establishment of that liberty, for which my father shed his blood you will not, you can not, refuse. Although a destitute young man of Eighteen, I reste asured of generious patronage, in your patriottic soul.

Then Hond. Sir, to one who pants to shed his blood, and to one, whose soul Burnes to raise a monument of heroism to his Country's fame, grante him Kinde Sir, but Small the means, & he presumes to raise them to as yet unheard of glory. No hills, no dailes, no ballus[trades] shell impeed his course.

With the Greatest Respect I am Hond. Sir
Yr. Very Obd. Hbl. Servent

BENJ W STUART

The acquisition of the Louisiana territory by the United States in 1803 prompted a number of young men to apply for the new governmental positions needed to administer that vast region. The following application was forwarded by Jefferson to the Treasury Department. The reason he did not ignore it as he did most other such letters may have been a piece of information that the writer, James Law, included: that he could "produce Recommendations from some of the Principle Republican Citizens" of Pennsylvania. In virtually all appointments for patronage positions, Republican credentials were absolutely necessary; Jefferson had decreed that no Federalists would be appointed until Republicans achieved parity in governmental positions. The fact that Law's father had died in the battle of Brandywine during the Revolutionary War would have been a recommendation to either political party.*

It may seem surprising that Law was a teacher; his spelling and punctuation are embarrassingly poor. Aside from the phonetic spelling, however, his letter is reasonably well written, particularly for one who was self-educated. Country schools at this time taught little more than the three R's, and he appeared to be well enough qualified for this—spelling excluded.

---

* According to Robert M. Johnstone, Jr., Jefferson had four criteria for selecting appointees to vacancies: "evidence of sound Republican sentiments; a record of military service, preferably in the Revolution; proper geographical distribution of offices; and a reputation for respectability and standing in the community." "The Presidency," in Merrill D. Peterson, ed., *Thomas Jefferson, a Reference Biography* (New York: Charles Scribner's Sons, 1986), 357.

New Jersey State Somerset County Near Princeton
[9 November 1803]

WORTHY SIR,
  You will perhaps be surprised at receiving this leter from
a person whome you have never so mutch as heard of before,
but I hope you will excuse my freedom as I had no other way
to introduce myself to your notice, and being encouraged by
the Character that I have heard you represented under that
is a benovelent friend to mankind and one who did not pay
attention to fortune, but to abilities and principal. I had no
person to make application for me I therefor Concluded to
make application to you myself in this maner and leave it to
your Honour whether you thought me worthy of your attention or not. If you think me worthy of your notice I Can
produce Recommendations from some of the Principle
Republican Citizens of the State of my good Conduct and
fidelity.
  I am now in my twenty sixth year a Pennsylvanian by
Birth: I left my father three months before I seen the light.
He fell at Brandywine fighting for his Countrys rights which
you are now maintaining to the satisfaction of a great majority of the American Citizens. I am the only Child and had the
misfortune to loase my surviving parent at five years of age.
I was put to a trade but not being able to folow it after I had
learned it on account of my health: I was then without Learning or any way to maintain my self but by Perticular attention I learned to write a tolerable hand and got acquainted
with figures and was soon Capable of teatching a small school
which I now folow for a Living.
  I have from my earliest Days been fond of acquiring
knowledge and wishing if it was posable to attain to something greater than a Country Schoolmaster. I did not know
to whome I Could apply with more hopes of success than to
you Sir who has so mutch in your power and who I belive
from every information to be a friend to the unfortunate and
virtuous. I have nothing to recommend me to you or any

other person but my Character and behaviour and I am proud to say that I have ever suported a good Character. By the Late traty with France I supose there will be a Number of young men who may get into imp[l]oy in the Louisana Country or in the Indian department as I find by your speech to Congress that you intend establishing trading houses among them. Perhaps Sir I might be Capable of acting in some of them places to the advantage of Country. If you Sir should see fit to put me into some small post or office whare I might make a living and acquire knowledg and Reputation, I should indevour as far as my abilities would permit to gain the aprobation of my patron by my fidelity and appications to business. If it is posable for you to do anything for me in that way I shall try to express my gratitud beter by my actions than by my words.

If you think me worthy of your attention a line will be attended to as soon as recieved. In Hopes of your approbation I Remain your

Humble Servant
JAMES LAW

The following letter purports to be written by a four-year-old boy, requesting a future appointment as a midshipman in the navy. What is surprising about Jefferson's reply is the age at which it *was* possible to apply for such a commission.

Annapolis March 4t. 1805.

DEAR SIR,

Having had the honour of being named after You by my Father, and having now arrived at the Age of four Years old, permit me to congratulate You on your being again elected the President of the United States. Your Election having been secured to You by the Unanimous Voice of fourteen States, and almost by the Unanimous Voice of Maryland must be particularly gratifying to Your feelings. Long may you live to retain Your Faculties, and in the hearts of your fellow Citizens to be the President of the United States. An Administration so wisely conducted since You have been at the head of it no doubt must as long as you live secure to You, the good Wishes of Your Citizens.

Could it be possible to give a Youth of my Age the appointment of a Midshipman in the Navy. It would be very gratifying to me, and when I arrive at a proper Age, would then come forward and fill the Station in the Service of my Country.

> Permit me to Subscribe myself
> With the most profound Respect
> Yr. Obt. Servt.
> THOMAS JEFFERSON GASSAWAY.

The president replied:

> Colo. [John] Gassaway
> Washington Mar. 12. 05.

SIR

I have received a letter, which I presume I may consider as coming from yourself, proposing that your son, of 4. years old only may recieve the appointment of a Midshipman. After acknoliging my sense of the kind disposition manifested in the name given him it is my duty to observe that the earliest period at which midshipmen are recieved is about 10. years of age, when they have learned to read, write, and the first rudiments of arithmetic. Until that period therefore nothing of this kind can be done. Accept my salutations and respects.

> TH: JEFFERSON

Some of the requests received for governmental appointments were in reality expressions of the fantasy lives of men trapped by obscurity and unhappiness. Writing to the president was like buying a lottery ticket to adventure, excitement, travel, and a new way of life. The following letter is as revealing for what it fails to say as for what it states. The writer lives with his wife on his father's farm in southeastern New Hampshire, forced to do work he dislikes and is physically unsuited for. He obviously longs for independence from his father, but his letter ends by suggesting some of the reasons he has failed to achieve it. His greatest fear is that his request to Jefferson for a governmental position will somehow be made public and he will be considered a fool by his neighbors.

Pelham [New Hampshire] February 14th 1806

His excellency Th. Jefferson President of the U. States

EXCELLENT SIR,

The person who now addresses you is a Young Man, inhabitant of Pelham N.H. My design in addressing your Excellency will appear by the following letter. But before I proceed on my main design, I will give you a short account of my life.

I was born in the Town of which am an inhabitant AD 1780, of honest and reputable parents. My father possesses a considerable farm for this neighborhood, which was new when he began upon it, & being always in debt he got but a comfortable living. It was his desire that I should labor with him on the farm, which I did untill about sixteen when I received about a Years schooling, which is the greater part of educational advantages I ever received; Since which time have married, & live & labor on the farm with my father.

Nature never favoured me with that athletic Constitution, which admits of very hard labor, & as very hard labor is the only means I now posess of acquiring property, I see but very little prospect unless I can get into some other business, but that myself and family must remain indigent & obscure. My object in now addressing you is to enquire whether it will not be advantageous to the United States, & Satisfactory to Your Excellency to employ me in some of the inferior offices of Government, to which a competent Salary is appropriated, that by prudence & economy I may raise myself & family above the power of want. Was my military figure commanding, I should request an appointment in the Army of the United States, But this is by no means the Case. I might however by practise & perseverence overcome some of my natural difficulties, & make a decent military officer, but I should prefer a civil appointment in any office & in any place, to which your Excellency may think my abilities competent. I have not the Temerity to request an office of any great responsibility, my highest wish would be gratified by an office, which would allow me to show my good qualities, if I have any. . . .

No mortal to my knowledge except myself ever saw or knew one syllable of this letter. You Sir on reading it will immediately know what use to make of it. I know you will not delight in torturing the feelings of inexperience. My mind will be filled with very great anxiety untill I know the fate of this letter, & could a few moments be spared from those important concearns which occupy your attention, just to inform me, with what feelings you receive this letter, it will give me inexpressable satisfaction. Should you view this as an idle attempt of one who ought to remain in obscurity, after informing me you will let it sink into the deepest oblivion. But I fondly anticipate the pleasaure of hearing the call of my executive to partake of the dangers, fatigues & honors, of a public life.

There is a Post office in this Town, Pelham N.H., to which if you direct a line, I shall soon to receive it.

I long for an opportunity to be usher'd into the world,

where I can have a view of those book[s] which contain those dark principals of Science, which I long to know. I long for an opportunity to raise myself into honest fame—to be usefull to my Country & to raise myself & family above t[he] power of Want. Pardon Grammatical errors, & forgive mistakes. I have heard it said that great men are apt to be forgetfull. I hope that forgetfullness will not be the cause of any injury to me, do let this be remembered by you at least a short time. But Sir I have written enough, to determine you to grant my request, or to refuse it. So excellent Sir permit me to Subscribe myself your devoted friend & Servant.

Asa Gage Jr.

P.S. If you should wish to know any more particulars respecting me, I should be happy to inform you & perhaps I could obtain some others to be my sponser.

It is comforting to discover that the Jefferson administration had its whistle-blower, if only a modest one. Charles Steele, a messenger at the War Department, was so outraged at being peremptorily fired that he wrote a blistering catalogue of alleged abuses by his boss, William Simmons, head of the department's accounting office.

Steele began writing his letter October 1, 1806, but he did not finish it until three and a half months later, probably because he held the letter for some time, trying to decide what to do with it. Although his indictment is addressed "To the Publick at Large," it was finally sent to the president.

Washington City October 1st. 1806

To the Publick at Large—

Wm. Simmons has turned his Messenger out of Office. What for? Not for neglect of his duty in the office as A Messenger nor for neglect of Wm. Simmons own privet duty

which all the naibours knows how I work for him and Cries
out shame. He never gave me any notice. I knew nothing
about it till two or three days before Quarter day—I went to
ask him for some wood; he then told me he did not no whether
it was worth while to give me any, that he must get an other
Messenger.*

I then asked him his Reason, if I had done any thing Amis
in the Office or if I did not do my duty in the office as the
Rest of the Messengers. He said I did. I then asked him if he
ever asked me to do any thing for him by day or by night
that I did not do. He said no there was nothing but I did that
he asked me, but he said his Spirit was so grate that he Could
not ask me to do what he wanted me to do, that he would
get one and make the Bargan with him, what he must do for
him before he would take him in the office. He said that it
was my duty to be every Morning at his house before I went
to the office and work about his house and Likewise every
afternooon and do what he had to do. He said he expected
the same of my wife to assist doing the work of his house. I
said Mr. Simmons I have done a grate deel of work for you
since I have been in the office and I am willing to do any
thing now. I take it very hard Mr. Simmons to be turned out
of office with out A fault at this time of the year. If you had
of given me three Months or till spring I should not care but
he said it was too Late. . . .

I have been in the office since 1799 and never had a word
with him in anger and did all that ever he asked me to do. I
always thought him a friend of mine but now I find him to
the Contrary. He is an enemy to me there fore I think its
Proper to let the Publick know what for a Carictor he is.

First when he moved to the City of Washington he Charged
the Publick fifty Dollars for Damage of furniture when there
was not fifty dollars Damage. I Can sware because I helpt
him to Pack and on pack them. When the Publick found all

* Quarter day was the beginning of a three-month work contract.

the heads of Departments and Clerks Horses in hay while doing duty at the office, the Secretary of War and Simmons had A stable together for there Departments and Bought hay together. Simmons, when the office was out, would take the key and at night would send his Black man with fore or five horses to the stable and feed them on the Publick hay all night and then take them out early in the Morning and send the key to my house so that no body would take notice of it, and send to my house and take one Load of Publick Cole after the other for his use.

When I left his house and moved to his other for his Mother to move in, I had a bout Sixty Bushels of Cole and about two Cords of wood and better which he kept for his Mother the Poor widdow as he Calls her. When he Bought wood for me he would generally Purchase for himself too and take two or three Cart Lods of mine to his house. When he would Purchase Cole for the Office he would for himself also and send A Bout one hundred Bushels of the Publick Cole to his house.

He Received one Thousand Dollars a year for the use of his office. He kept that money to buy Lots and build and let his office Suffer. He would buy fethers instead of quills, twine in stead of tape, keep all Locked up. If a Clark wanted a quill or paper he must ask pleased to give me a sheet of paper or a quill. He Could send me home to his house with Lodes for the use of his family and had to be saven because he made use of the money. He had to get a note Discounted every Month all most to keep up his Credit; one note Discounted to take up the other.

He Caught the naibours fouls and Ducks. Some he would keep and some he would send to his Mothers. He Caught a Bullock, sawed of[f] his horns, filed out the Brand on his horns, fed him awhile and made his black Man kill him in his horse stable. He gave the Black man a small hatchet to nock him down. He hollered Repeat your Blows, Repeat your Blows you damn black son of a bitch. Make hast and get the hide off. He took A handsaw from the office belonging to some of the Carpenters that was at work there. He made his Black man go to Samuel Davidsons fence, take the Rales to fence in his lot, buy things for the office and take them home for his own use.

He would get Drunk and stay two or three days from the Office and betend to be sick. All the while he was Drunk sick. He is guilty of many durty tricks which I could mention but I Conceive there is plenty so I leave the Publick to judge—the Above is just and true.

CHS. STEELE

The A bove I intend to put in the publick p[r]int because he is not fitt to hold that office. I hope your honour will excuse me for the Liberty I have taken and Consider the above Carictor.

January 17th. 1807

If Simmons learned of Steele's letter it may have caused him some embarrassment, but it did not cost him his job. He remained in office the entire eight years of Jefferson's presidency.[20]

3

Youth

"That treasure for which his soul pants"

THE Great American Dream of rising from poverty to wealth and fame, which had first been distilled in the nation's consciousness by Ben Franklin's Poor Richard, found renewed impetus during the presidency of Thomas Jefferson. Young apprentices, mechanics, and farmers saw in Jeffersonian democracy the vision of a better life, and they recognized, as Franklin had, that the way to a higher calling was through education.

They also knew that the president of the United States was an advocate of state-supported schools and of educational opportunities for the poor. In *Notes on the State of Virginia,* a work widely quoted in newspapers and magazines, Jefferson called for a universal-educational system that would select bright students from the laboring classes and give them an education at state expense. "By that part of our plan which prescribes the selection of the youths of genius from among the classes of the poor," he wrote, "we hope to avail the state of those talents which nature has sown as liberally among the poor as the rich, but which perish without use if not sought for and cultivated."[1] Such a plan was to remain a chimera for generations, but the man who proposed it was seen by many young men as a potential patron who would make the dream of education a reality.

The aspirations of America's young men are reflected in the letters written to Jefferson requesting books, tuition money, or educational advice. (Jefferson received no such requests from women, for daughters of poor farmers and mechanics had little opportunity or motivation to seek a liberal education. As letters in this collection will show, there were many "ladies' academies" for the daughters of those who could afford the tuition.) Before institutionalized public education gained a foothold in America in the mid-nineteenth century, patronage was still one of the main hopes for an education by a poor but ambitious young man. If he could secure the sponsorship of an affluent relative or friend, he might have his schooling subsidized. When all else failed, many young men appealed to the patron of last resort, the president of the United States, a man known for his generosity.

Lewis Mayer, an eighteen-year-old saddler's apprentice, is typical of the young men who poured out their ambitions to better themselves through education. "A burning desire vibrates in my breast," Mayer wrote, and he described this agitation to Jefferson in what he must have considered an appropriate length for one who aspired to a writing career— eight folio pages.

He insists, in his opening paragraphs, that he has abandoned all titles of rank and privilege—no doubt to show his independence—but it demonstrates the appeal that republican egalitarianism had for the nation's aspiring youth. His stilted diction is obviously an attempt to demonstrate literary talent.

Frederickstown (Maryland) Feb. 21th. 1802

Thomas Jefferson L.L.D.
President of the A[merican] P[hilosophical] S[ociety]
and President of the United States of America.

ILLUSTRIOUS PATRON

Permit, I pray, an unfortunate youth to approach your
pressence, and expostulate with a freedom, which nothing
but his knowledge of your benevolent character could induce
him to take. I beg leave to address you in the plain style of a
simple unpollished youth; and hence my first request is, that,
the usual compliments paid to persons in high stations, may
be dispensed with. I beg pardon if the rusticity of my manners should be offensive to the refined policy of well bred
characters. I am sensible of the respect which is due to the
chief magistrate of the Union, and beg leave to assure you of
my profound esteem for your character in every station of
life, which you have held, wether in a public or private capacity.
You will, perhaps, smile at this simple appology; but a regard
to my local condition will obviate displeasure.

My esteem for your character is not lessened by a disre-
gard of personal distinctions. I consider such distinctions
derogatory to the honour of the President of a brave, free
and enlighten'd people: the titles of "Lord" and "Excellency"
may delight an aristocratic ear; but the dignity of a free republic
is wounded by the expression: the illustrious names of
"Patriot" and "Sage" are more gratefull to a great soul, and
create a more sublime idea than all the pompous train of
hereditary titles can inspire. . . .

My nativity is Lancaster in Pennsylvania. I was born to
no patrimonial estate. My father, George Lewis Mayer, was
a mechanic; he was an emigrant from Germany and was well
versed in the German & French, and indifferently in the Latin
& English languages: his fortune was low, and he left this
earthly stage when the morning of my days scarce had dawned.
My mother (left alone) with five helpless orphans, was not

in a condition to give her children a proper education; she design'd me for a mechanical profession, and to such I am now apprenticed; but, perhaps to my missfortune, the narrow compass of mechanism is a province too small to admit the contemplated prospects of my mind. I have an aversion to manual labour: altho' my time is occupied by this duty, the speculative powers of my mind are expanded over a wide field of scientific contemplation, and the intellects are closed against all other than literary improvement: my natural genius prompts my soul to these pursuits: a burning desire vibrates in my breast: the obstacles which Fortune has oppos'd to it, can only retard its progress; but all the torrents of adversity can not extinguish the flame.

To the study of Literature are devoted all my leisure hours: but these are few; my means small, and my improvement in proportion. The English language, Geography, and that part of Astronomy which constitutes the link between the two sciences, Eloquence, and Politics are my favourite studies. In the English language & Geography I acquire improvements with most facility; in Politics & Eloquence I am dilatory. In the study of the latter I labour under some natural impediments, which are, a defect in my pronounciation, and a too great sensibility which, too often, produces an ill-tim'd blush: but, I flatter myself that, these obstacles are vincible; and, from an instance, which the pages of history unfold, I have the most flattering prospects of future excellence. . . .

The great aim of my ambition is to cast my mite into the transatlantic scale of literature; but, unfortunately, poverty excludes me from a participation in the toils for American glory: therefore do I lay my case before you, and pray for your assistance. I am destitute of money, books and freinds; and have not the means of procuring them. I have wealthy relations, but these, occupied entirely by the mechanical and commercial habits of life, are not disposed to encourage eny tendency but that which relates to lucrative gain. If your character were only politically great, I would despair of success; but those virtues, which dignify your social character, give me the highest encouragement. . . .

It can not be unknown to you, that, a genious should not be mar'd by the opposition of a duty which is foreign to its views: to hold in one view two objects, diametrically opposed to one-another, will destroy both, and to force a genius to inimical pursuits is an impossibility. Hence the inference is obvious, that, as my future prosperity & happiness are objects of consideration, I must abandon, entirely, the mechanical habits of life, and apply my time to the study of the musses only. I could with inexpressible delight, renouce Mechanism with all its promised advantages, if Fortune would conde- scend to lead my steps in the path of Literature.

Another principle no less conclusive, argues the expe- diency of excuting immeadietly my contemplated design. I am now near the period of my nineteenth year; an age wherin the intellectual powers are most susceptible of improvement, and the passions most glowing. At a more advanced age, when the mental faculties will have recieved the taint of man- hood, they will not, with great facility, acquire new ideas; and the pride of that fluctuating state is not easily subdued to subordination and colledge discipline. This, then, is the favourable moment which should not be neglected. . . .

My deficiency in books is one of the principal obstacles to my literary progress: Morse's Geography abridg'd; the sec- ond part of Webster's Institute; and a few other books of less value, constitute my whole library: I need not observe, that, in such a predicament, my improvement must be slowly pro- gressive.[2] These guides lead me through the outlines only of those sciences, and then lead me in an abys of darkness, with no other light than that which reason affords. . . .

Allready do I anticipate the sweets of Literature: the idea of Learning diffuses inefable pleasures in my mind; excites the most gratefull feelings; and fills it with a theme which words can not illustrate. My soul hovers over the literary stage; my imagination dwells on your patronage; my happi-

ness stands on a precipice: Pause! illustrious sir! Pause a
moment befor you decide their fate! Reflect that your country's service and my happiness are at stake; let not an unjust
diffidence supercede the more noble principles of Patriotism
and Charity; reject not the prayer of an unfortunate youth;
but open your bosom to his affliction, and participate in his
missfortunes by a small sacrifise of that wealth wherewith it
has pleased Providence to bless you: the object is great, and
the gratefull remembrance of so noble an act will be ample
reward. I am, with the

most profound respect,
Your obedient humble Servant
LEWIS MAYER

P.S. I am not able to defray the expence of postage of this
address. I beg pardon for its length. My place of residence is
at the house of Mr. Jacob Heiner Junr. Saddler.

The following two young men also asked Jefferson's aid
in getting an education. Like Mayer, they were apprentices
with little schooling, but with an eager desire to break the
generational lockstep of working as a tradesman. The first
letter, from a fourteen-year-old boy, illustrates the frustra-
tions and despair produced by the medieval apprenticeship
system of vocational education engrafted on the political
egalitarianism of the new American republic. The ideals of
American democracy, that all men are created equal, had
planted in the hearts of bright, sensitive young men the perception that being apprenticed by legal contract to a master
craftsman, who had total control over how you worked and
how you lived, was tyranny. It precluded the possibility of
intellectual upward mobility, because many masters were
unsympathetic to abstract learning and refused to provide
their apprentices with even the bare rudiments of reading

and writing that their contracts called for. Republican ideas profoundly altered the institution of apprenticeship in America. The authority of masters was eroded, and apprentices became more independent and freethinking.[3]

Young Samuel Holmes at least had the advantage of being apprenticed to a printer where he would become literate, but, like Ben Franklin, he seethes with the desire to make more of himself.

Brooklyn May 17th 1803

To Thomas Jefferson Esqr:
President of the United States of America.

Dear Sir,

For some time past I have been endeavouring to find out Some method by which I might obtain Learning. At length I have (as I knew not of any so likely method by which I could acquire it) [decided] to write to You.

Sir—In the first place I will give You a short detail of the Circumstances of myself and then the reasons which induced me to take the Liberty of writing to You.

1stly. My father is poor; and is my only parent thats is living. He is old and is now I expect among the Indians, there sent by the Baptist Misionary Society of New-York.[4] He has given me but a little Learning, though as much as he possibly could afford. At twelve Years of age I was bound an apprentice to the Printing business wher I still remain.

2dly. But Learning is my object, the sole cause of this letter, and what renders me unhappy because I cannot attain it. Finally, (O do consent) it is to ask the boon of You.

Excuse me dear Sir if what I am saying is wrong. If Fortune will not smile when You receive these few simple lines (simple, for perfection cannot be expected from a boy of only 14 Years of age, with no more Learning than barely to read and write.) then will I call myself the happiest of beings, but if not, why I suppose I must bear it with patience as Job did, when he felt the rod yet blessed God.* That this request may succeed, will from this time to the time I shall receive an answer, (for do please to write a few words in return, if not I shall be more wretched than ever) be most earnestly prayed for. O God Interfere!

Dear Sir if You will but consider that my relations are poor and not able to grant such a request, and knew my thirst for Learning You would not think my asking it of you strange. I cannot ask you in any grand style which perhaps might be rather more agreeable to You, for I am Yet too young. And again I repeat it, if I have said any thing improper please to forgive me—What more can I say? Why my dear sir, no more than the Glorious word Learning. Learning the greatest blessing, the only ornament and jewel of man's life—and to conclude that I remain now Your unhappy, but when at the arrival of the answer with the transporting Consent! Then Your O ever happy Friend and

Humble Servant—
SAMUEL L. HOLMES

P.S. Please to excuse me for the manner in which this Letter is wrote as the time I had to write it in was in the working hours. Please to write a few words in return and direct to

Samuel L. Holmes
at Mr. Thomas Hirks Printing Office
Brooklyn Long Island

Eben French is another apprentice whose aspirations collide with the brute realities of a family shattered by a father's death, and with it the hopes for a "classical education." Like young Samuel Holmes, three years as an apprentice have

---

*From the rhyming alphabet in *The New England Primer,* 1727, under the letter J: "Job feels the Rod Yet blesses GOD."

produced a strong desire to escape the tradesman's life through education.

Boston, Oct. 29, 1804.

His Excellency Thomas Jefferson Esq.

HONORED & RESPECTED SR,

You will forgive an illiterate youth, whose ambition, perhaps, may lead him beyond the steps of modesty, in asking of you a favor which perhaps, may never be in his power to repay. I was the son of a poor, though respectable tradesman in this town, who has long since paid the debt of nature. As my mother had nought to depend on except that which she earned by her daily labor, two brothers of us, out of four, fell into the hands of an uncle, an honest upright, man, who has been a father to us, and did his means accord with his will, I should have no occasion, Sir of addressing you, at this time.

My mind was ever bent on a classical education, & since I have commenced my apprenticeship, which is now three years since, I have had a more ardend wish than ever to obtain that education. Of all my friends not one possesses the power to assist me. Could I find a benefactor, my eyes should never be closed in sleep until a prayer was addressed to God for his welfare & prosperity—And gratitude towards my benefactor should ever be a predominent feature in my character.

I have made bold Sir, to address you, hoping I shall give no offence, and if you can find in your heart, a wish to assist a youth to obtain that, which fortune has denied him—He will ever conceive himself your debtor, even should it lay in his power at any future period to repay You to the utmost farthing.

I am sir, with Respect

Your Excellency's Most
Obedient Humble Servant
EBEN FRENCH

P.S. Condiscend to return an answer and confer a favor, which shall never be erased from my memory.

A quiet revolution in higher education was just starting in New England during Jefferson's presidency. Before 1800, college education had been restricted to a wealthy class of farmers, merchants, and businessmen, who attended Harvard, Princeton, and Yale. By the end of the first quarter of the nineteenth century, however, eight new colleges had been founded, including Dartmouth, Brown, Williams, and Amherst, and to these institutions streamed an unprecedented number of impoverished students. As many as one-fourth of the students enrolled in these new schools were the sons of poor farmers, tradesmen, or clergy who could not afford the costs of a higher education. Such students found money for tuition from such sources as loans and gifts from friends and relatives, but also increasingly from the students' own labors, in jobs that forced them to interrupt their educations. The student bodies of these colleges slowly changed; the teenaged youths of a previous generation were now mixed with mature young men who had returned to college after several years of work to earn their expenses.[5]

Levi Hurt and Thomas Skidmore came from this new underclass of students; they have managed to stay in school for a time, but their money, and their resources for obtaining it, have run out and they now make one final appeal to the president for help before being forced to drop out of school and go to work.

Preston (Con) 18th May—1801

HON'D SIR—

Permit me a moment to solicit your attention from the affairs of a great nation to the situation of an unfortunate young man. Nothing but a profound sense of the generosity of your character, and a conviction of the absolute necessity of the measure could persuade me to make this almost desperate attempt to recover from the embarrassed state of my affairs.

My father the Revd. Levi Hurt of Preston (Con) gave me early, a domestic education, and at the age of 14 (in the year 98) I was entered freshman into Rhode Island College.* His kind solicitude for my welfare assisted me through my first year; at the commencement of my second he informed me he could help me no longer, but if by my own exertions I could continue in College it was his desire that I should. An anxious desire of improvement in science and relying on my youth determined me to pursue my studies. I am now entering on the last term of my Junior year and find myself in debt to the amount of one hundred and fifty Dollars, to borrow which sum is the object of my present address to you.

If you should be pleased to answer my wishes I bind myself by every tie of gratitude & honour to repay the sum in the following manner Viz—fifty Dollars—1st of April, 1803—fifty Dolls—1st October, 1803 and the remaining fifty the 1st of April 1804. I name these periods knowing it will be in my power to fulfill my engagement. If you should see fit to assist me please to ⟨write⟩ to *Providence* (R.I.) where I shall await y⟨our⟩ answer. Permit me Sir to mingle my prayer with those of a great people that your life may be long, useful, & happy.

I am Sir your Obedient humble Servant
Levi Hurt Jun.

P.S. As my receiving a Letter from you Sir, would be a matter of wonder will you be so good as not to frank your answer if you should see fit to comply with my request.

Levi Hurt Jun.

---

*Rhode Island College, founded 1764, is now Brown University.

Weston, (in Fairfield County and State of Connecticut)
Monday June 6th. AD 1808.

To Thomas Jefferson Esquire,

Sir,

The occasion of this letter to you from a youth who is
totally unacquainted with your person may indeed incite your
astonishment. I fear that I may incur the epithet of presum-
tion by thus making known to your Excellency the motives
which prompt me thus to address you. But I trust you will
do me the justice to believe that what I allege as the motives
for thus intruding myself into your notice, are founded in
sincerity and candor. . . .

A liberal education cannot be obtained without pecuniary
assistance; and, unhappily for me, I am destitute of this aid.
My Father, early perceiving my inclination to attend to the
sciences, was anxious to have me pursue them; but finding
himself wholly unable to afford the requisite aid for this object,
he told me, one day, that if I could, without his assistance,
obtain that education which I so ardently desired, I should be
welcome to the time that would elapse before I could accomplish my purpose. Since this declaration I have endeavored
to obtain the education I desired; but the difficulty I find in
procuring pecuniary assistance has retarded my progress
materially and threatens to frustrate all my attempts. . . .

I am Now at an Academy in this town gaining all the
instruction of which I am susceptible; but alas! I foresee that
I cannot support myself here longer than this quarter, which
expires in the month of July following, unless your Charitable hand can afford me some assistance. "And why should
you afford me any assistance?" perhaps you will say; "Why
bestow aid on a stranger, a person in obscurity without
knowing what use he will make of it?" But again I repeat it;
I reiterate, that the sole object for which I ask this assistance
is only to enable me to obtain a classical learning; and not to
gratify the mercenary views of myself or any one else. No

one indeed knows that I am writing this or ever intended it. It is my own free act without any influence from any person or consideration but that of an ardent, laudable desire to obtain that instruction, which is, in a manner, the "life of the soul."

Pardon the liberty that a youth of seventeen, has taken, in thus (I fear you will say) audaciously presuming to address You, Sir, the Chief Magistrate of the nation. Look on this production with an eye of charity and do not, I intreat you, draw an unfavorable conclusion from its contents. Consider it as the effusion of an illiterate and obscure youth; but a youth who wishes to wipe the reproach of ignorance and obscurity from his eyes; who anticipates with anxiety the dawn of a happy stage of life, from the hope of attaining that treasure for which his soul pants. And, if agreeably to your will and pleasure, you think proper to grant me but a trifling subsidy, be assured, Sir that I will accept it with the warmest gratitude and forever remain—

> Your most faithful obedient and humble servant,
> THOMAS SKIDMORE

Note. As soon as you receive this, if it is agreeable to your pleasure, I wish you to write to me and on the outside of the letter inscribe these words "To be left at Bridgeport post office."

> Yours &c—THOMAS SKIDMORE

If there was any single way of wheedling a response from Jefferson, it was to ask him about books—not for money to buy them, but for information about them. He owned one of the largest private libraries in the nation, and throughout his life he was an omnivorous reader, on a wide variety of subjects. Few realms of human knowledge were foreign to him. Jefferson did not respond to the following letter from Samuel Demaree, a young Kentuckian with a crippled arm and priggish morals, but he did to later ones. Altogether, he wrote three replies to letters from Demaree, two of them after his presidency. All of them were about language or books. Demaree later published a newspaper in Kentucky, the Danville *Informant,* from 1805 to 1810.

Harrodsburgh (Ky.) Jan 6th 1802

Honble Th. Jefferson, P[resident] U.S.

Dear Sir,

Reflecting on the happy situation of America—that her Rulers are not inaccessible tyrants nor bloody despots; but patriots, friends of mankind, and of the unfortunate; examples to the world & patrons of science, I am emboldened to communicate a few of my wishes even to our chief magistrate, which however defective in form and matter, I hope you will not attribute to any unworthy motives.

For your satisfaction I would just inform you, I am the son of a a poor but independent *farmer;* in the dispensations of divine Providence, I am nearly deprived of the use of my right arm which consequently prevents me from engaging in the peacible employment of husbandry, and almost forces me to seek the tempestous road of public life: which I will gladly do if I may be of service to my country.

It must be painful to every patriot, to see the negligence and supineness of the youth here—how ignorance and vice triumph over reason and knowledge! Pardon me if I entreat you, if possible, by some method or other to inspire my fellow youth with application and virtue. I forbear saying anything about our masters lest for want of penetration I might mistake: but I would fain see them more concerned for the advancement of their pupils, and the improvement of science.

I am particularly unfortunate in a way of precuring Books. No peculiar friend of extensive information to whom I might apply for direction in the purchasing of books—there are many branches of the sciences, and different authors have written on the same branch—so expensive that I cannot buy them all, and ⟨I⟩ know not which branch, and what author thereon, is preferable: I therefore humbly request you to send me the names of those books which would make the cheapest and most useful *library** for an individual citizen. From your extensive knowledge of books I was induced to apply to you, and from your goodness as a literary character I hope you will indulge me a little in this request. If you are so good as to take notice of this, I entreat you to add what directions and information you may think proper, and I will cheerfully attend to them: but if [I] have erred (as I possibly may) and you should not think it worthy of attention, at least pardon me for intruding upon you thus—my intention I trust is philanthropic.

If you should grant my request I will rejoice, if not, I can but bemoan my ignorance and misfortune: yet I hope to remain a sincere patriot and admirer of your conduct hitherto and as long as you shall be worthy, which I hope will be untill you descend with honor to the grave.

Yours affectionately,
Saml. R. Demaree

* What Authors on Rhetoric, Logic, Philosophy, Astronomy &c by name if you please, *Simson's* or *Barrow's* Euclid—S. R. D.†

John Norvell also requested information about books. His letter coaxed a reply from Jefferson by asking how to obtain "sound political knowledge," but he also received one of the most important statements about the American press that Jefferson ever wrote.

† Robert Simson, *The Elements of Euclid* (Glasgow, 1756); Isaac Barrow, *Euclid's Elements* (London, 1660). Both of these works were published in a number of editions.

Danville, K[y]. May 9, 1807.

VENERABLE REPUBLICAN,

Some benevolent writer observes, that happy is the person who has an instructor to point out to him those books which ought, and those which ought not to be read, and the manner in which they ought to be read. Feeling the force of the observation, and believing that you would take pleasure in giving good advice, I take the liberty to ask your opinions respecting some subjects, of which no person, perhaps, has a greater knowledge than yourself.

It is well known that your time is employed in more important and beneficial concerns, but it is fondly hoped, that you will find a leisure moment to confer a benefit and favor on an individual.

I should be glad to have your advise of the proper method to be pursued in the acquisition of sound political knowledge. Is it essential that much history should be read? And if it be, be so kind as to mention those authors which should be read; as likewise those writers on political subjects, who may be studied to greatest advantage. And any other advise on those points would be gratefully acknowledged.

It was a maxim of the great and good Dr. Franklin, that "time is money," and my situation, being such as enables me to devote but a small portion of time and attention to books, has been the principle cause of my taking the liberty to trouble you.

It would be a great favor, too, to have your opinion of the manner in which a newspaper, to be most extensively beneficial, should be conducted, as I expect to become the publisher of one for a few years.

Accept venerable patriot, my warmest wishes for your happiness.

JOHN NORVELL

Jefferson's reply to Norvell has been frequently quoted because it expresses his views on two important subjects, British history and the American press. His opinion that "nothing can now be believed which is seen in a newspaper" was the result of relentless, scurrilous attacks on him and his Republican administration by the Federalist press. In the history of American journalism the Jefferson era marked a low point in objectivity and truthful reporting. The newspaper wars between Republican and Federalist editors were a no-holds-barred slugfest, with lie and libel the favorite weapons on both sides.

Why Jefferson chose to write this long, thoughtful response to a stranger can only be guessed at. Norvell's letter seemed to have caught him at a moment when he was particularly sensitive to what he considered to be distortions in British history by a gifted philosopher, David Hume, and to the continuing assault on the presidency by Federalist newspapers during the Burr conspiracy trial taking place at this time.

Mr. John Norvell
Washington. June 11. 07.

Sir

Your letter of May 9. has been duly recieved. The subject it proposes would require time & space for even moderate development. My occupations limit me to a very short notice of them. I think there does not exist a good elementary work on the organization of society into civil government: I mean a work which presents in one full & comprehensive view the system of principles on which such an organization should be founded according to the rights of nature. For want of a single work of that character, I should recommend Locke on Government, Sidney, Priestley's Essay on the First Principles of Government, Chipman's Principles of Government & the Federalist. Adding perhaps Beccaria on crimes & punishments because of the demonstrative manner in which he has treated that branch of the subject. If your views of political enquiry go further to the subjects of money & commerce, Smith's Wealth of Nations is the best book to be read, unless Say's Political Economy can be had, which treats the same subjects on the same principles, but in a shorter compass & more lucid manner.* But I believe this work has not been translated into our language.

History in general only informs us what bad government is, but as we have employed some of the best materials of the British constitution in the construction of our own government, a knolege of British history becomes useful to the American politician. There is however no general history of that country which can be recommended. The elegant one of Hume seems intended to disguise & discredit the good principles of the government, and is so plausible & pleasing in it's style & manner, as to instil it's errors & heresies insensibly into the minds of unwary readers. Baxter has performed a good operation on it. He has taken the text of Hume as his ground work, abridging it by the omission of some details of little interest, and wherever he has found him endeavoring to mislead, by either the suppression of a truth or by giving it a false colouring, he has changed the text to what it should be, so that we may properly call it Hume's history republicanised. He has moreover continued the history (but indifferently) from where Hume left it, to the year 1800.**

* John Locke, *Two Treatises on Government* (London 1789); Algernon Sydney, *Discourses Concerning Government* (London, 1763); Joseph Priestley, *An Essay on the First Principles of Government* (London, 1768); Nathaniel Chipman, *Sketches of the Principles of Government* (Rutland, Vt., 1793); *The Federalist: a Collection of Essays;* 2 vols. (New York, 1788); Cesare Bonesana, Marchesi di Beccaria, *An Essay on Crimes & Punishments,* translated from the Italian (London, 1767); Adam Smith, *An Inquiry into the Nature and Causes of the Wealth of Nations,* 3 vols. (London, 1776); Jean-Baptiste Say, *Traite d'Economie Politique* (Paris, 1803). Say's Law, that the supply of goods is always matched by their demand, was the historical authority for supply-side economists of the 1980's.
** David Hume, *The History of England,* 8 vols. (Edinburgh, 1754–59); John Baxter, *A New and Impartial History of England* (London, n.d. [c. 1796–1801]). Jefferson has been accused of attempting to censor Hume's *History of England* by promoting Baxter's *His-*

The work is not popular in England, because it is republican, & but a few copies have ever reached America. It is a single 4to. [quarto] volume. Adding to this Ludlow's memoirs, Mrs. McCauley's & Belknap's histories, a sufficient view will be presented of the free principles of the English constitution.*

To your request of my opinion of the manner in which a newspaper should be conducted so as to be most useful, I should answer 'by restraining it to true facts & sound principles only.' Yet I fear such a paper would find few subscribers. It is a melancholy truth that a suppression of the press could not more compleatly deprive the nation of it's benefits, than is done by it's abandoned prostitution to falsehood. Nothing can now be believed which is seen in a newspaper. Truth itself becomes suspicious by being put into that polluted vehicle. The real extent of this state of misinformation is known only to those who are in situations to confront facts within their knolege with the lies of the day. I really look with commiseration over the great body of my fellow citizens, who, reading newspapers live & die in the belief that they have known something of what has been passing in the world in their time. Whereas the accounts they have read in newspapers are just as true a history of any other period of the world as of the present, except that the real names of the

tory, a republicanized version of Hume, which "gives you the text of Hume, purely and verbally, till he comes to some misrepresentation or omission . . . then he alters the text silently, makes it what truth and candor say it should be, and resumes the original text again, as soon as it becomes innocent, without having warned you of your rescue from misguidance." Jefferson believed Hume's *History* was so well written that its Tory bias would be seductive to Americans. (Jefferson to Matthew Carey, 22 November 1818.) See Leonard Levy, "Civil Liberties," in Merrill D. Peterson, ed., *Thomas Jefferson, A Reference Biography* (New York: Charles Scribner's Sons, 1986), 339.

* Edmund Ludlow, *Memoirs of Edmund Ludlow, Esq.,* 2 vols. (Bern, 1698–99); Catharine Macaulay, *The History of England,* 9 vols. (London, 1763–83); Jeremy Belknap, *The History of New Hampshire,* 3 vols. (Philadelphia, Boston, 1784–92). Belknap's *History,* which included the colonial period, was a Whig interpretation of British Parliament and a defense of American republican government. He was one of the founders of the Massachusetts Historical Society.

day are affixed to their fables. General facts may indeed be collected from them, such as that Europe is now at war, that Bonaparte has been a successful warrior, that he has subjected a great portion of Europe to his will &c. &c. but no details can be relied on. I will add that the man who never looks into a newspaper is better informed than he who reads them: inasmuch as he who knows nothing is nearer to truth than he whose mind is filled with falsehoods & errors. He who reads nothing will still learn the great facts, and the details are all false.

Perhaps an editor might begin a reformation in some such way as this. Divide his paper into 4. chapters, heading the 1st. Truths. 2d. Probabilities. 3d. Possibilities. 4th. Lies. The 1st chapter would be very short, as it would contain little more than authentic papers, and information from such sources as the editor would be willing to risk his own reputation for their truth. The 2d. would contain what, from a mature consideration of all circumstances, his judgment should conclude to be probably true. This however should rather contain too little than too much. The 3d. & 4th. should be professedly for those readers who would rather have lies for their money than the blank paper they would occupy.

Such an editor too would have to set his face against the demoralising practice of feeding the public mind habitually on slander, & the depravity of taste which this nauseous aliment induces. Defamation is becoming a necessary of life: insomuch that a dish of tea, in the morning or evening, cannot be digested without this stimulent. Even those who do not believe these abominations, still read them with complacence to their auditors, and instead of the abhorrence and indignation which should fill a virtuous mind, betray a secret pleasure in the possibility some may believe them, tho they do not themselves. It seems to escape them that it is not he who prints, but he who pays for printing a slander, who is it's real author.

These thoughts on the subjects of your letter are hazarded

at your request. Repeated instances of the publication of what has not been intended for the public eye, and the malignity with which political enemies torture every sentence from me into meanings imagined by their own wickedness only, justify my expressing a sollicitude that this hasty communication may in no wise be permitted to find it's way into the public papers. Not fearing these political bull-dogs, I yet avoid putting myself in the way of being baited by them, and do not wish to volunteer away that portion of tranquility which a firm execution of my duties will permit me to enjoy.

I tender you my salutations & best wishes for your success.

TH: JEFFERSON

Norvell, who was only seventeen years old when he wrote to Jefferson, did go on to become a newspaperman, and a highly successful one. He learned the journalistic trade in Maryland, studied law as well, and in 1817 purchased the Lexington *Kentucky Gazette*. Two years later he bought an interest in the Philadelphia *Franklin Gazette*. Norvell then moved to the Midwest, became involved in Michigan politics, and ultimately served as U.S. senator from that state from 1837 to 1841. He kept faith with Jefferson's request not to print his letter; Norvell held it until after the former president's death on the Fourth of July, 1826, then printed it in the *Aurora and Franklin Gazette* on September 9, 1826.[6]

THE following young man, an orphaned merchant's apprentice, asked Jefferson's help in achieving his ambition to go to sea. He was certainly naive, however, in expecting the president to supply money to a boy under eighteen to break his apprenticeship indenture in order to become a sailor.

Boston July 14 1806

S<small>R</small>,

A lad or a young man presumes to adress you & request such a favour as probably never was asked of you or perhaps an[y] one else before. I am a lad living in this town with a respectable Merchant. Being peculiarly unfortunate while very young in losing both my Parents, I am indebted to a very distant relation for clothing & Board (as it is not the Custom in this place for Merchants to allow their apprentices Anything untill they become eighteen or nineteen years old). My relation is not in Circumstances if she were willing to advance me even a very small sum, for me to Risque as an adventure to Sea, which always has been my wish. Under these Circumstances I have presumed to adress you & to request a Small sum for the above purpose, k[n]owing you to be very Rich, & a part of a days service of yours to goverment given to one of you[r] Subjects in a short time with good luck might make a rich man.

If you should feel disposed to comply you would lay me under Eternal obligations, who would esteem it an honor to subscribe himself your Well Wisher & Humble Servant—

L<small>ACOSTA</small> S H<small>ARRIS</small>

A precocious boy of fifteen, bold enough to criticize Jefferson's politics, but not enough to sign his name, sent the following letter. This is the second of two letters he wrote; it is a catalogue of Federalist attacks on the president during his first term in office. Jefferson wrote after the endorsement, "abuse."

Petersburg Va., May 9th. 1802

Thomas Jefferson Esqr.

SIR

Some time in February last I wrote to you to which I beg Responce concerning the opinion I then entertained of You and your proceedings. Since then I have waited with impatience for either a private or public Declaration of what you and your Tribe of foreign outcasts really had as a Heart—but that Declaration has not yet appeared. But you and your jacobine-Democratic Tribe of Sycophants still continue to carry on your hellish Deeds—which I pray God may not prove the Destruction of this Country—which all the powers of that warlike Nation Britain could not do. Even Tommy Jeffersons *Bosom Freind France* endeavoured to injure us, but by the prudent Conduct of your predecessor John Adams—their Designs were frustrated—even since they have set you by their midnight Machinations, into the presidential chair. . . .

I address you for your own Sake as well as for the Sake of our country—to reform your conduct like a true Repentant and let the Americans—more particularly the Virginians see they were not mistaken in the choice of a President, for Sir if you do not—I could almost venture to swear that in the course of two Years or perhaps less Time you have not one real Friend—for those you have here and in Richmond are daily—nay hourly forsaking you. Even Callender whom you always upheld has entirely forsaken your cause.* Had I seen such a Letter as this addressed to You twelve Months ago—I should have thought the Writer insane—but Sir when you consider the many Hardships We are likely to undergo—nay are now suffering—I say of you consider that all the evils we endure originate from your imprudence. You cannot

*James Thomson Callender is the newspaper editor who publicized the story that Jefferson kept a black mistress, Sally Hemings, at Monticello and fathered five children by her. Callender originally supported the Republicans but turned against them when he felt he had been slighted by Jefferson.

for a moment blame me—with either imprudence or pre-sumption. In hopes that the feeble Efforts of a youth of fif-teen—may in some Measure assist in the Reformation of the conduct of the President of the United States—I beg leave to subscribe myself

A Lover of his Country

In reading the following letter, one wonders whether the young man who wrote it was indirectly offering sexual favors to the president of the United States. There are a number of hints that this may have been the case. He was, he writes, to be "received by some Gentlemen with great pleasure" in Washington, to have the cost of his voyage from England paid for, and get "an annual pension" for doing no particular work. The only reason he gives for expecting this bountiful treatment is his "polite Education." His letter is full of pas-sionate rhetoric—"I fly to you," "throbbing bosom," and "dear to my heart." There is also the unnecessary assurance of dis-cretion—the "greatest propriety."

On the other hand, the age was awash with sentimental language, as many of the letters in this collection demon-strate, and a young man educated at Oxford or Cambridge may have been merely writing in the fashionable idiom of his day. There is no record that Jefferson ever responded to the letter.

[received 5 April 1803]

Mr. President

I am an unfortuante young Man lately arrived from Eng-land—I came over to this Country, having first received a polite Education in one of the first seminaries of my native soil. What chiefly influenced me to take this step, was 1st because I imagine that a change of climate would greatly contribute to repair my constitution, which long study had somewhat injured—& 2dly. because I received intelligence from some member of the College in which I was educated, that in the vicinity of Washington I should be received by some Gentlemen with great pleasure, have the expenses of my voyage defrayed & an annual pension of £75. I set sail in consequence in a vessel bound to New York. The Captain's demands were forty Guineas. On making the land of *Liberty* I had not a greater sum than £10—which was scarcely sufficient to pay the expenses of my journey from New-York to Washington.

At length I reached the city—But alas! how were my expectations frustrated, when I found that the reception I experienced, was quite in opposition to that whch had been represented to me before my departure from Europe.

Mr. President—for a young man to find himself in a foreign land without friends—without money, is a situation truly deplorable—but for a Person destitute of friends & money to experience ingratitude from those—whom he expected at least would treat him with civility, is a situation which cannot be conceived, unless by those who feel it. Such, Mr. President is my present unfortunate state. I am perhaps destined by Fate to suffer misfortunes—I know not—but I am certain at least that You are able & I feel myself convinced that You are willing to assist me in my deplorable condition. You have a noble & generous Heart—and since generosity resides in Your Bosom, You cannot read my misfortunes, without feeling compassion. I fly to You, because I know that You take delight in succouring the miserable. Cast on me, I beseech You, a propitious glance.

Mr. President

By the love of Your Country—by all that is sacred & all that is dear to You give relief to an *unfortunate*. If such is Your conduct, You will forever be dear to my heart. I shall love, reverence, & esteem You as a father—and certainly with the greatest propriety.

To conclude Mr. President

I request, entreat & beseech You to pour into my throbbing bosom the balm of consolation by assisting me in a manner becoming You the greatest ornament of a free, an independent Nation.

I am Mr. President

> Your most Humble but unfortunate Servant
> W F HARLE

Many of the letters Jefferson received from young men were unrestrained expressions of adulation. The following letter, sent when Jefferson was leaving office after two terms as president, was a request for his secret of success. Curiously, the writer signs only his initials, presumably because his family was known to Jefferson. After the endorsement, Jefferson wrote "respectful."

The letter begins with an address to "the Father and Protector of youth" who is "the brightest example of the effect of industry combined with talent." Jefferson has shown to the world "that in an Elective Government it is possible to be raised to the highest stations without having deviated from the faith, of virtue and honor." It continues:

> Charleston (So. Car.) 21st March 1809

... When I beheld you in the exercise of your Official duties, it was impossible that I could avoid feeling an anxious wish that I could have marked out to me, the outlines of the path you trod to greatness. Not, that ever my soaring ambition could ascend to the height, which you have so lately voluntarily left. Not that even in the pleasing dreams of anticipation, this Golden prospect was ever presented to my mind. No—my views were more confined. I would pursue the same cause which you have done, and strive to ascend as high as industry and virtue will exalt me. When I behold a great Man I am always induced to believe that he has become so by pursuing an uncommon road, for how many thousands who tread the beaten path, and who add the most persevering industry, to natural vigor of mind, perish in obscurity. Fully convinced of this, I am induced to request that you would point out ot me the way to Glory—You have been a successful traveller there. You then can surely direct me.

In History we admire the characters of eminent Statesmen and renouned Heroes, but we have not seen recorded the *private plans* they followed in order to become so. We are told indeed how Demosthenes, and a few others acted, but these accounts are either too romantic for belief, or by no means satisfactory. It is from living characters therefore that we must seek this information. And Sir, if all the great Men of Antiquity could this moment rise from their Graves, and dwell in our Country, I yet would make the inquiry of you.

I have not explained the motives of this application. It may not be *now* proper for me to inform you of my name. It will be sufficient to say that I am a Young Man whose character in his native State has not yet been clouded by the breath of Calumny. Perhaps Sir, my name might be an advantage to me. But disdaining to receive any favor through the merits of my Ancestors, I am induced to rest my claims upon your kindness alone. It is not impossible but that at some future period I may have the happiness of returning my acknowledgments in Person. Should you be disposed to gratify me in this my request you will please direct to A. U. at this place.

> I am Honored Sir, with
> every sentiment of Esteem
> Your most obt, servt.

Of all the patriotic letters Jefferson received, none was more so than this one from an anonymous fifteen-year-old Philadelphian. His youthful enthusiasm compensated for his slender mastery of the language.

Philadelphia,
[received 31 July 1806]

To his Excelency Thomas Jefferson Esq.

SIR.

It is A Boy of 15 years Old Address to You the following lines. I feel A Strong regard for my Country's welfair.

I think if I had A been Presendent at the time them opposen Set of People (I allude to the Brittish) appeared before Newyork I Should A been for rasing all the Naval force in the United States and opposed thire proceeding's. My Father is an Englishman Born. Ever Sence I had any knowledge of Nation affaires I dispised them tirents as there are. I often read of the American War. I fear they Never will Come hear Again. I think if they Should I take up armes boy as I am in my Country's Defence. If every one was as true to thier Country as me I think the Contest last war would not of been of so long Duration. Conquer or Die is my Wash Word.

A True American though a Youth

Huza to the Constetuon
Huza to the Repubeck
Huza Fredom Independence
Huza to all America.

PS. Sir Excuse the spelling.

4

Women

"Our sex being very prone to importunity"

IN the paternalistic culture of early nineteenth-century America, men often found it difficult—or impossible—to ask for aid, because other men interpreted it as a sign of weakness and failure. Women, on the other hand, were bred to dependency; as daughters they were little more than servants, and as wives mere housekeepers. Women had to ask— often beg—for their needs, first from a father, then a husband. It is little wonder then, that more women requested aid than men.

For these women, it was not enough to ask directly for money or a job; they felt it necessary to touch the sensibilities of the reader by invoking images of widowed mothers, drowned sons, hungry babes, suffering parents, or destitute families. This was the stuff of sentimental fiction, which women of every age and class in early nineteenth-century America devoured eagerly from books in lending libraries or in magazines. Epistolary novels modeled after Samuel Richardson's *Pamela* and *Clarissa* were particularly influential because they provided a pattern for a young woman's letter-writing style. The American epistolary novelists, most of them women, elicited sympathetic tears with plots involving catastrophic losses, attempted seductions, and tragic deaths, narrated in a diction exquisitely tender and pathetic. This language of sentimentality found its way inevitably into the private letters of the readers of these novels.[1] It can be seen in the diction of much of the unsolicited correspondence written to Jefferson, but especially in the letters from women.

The willingness of women to entreat when men remained silent, and the language of sensibility characteristic of these solicitations are both demonstrated in a letter from a farmer's wife, Jane Savary. Because women were "very prone to importunity," she was not only willing to ask Jefferson for money to save the family farm, but she also requested a job for her son-in-law and offered to sell a slave. She was aware, however, that her family would disapprove of the "bold act" of asking the president for help; therefore, like a number of other women, she wrote secretly.

Mont-azile, Prince Georges, Maryland
21 February 1807

Sir
　. . . My husband, Peter Savary who for a great many years past, has always with good success conducted his farm, which is a property estimated at about £5,000, so as to save it from any incumbrance, being now far advanced in age, his endeavours have not been lately Crowned with the same good fortune. The crops have been scanty, our Stock reduced by sickness and although we have denied ourselves some small luxaries our family were formerly used to, yet he has not been able to defend himself from seeing his debts accumulate to the amount of about $1,500. The greatest part of these, judgement has been obtained against him and he is threat-

ened every day to see his property sold by the Sheriff perhaps for half the value. He is a stranger in this Country and can or will apply to nobody. These gloomy thoughts prey upon his mind, and he is pining away visibly.

In this circumstance I thought that a bold act projected by me alone and unknown to any body, and charging myself with all the consequences if I act improperly, which I as a woman am not able to discern, particularly in a case where distress of mind deprives me of the power of reflection. The favor I come to sollicit of you Sir is great, great for *me,* but gratitude shall erect a monument in my bosom, which no time shall decay, no power overthrow. I can expect no compliance from my friends and acquaintances these being either unwilling or unable, therefore must rest my only resource in your exorable and beneficent heart that flies to the relief of the distressed.

Our farm if well managed, can clear 4 and 500$ a year very easily, which our meadow alone annually produces. Thereby you will please to observe, that in the mediocrity we live, we can be very well contented. Our family only consists of 5. Persons my Husband, myself, my daughter, and son in Law, a Gentleman from Poland, who after the Revolution of his Country travelled through great many Countries and at last sought an abode in the regions of Columbian Liberty, and after an unfortunate trial in trade was obliged to retire to a farmers life. Besides we have an Italian young Lady, a refugee from St. Domingo, whose husband was massacred there.*

If the farm is sold our repose is disturbed, and we see no way of support with the small residue that would come to us. Therefore I undertake to fly to your clemency for Protection, and humbly pray to save us from ruin. It is in your

---

* She refers to the virtual annihilation of the French army in 1802 by warfare and disease after it failed to capture Santo Domingo from native forces led by Toussaint L'Ouverture.

power I know it, and such a deed for which I come to crave your kindness will enable us to continue our industry for the sustenance of ourselves as we have been used to. It is, Sir, to advance us the Sum of 1200 or 1500$, for which we will make an annual payment of $4 or 500—which with redoubled activity and after having once extricated ourselves from the Labyrinth of sneaking Debts, Suits & judgments, which are always attended with gnawing expences, it will be a very easy thing to shew ourselves just and accurate to our promise.

I would have prevailed on my husband to address you on this subject himself, did I not know that his present weak state of Health will not permit him to use any mental exertions. But should you, which I fervently hope (as it is my only one), graciously grant my humble request, he will not loose a moment to give you the necessary Security for such a benign act, to which I shall myself in particular attend to as being the premum mobile of it.

The bearer, our Servant Tully, a Boy about 24 years old a capital waiter and excellent Carriage driver, has order to find himself a master for $500—which he is well worth. Should you be in want of such a character, he is at your service for the above sum. A favor I have to add to the foregoing is to excuse my forwardness, and the trouble I occasion you, and to bury it in oblivion. Having already the pen in my hand, and our sex being very prone to importunity, I request another favor of you not for my self but for my Son in Law. He is a young Polander as I have already mentioned of a very good family, speaks and writes several living languages to perfection as I am informed, and is fully penetrated with veneration for your merits and reputation. He wishes an opportunity to employ his talents more usefully than on a farm, and to have at the same time a comfortable living. Can his services be any ways acceptable to you? He holds them entirely devoted to you.

In hopes of a favorable answer, I raise my hands up to

heaven and pray for your health and life and will always call
my self as I have always done heretofore

> Your Excellency's
> Most Obedient and
> Most humble Servant
> JANE SAVARY

Anna McKnight also wrote Jefferson without the knowledge of her husband and she, too, faced the loss of her home.
Unlike Jane Savary, she is unwilling to sell her two slaves.

Darkesville, Berkel[ey] County [Va.] October 29 1802*

To the first and best of Men

SIR

Permit & Pardon a female Now in humble Life & one that
was Bred up & for Many years has Lived in Eas & affluances
tho Now at the Eage of '73 is in a fair way to be Reduced to
Extream want to Lay her distress Before her Beloved President. My husband Mr Robort McKnight was true a harted
DemoCrat as the[y] Call him, as Ever lived & as honest a
Man & by his Polictks has been thrown out of all Business
& by his good Nature in being sacurity for a friend has Put
our Little Movable Property in the Power of the shariff which
Consists of 2 slaves & some furniture. My slaves are as My
Children & if I Could Procure 5 hundred Dollars I can secure
all I have sir, 2 houses & Lots in this Place which is 3 Miles
from the Sulfer Spring, one of which I would Morgage or
indeed give a Clear deed of for the Money. It Rents for 90
Dollars. If I can Procure this sum by the first of Desember it
will be a great Blessing to me.

No one on earth Knows of My writing. If My persumtion

* Darkesville is now in West Virginia.

is too Great distress alone and the exalted oppinion I have of your Exalancy Must Plead for [me] & you sir Can throw it in the fire. If I am honnord with any Notice Mr. Wm. Sumervill Post Master in this County will send it [to] me safe. My Husband is a very Macanicle Charractar having Been Breed a Mill Write in his youth. If your work, & where fit, would have ocation as for such a Person to superintend, an honister & more faithfull Man I am sure you sir Could Not imploy. PerMitt me once more to implore your Pardon & to have the honnor to subscribe My Self your sincear tho humble friend & servt.

ANNA McKNIGHT

Mary Osborne wrote two letters to Jefferson; the first, requesting money for her mother, was signed with an assumed name—an anagram of her own—and was delivered in person to his office. It, too, was written without the knowledge of the one she was attempting to help. The second was a request for money for her sister and brother-in-law. Mary Osborne, like Mary Ingraham, Jane Savary, Anna McKnight, and other women who wrote to Jefferson, requested aid, not for herself, but for a husband or close relative. Women's traditional role of caretaker—mother to the young, nurse to the ill, companion to the aged—is seen repeatedly in these appeals for help, not for the writer herself, but for a close family member.[2]

City of Washington Dec 29 [1803]

Mr. Jefferson

SIR

You who have studied your peopels happiness and so generaly bestowed it will no dought be surprised to be individually asked for assistance and from an intire stranger. The motives which induce me to so an action as appl[y]ing to one in the station Mr. Jefferson holds, if I was to relate particularly would plead my pardon for so bold an intersession.

A daughter beges for a widowed mother whose misfortuns have bean many and who has long suferd bodly and mentily with a tender family whose sex will not permit them to seak a livly hood from under her protection. My Mother keeping a shop of Ladys goods and as the summer being very dull and this faul unhealthy in conciquence my Mother could not intirely pay her Merchant and as this is the only seson of year which bisness can be done with the help of som friend my Mother could free her self from all incomberence and doe very well at her imployment.

The many liberal bestowments Mr. Jefferson has give in incoragin arts and industry and his munificence to the unfortunate has made me hope and dare ⟨ask⟩ him to be my mothers friend and if Mr. J————n can put so much confidence ⟨in the⟩ word and honasty of a femail and Lend my mother five hundred dollars for ⟨. . .⟩ Months for with in that time it shall be returned. It will inabel my ⟨mothe⟩r with industry and the incom of a small property establish her self in her bisness and free her self from all det. If Mr. Jefferson can make it convenint and find satisfaction in granting my reqest and make a mother and family comfortable and happy he will never have cause to repent a bounty and charity which will never be forgot and ever greatfull for and punctuably returnt.

I am sencibel I have broke throw thos ruls surscrib to my sex and actud undutifull with out my Mothers knowledg and unnone to any person solisited Mr. J————n friendship and for fear of miscarage asked it in a fictitious name. If ancred [answered it] shall be known.

If Mr. Jefferson is so Beneficient as to grant the above favour he will please to ancerit this week and direck it to

Susana P Roboson
City of Washington

PS Mr. Jefferson will blame but if he new my unhappy resons for so bold a solisitation which principels and sentiment makes shuder at he would pity, pardon and grant and with the hope he will, I conclude a letter which I am sencibel the manar is not proper but the motives great.

With Obd. & Rspct.

S P ROBOSON

Haver de Grace [Md.] Oct 12th AD 1808

RESPECTED SIR

I forbear makeing an apology for this letter and its contents, As I am concious the attempt to make it appear in A more favourable light than your judgement will, is unnecessary. I wish truth to be my only eloquence in pleading my Success and pardon. The one who now dares to address Mr. Jefferson is a female; and candour would bleed! if I did not add it's not the first time. Mr. Jefferson no doubt will recollect the recipt of a letter near five years ago begeing the loan of five Hundred Dollars with the Signature of S Roboson which in truth is not my name, though the world might condemn me for so bold an attempt. Yet I have no painful reflections arising from it, only that of concealing my real name. Can I blush for seeking and asking relief? No I believe the benevolent Soul finds a happiness equal with the one that partakes his bounty, and would not hesitate to ask a favour when needing one.

And on this presumption I have once dared to importune for assistance from one that I hope will have the will and power to grant my request, as I never thought Mr. J['s] silence to my former letter arose from either but from A fear of imposit[i]on, Which Heaven is my witness is not my design. Would my situation in life permit I would appear personlly to Mr. Jefferson and I can't doubt but he would allow my claims to his humanity in the present case.

My first application to Mr. J was in behalf of a beloved Mother who it has pleased God to take to a better World. Since that period I have lived in this County with A Sister whose husband has been unfortunate from a partnership and her portion which she received at her marriage became a sacrifice as well as his. It is for them that I now solicit Charity, yes a bounty that will never be forgotten by me, which I do no[t] wish nor could not ask if I had not a prospect of returning it. In the space of 12 Months from this I shall inherit a small portion from the wreck of my Mothers estate and the only pleasure I can have from it will [be] from its afording the means of living to my disstred [distressed] Sister. Her Husband has heard favourable accounts of the state of Ohio and is desirous of removeing their but is destitute of the means and as I have every reason to think it will be for the better for them, I can not forbear makeing every exertion to assist them which again induces me to seek Friendship from your hand, which Heaven enable you to bestow.

The sum I ask is Fifty Dollars which as I have already said will be a Charity nevery to be forgotten and faithfully returnd in the course of Twelve Months. The errors of this as well as my former letter I am sensible are very great but I hope they will be look'd over, and their real motive & design viewed in a light that will do justice to there intention, and to [a] heart that shuders at what its done in daring to wright to its sovereign. Allowing the expression, I cease farther intruding on the patience of Mr. Jefferson relying on his wisdom and mercy for a propitious answere. Even if M J does not find it proper to grant my request a letter with only three words in it, signifing, the receipt of this will be received with greatude, as it will releive me from the anxiety of fearing my letter had fell in other hands, which I have often feard had happend to the one I have mentioned. Should Mr J grant my petition he will please to direct it to Miss Mary Osborne (which is my real name) Haver de Grace Post office, and I would beg the favour soon, as my Brother thinks of going out this faul.

I intreat pardon

> With Respect
> MARY OSBORNE

The pathetic living conditions described by Betsy Beauchamp in the following letter were also the indirect result of her concern for another family member—her brother, a merchant seaman who had formerly been in the U.S. naval service. Her appeal, however, is for help for her entire family. The British impressment of American merchant seamen was a foreign-policy problem familiar to Jefferson, for it plagued him throughout his presidency. There is no record of his responding to the letter, but in cases such as this where a small amount of money was requested, he often sent it and recorded the gift in his pocket memorandum book simply as "charity."

> [Alexandria, Va.]
> March the 11 day 1806

HONOURED SIR

I am under the obligation to inform you that I am in a distressed situation at present and has ben for three weeks and still grows wors with me for I cant get now work a tal to do and am a suffering for vituals and fire wood. We have maide out all this winter until now. I have aplyd to the Corporation [municipal government] and they say that I and my poor old mother and my sickley husband and my Children, I have foure of them, O honoured sir how it hurts my feelings to think they said I must go to the poore house when my hands does not refuse to work, if I could get it to do for a

suport of life. I Came over heare to Alexandrea upon the
account of my brother Isack Moore being impresed by the
English the first voige he went after he was out of Amarica
sirvice and has ben there going on three yeare. I got a protection and sent it on for him and I trust in god and threw
the wish and proposa[l]s you have maid for the Amaricans,
honoured sir, he will be Cleared.* It is my desire to leave this
place for we have all sufferd a great deal here, sicknes &
poverty. There fore I send to you with tears my dear an
hounere[d] master hoping you will be pleased to think of a
poor distresed woman wors than I have wrote. I humble beg
if you will be pleased to give me something to get me some
provition and pay my pasag a Cros the bay, for there is a
pasag here that we Could get on Thirsday or on Friday if we
were able to pay our pasag. There foure if you will be pleased
send me something [to] Cary me a way I will give ten thou-
san thanks and I hope that God will be your protector threw
life.

BETSY BEAUCHAMP

Honoured master be pleased to excuse me for inter[rupting]
your honour with these lines. It is suffering has made me do
it honoured sir. If it is you[r] good will and pleas[ure] to help
me be pleased to put in a letter my honoured sir.

Like Betsy Beauchamp, Maria Digges dedicated herself to
the care of a brother at the cost of her own economic security. She was a "once happy Freind" to Jefferson, apparently
during his early years as a student or practicing lawyer at
Williamsburg. He refers in his correspondence to purchasing

---

* "Protection" refers to documents proving U.S. citizenship which American sailors
were forced to produce to prevent being impressed from U.S. ships by British boarding
parties. See Harold D. Langley, *Social Reform in the United States Navy 1798–1862* (Chicago: University of Chicago Press, 1967), 89.

a book from a Molly Digges, who may have been Maria or one of her sisters.[3]

Williamsburg Octobr 25 1801

DEAR SIR

Permit me to Congratulate you on being Chose President of my Country. I sencerely Pray every Blessing may Attend you. I Intended to have done my self this Honr before this, but have been very Ill for ten Weeks and have just lost my Dear and only Sister. My other Sister I lost about ten Months. Immagination cannot furnish Ideas Strong Enough to Paint my Distrest and Melancholy Situation. Add to this My Dear only Brother in a Derainged state quite unable to Assist him self on what I can do for him wch is scarse enough to Exist on. Permit my Dear Freind to Ask your Freindship and Attention. I think I am to well Acquainted with the goodness of your Heart, your tender Sensibility, to doubt your sending me a little Assistance. That Being who is a Freind [to] all will reward you.

You will Pitty and feele whin I tell you my Dearest [brother] turned out a Volintear for [h]is Country before he was six-tene, behaved so Well that he got a Captains Commision at Eighteene, Commanded the Garison at this Town with great Apploi⟨ance⟩ and Raised five Countes of Solders for his Countrey. All our Old Freind[s] were very fond of him, but an unlucky affair distrest him. Col. Porte[r]field Struck one of his Solders wch my Brother resented so much that he gave the Col a Challenge wch Obliged him Ether to Arsk Pardon or *resine.** Poor Dear Youth full of Fire, Chose the latter, but

---

* Colonel Charles Porterfield was one of the heroes of the battle of Camden, South Carolina. He died on 10 January 1781 of wounds received in that battle. See Jefferson to George Washington, with a Narrative of the Battle of Camden, 3 September 1780, John Catanzariti et al, eds., *The Papers of Thomas Jefferson,* 3:596. Maria Digges does not give the name of her brother, but he was possibly Edward Digges (also spelled Diggs), who is listed as a captain in the Virginia State Garrison Regiment, and who died about 1816 in Williamsburg. John H. Gwathmey, *Historical Register of Virginians in the Revolution* (Richmond, Va.: Dietz Press, 1938.)

the Gov[ernor] and Counsiler gave him a Captains Comisions in Col Mo[. . .]s Rigiment. Alass that was not filled before Peace so that this young *Man,* had not only lost his time at College but spent his little in raiseing his Men. He Parted with what he could in defence of liberty and wee three Sisters distressed our selves in lending him, Expecting he would be an Honr to his Country.

I Sir have Mintained him for ten Years. His Reson could not bare his Misfortunes. To see us distrest and his Inabillity to Assist was too too much a Melancholy State. He is now left to my Poor Exertions. A Word from you Sir Perhaps may Get the Honble Congress ⟨to⟩ do something to Assist him. . . .

Pray Sir Assist your once happy Freind get something done. I live in a Cottage that I feare will Crush us, and have it not in my Power to Mend. One Hundred Dolalars would mend it so as to make it habitable but I feare being troublesom. Forgive and beleive me your much obliged Fr[ien]d with great Rispect and Warme Freindship your

> Huml. Servt.
> MARIA DIGGES

Hast let there be Musick all thrugh the land
Around your Home may Laurels twine
And evry Voice be tuned to Love and *Peace*
⟨Will⟩ our Worthy President do me the Honr of an Epistle?
M D bleses her self on haveing Mr. Jefferson her Freind.

One of the few women asking aid for herself was Susannah Febvrier, whose husband sailed for Martinique, leaving her alone with two children and no funds. Her appeal is a direct request for money, without any attempt to tug at the president's sensibilities with references to hungry babes and a mother's tears.

Her use of the term "lordship," like Mary Osborne's use

of "sovereign," was not uncommon among less-educated writers. Prerevolutionary forms of address, which equated high governmental service with aristocracy, died slowly in the new democracy.

George Town January 8th 1805

Sir

Please to excuse me for troubling you but my reason for troubling you Sir, is to beg you would be so kind as to helpe me to a little money. I am in Greate distress and have two Children in my armes without any means to Supporte them and rent to pay which I am not able to doe at preasent. My husband was obliged [to] Give all his property up to his Creditors last Spring and finding him Self reduced to such extreem poverty he returned to Martinique where he processes Some property, and from whence he promisd to Send me money to releave me from my distress, but I have not yet received any thing from him. I was Sick all last Summer which prevented me from earning any thing to Supporte my Self and infants with this winter, and in my Greaf and trouble I thought your Condesending Goodness might Perhapes helpe me to something. I Cannot well express myself to you Sir as I am not acquainted with such importance. If the dictates of my letter are wrong I hope your lordship will excuse me. I am Sir your most obedient Servent

Susannah Febvrier

Jefferson quite possibly sent Susannah Febvrier some money; the following year, April 16, 1806, she wrote again, asking for a ten-dollar loan. She was living in Washington, "near your house," and now called herself "an unfortunate widow woman." Her husband apparently died at Martinique.

Susannah Febvrier's husband may have intended to return to her, but the woman who wrote the letter that follows was the victim of seduction and abandonment—a story as old as humankind.

Petersburg [Va.] March 8th 1808.

DEAR SIR

Perhaps you will be Suppriseed to receive a letter from one that you probaly never heard of before, but when you come to know the nature of my business, I hope will Pardon me for my boldness.

I will relate to you my unfortunate situation in a concise manner as possible.

I was born at Lexington in Kentucky of Poor but honest Parents, had a tolerable education for my rank in life, as my mother doted on me and I was thought a great beauty but alass! the Scene is changed. My body is a perfect Skeleton now and the lord I hope will spare me to see them again. Oh! the Perfidy of mankind! Will it never cease?

Suffice it to say that I was seduced by a young man of fortune, as he pretended to be for he always had plenty of money, but my father would not consent of his proposals as he never liked a man from the town, as this man told us that he lived in Baltimore. His name is James Hargrave. We arrived in Petersburg last September and lived as man and wife until about 20th last December when on pretence of business in Philadelphia he left me and said would be back in a fortnight and I have great reasons to suspect will never return. He left me about 12 dollars which I have nearly exhausted. Honored sir if you have any compassion for a Penitent that wishes to return to her distracted Parents by sending money, as much as you think will do, she will consecrate her remaining life to your goodness.

Your fellow being
MARY L. MINOR

Many of the women who wrote to Jefferson were widows. This is not surprising, because some 10 percent of the women in early America were widowed.[4] In addition, the Revolutionary War had produced a class of women seeking war-widows' benefits from the goverment; many of these women appealed to the president for redress.

The loss of a husband could be a catastrophe for women of this period. They were ill prepared for a sudden thrust into a world of independent responsibility. Often with large families to support, and no experience in working outside of the home, with little or no formal education, and less self-confidence, they were extremely vulnerable to a slide into deprivation and want.

A number of these appeals for help came from widows living in the District of Columbia—Washington, Georgetown, and Alexandria. The Washington area had become a magnet for families hoping to find work in the new capital. Those that failed often became destitute. The following two letters are typical of the condition in which many women found themselves at the death of a husband. For many, the only hope was to abandon the city and return to their family in the country.

George Town—Saturday Morning March 9th. 1805.

Mrs. Mary Bond, an unfortunate woman, left a widow, with four small Children, pleads great poverty, makes application most humbly to Mr. Jefferson, President of the United States, for a little assistance, being this present time, without one single cent; and what is an addition to her destress'd situation, in a strange Place, and without one friend, to render her the least service, although she solicits every comfort in life, for she now wishes to incist, that with the help of a little money, will carry her into the Country, to her friends, whom she is in hopes, will do something for her, in her very unhappy situation.

Concludes beging leave to subscribe herself—

Your Obnt. Servant

MARY BOND

City Washington July 6th. 1803

HONORABLE SIR,

My present Situation oblidges me to Write these few lines to you hopeing your Honour will be so kind and so Considerate as to help me in my Distressed Situation. My Husband now deceased, was in the Service for Some time; he was a Serjent. His name was Heator. I am Quite destitute & my Little Effects are Appraised and to be sold for Rent, without Your Honour be so kind as to help me in my present Distress. I have a family of Young Helpless Children and I hope you will consider them and Grant me some present Assistance. And I in duty Bound will Ever pray.

MARY HEATOR

Widows who were forced to work found a limited number of occupations open to them. The jobs they were qualified for were extensions of the household tasks performed by married women—midwifery, nursing and teaching children, sewing, making clothing, housekeeping, and food preparation. They often worked as domestics in other families' homes, but also opened small shops, boarding houses, or taverns. Rarely did these occupations produce much more than a subsistence living.

The occupation to which many aspired, because it was one of the more lucrative businesses available to a woman, was mantua maker—the standard term for a seamstress who made

fancy dresses. Mantua making required a lengthy apprenticeship, but once mastered, it endowed a woman with a highly
paid skill that was always in demand. Training one's daughters to become mantua makers offered the promise of family
security to a number of impoverished widows.[5] Two such
women wrote to Jefferson. The first, a sixty-year-old widow
with three daughters, apologizes for her inferior education
before telling her story.

City Washington December 4th 1802

Honor'd Sir
President of the United States

   May my intretis prevail on your goodness to condesend
to notis this scrall. I beg your honor wold please to pardon
me, and let the cause that urges me to the ardent task apol-
ligise for the liberty I take. My lack of education and want of
abilitys, renders me uncapable of placing words with that
sence and stile proper to address so grate and worthy A President. From the public charractor your honor barse of humanity
and benevolant disposition assurse me a rely on your honours goodness and charity for my conduct. I take the liberty
with A humble fealing to relait my circumstanc.

   I am A stranger A widow upwards of sixty years of age.
My family consists of three daughters the yongest foreteen.
I travled with them from Redstone Old Fort to this place
with views to perfect them in branches of neadle work, man-
tumaking and other branches that might assist them to suport
in some genteale line of business.* I am happy to mention as
A truth that my daughters with honesty at hart do what they
can to assist me in compassing these advantages, but my low
surcumstances and the little oppertunity this place affords me
to git A living that it is with difficulty that I make out from
day to day. I am greived to know that near too years has

* Redstone Old Fort is now Brownsville, Pennsylvania.

relapst Since I came to this place and my Dear Children unperfected in any point of view. All our exertions to pay house rent and fire wood. I occupy A Small building; the rent is eighty dolars A yere. I feer from thes circomstances I shall be obliged to devide the family. It will reach the Childrens feelings very much and A grate trial to me. If I could know my self independent of rent it would be a happy release. If your honour will pleas to cintribit to they relief of A widow and orphins under these distressing circumstances, I shall be under grate obligations and thankfulness at harte and ever feal grateful for the happy change. One more earnest wish I beg to be indulged with; please to cause a line to be wrote desiding this matter to me and I will attend the post office to meet with it.

Thes with Sumision to your Superiority

AFFINITY MEGEATH

N B
I resid near the waroffice.*

Elizabeth Chester wrote in the fixed formula of the memorial, commonly used by petitioners who were unsure of how to write to government officials. The memorial was a popular form of conventional address for petitioning grievances.

---

* "On square bounded by I Street and Pennsylvania Avenue and Twenty-second and Twenty-third Streets, two two-story brick houses, one owned by Mr. Lowry and the other by Mr. Hodgson. In the one last mentioned, the War Office was kept in 1800 and 1801. It was destroyed by fire soon thereafter." This is the fire described in the petition by Agnes Jackson. Christian Hines, *Early Recollections of Washington City* (Washington, D.C.: 1860), quoted in Samuel C. Busby, *Pictures of the City of Washington in the Past* (Washington, D.C.: Wm. Ballantyne & Sons, 1898), 142–43.

City of Baltimore March the 15th. 1801

To his Excellency Thomas Jefferson Esqr,
President of the United States—

The Memorial of Elizabeth Chester
Most humbly Sheweth—

That Your Memorialist's Husband Samuel Chester formerly a Recruiting Officer last American War, during which time he had Enlisted 7,500 Men for the service of the United States and learned them their Exercise, and he has been Dead about 5 Months, left me destitute of house or home, as he had nothing himself. And Your Memorialist has been Advised to apply to Your Excellency for a little relief as She has One Daughter whom She has bound to the Milliner and Mantua Making business, has two Dollars a Week to pay for her Board which is more than I can do at present without some Assistance. She will be free in a Short time and may be able to Support me in my Old Days by her Trade.

Therefore Your Memorialist Craves some help from your Excellency, and she will ever pray

ELIZABETH CHESTER

Any commands directed to the post office Baltimore shall be duly attended to.

According to contemporary accounts, the fire described in the following letter started from a defective chimney in the house of the writer, Agnes Jackson. She reports that the fire began in the War Office and spread to her house. This disagreement about the cause of the blaze may be the reason why her claim for compensation had not been honored. The body of her husband, Jonathan Jackson, who had died that day, was removed from the house before the building was consumed by fire.[6]

Although the writer uses the formulaic style of the official petition in recounting her tale of personal calamity, her diction comes from the sentimental novel.

City of Washington
January 22d. 1802

The Petition of Agnes Jackson of the City of Washington humbly sheweth that in the 8th day of December 1800 when the War Office was burnt, notwithstanding the vigorous exertions of the Neighbours and Spectators to check the progress of the fire, her dwelling House was soon enveloped in flames and sunk in ruins. That a few hours previous to the fire she had sustained the greatest loss this world can inflict, namely a tender, affectionate and provident Husband, who lay in the House a cold and lifeless Corpse insensible of the conflicting passions and dangers that surrounded and rent the hearts of his loving Widow and tender offspring. And thus when she was bereft of the greatest comfort this World could bestow, and the cup of misery filled to the brim, deprived of the small remaining comfort, her House and home, and thrown upon an unthinking World to struggle and support a number of small Children.

Your Petitioner therefore implores your Excellency to compassionate her sufferings, and use your influence with the Grand Council of the Nation to make her such compensation for her losses as your Excellency shall in his wisdom and goodness think proper, and your Petitioner as in duty bound will pray &c.

The way Jefferson handled petitions that involved claims on the government is demonstrated in the case of another widow, Anna Young. Her father, Colonel John Durkee, had lost his right hand in the Revolutionary War Battle of Monmouth and died "a short time before the peace." Her mother and husband subsequently died also, and she was left with three small children. She had petitioned George Washington for "seven years half pay" due her father, but, because veterans' claims were paid by the individual states rather than the federal government, he had referred her to the member of Congress from Connecticut, where she lived.

Now, fifteen years later, she was still attempting to get the pension she felt was due her. She wrote a long letter to Jefferson, outlining her case, and he forwarded it to his secretary of war, Henry Dearborn, who responded in a note on the bottom on her letter: "On application to the Connecticut Gentleman in Congress, I was informed that no relief can be had in the case of Mrs. Young, that her case is so effectually foreclosed, as to render all further attempts in her favour vain." Jefferson then wrote her the following letter:

> Mrs. Anna Young,
> Norwich Connecticut
> Washington Feb. 4. 1802.

MADAM

Immediately on receipt of your letter of Jan. 21. I referred it to the Secretary at War, who was best acquainted with the subject of it, desiring him to investigate the nature of your claim, to see whether it could be effected, and to point out the course to be pursued. He accordingly has made a thorough enquiry into it, and assures me that yours is one of a class of cases which have been barred by two or three different laws of the United States, which would render vain any attempt to bring it forward.

It would have been more pleasing to me to have been able to assure you that your wishes could be fulfilled. But the laws being opposed to this, I can only relieve you from further useless pursuits, and assure you that my attentions have been duly bestowed on your case. Accept my best wishes and respects.

TH: JEFFERSON

Jefferson wrote a similar letter to Ann Welsh, of New London, Connecticut, the widow of a captain in the Revolutionary War and the sister to another captain who died in the war. Jefferson's letter not only dealt with her case, but also stated a legislative principle:

Mrs. Ann Welsh
Washington, March 12. 1805.

. . . The old Congress had engaged to give half pay for life to all their officers who should serve through the war. Those whom you represent, having fallen during the war, no right of half pay could arise in their case. After the war, the officers entitled to half pay commuted it for a fixed sum; but no one not entitled to half pay could be entitled to the commutation which was the equivalent for it. The merit of those you represent appears to have been great, but a legislature must act by general rules, and never do for one person what they would not do for every other under the same circumstances. To give the commutation in your case could not be done but under a previous general rule that they would give it to all officers who fell or died in their service during the war. This has never been done by any nation, and it would be a vast undertaking for ours. No one can say what it would add to the national debt. . . .

The following widow also had a claim against the government that went back to the Revolutionary War.

Pruntytown Febr. 18. 1808.
Harrison County [Va.]

SIR,
I have wrote to you in hopes of Some redress. I am a widow who has Suffered great losses by the public, apply to you Sir as a Gentleman of Honour in whose power I expect

its to assist me in a helpless and friendless Situation. Am at a great distance from my family, have been in hopes of seeing Col. Burr, to have ask'd his advice and assistance. I was of the Burr family, hoped his friendship, but that hope is o're.* I then intended seeing John G Jackson Representative for Harrison County to get him to speak for me. You Sir are at the helm of publick affairs, of the Honourable House, to you I have Sent my complaint. Have lost 900£ pounds by Privateers & 500 Dolr. We had Satificuts [certificuts] from the Officers, to the pay master Generals in Philadelphia. We lived in Newjersy. It was ferriages of the army, and forage for horses & Oxen, three hundred oxen that was to [pull] the brass fieldpeaces. We have Suffered many more losses, that I never expect. I hope from the Character I ever heard of you I have a hope you will consider my situation with two Small Children. Those who had our property, are the persons I should look to for help. I have no way without you Sir. Should please to look with pity on me and my little boys, one nine years old and the other only six.

Prisa. Kemble

My Dear Sir, I hope will consider how long we have been out of our money and was promised cash—Several times. If I could get some Store goods for clothing, it would be a good pay.

Beg you will excuse my troubleing as I have all ready told you my reason.

I wrote to a friend of [yours] to go to you for me but I have not heard from him—made me undertake for myself.

Am Sir your most humble Servent

Priscilla Kemble

* Her hope of assistance from Aaron Burr collapsed with the Burr conspiracy of 1806–7.

The plight of a widow who fell ill and was unable to work is described in the following letter.

Washington near the Six Buildings*
Nov. 15. 1804.

The President of the United States

MAY IT PLEASE YOUR EXCELLENCY

The Voice of Misfortune and Misery have presumed to enter the Apartment of Your Excellency:

'Tis not common Distress or patient suffering would have continued to have mourn'd in silence.

The Widow Noland a resident ner the Six Buildings, brought up in the tender lap of sensibility and introduced into this Country from England by the late Mr. Johnstones family as a superior Domestic, has now long suffered under a most severe indisposition, totally friendless and helpless save what common humanity may have drawn from the Citizens of her Vicinity.**

She is now stretched on her Sick-Bed surrounded by the cries of three most promising children, literally wanting food and raiment.

Her Caracter is well known to several Families in the Six and Seven Buildings for respectability of deportment when in health. If too many Pictures of distress are not crouded on your Excellency the Widow Noland and her three helpless infants may probably claim some temporary relief on Your Philantrophy.

Mr. Carton the Bearer, a respectable Citizen near the West-

---

* "On square between Pennsylvania Avenue and K and Twenty-first and Twenty-second Streets, the 'Six Buildings,' three stories high. ..." Busby, *Pictures of the City of Washington in the Past,* 144.

** "Mr. Johnstone" is possibly Zachariah Johnston (1742–1800), colleague of James Madison in the Virginia House of Delegates.

Market 40, has been kind enough to Interfere in behalf of this[6]*

Unfortunate Family

Sally Palmer told a story of the avarice of the physician who treated her late husband. Jefferson might have read this letter sympathetically, for he had a healthy contempt for most of the doctors of his age and for the medicine they practiced. Five years before receiving Palmer's letter Jefferson had written, "The state of medecine is worse than that of total ignorance. Could we divest ourselves of every thing we suppose we know in it, we should start from a higher ground and with fairer prospects."[7]

Hudson [N.Y.] 30th January 1804

HONERED SIR

I pray you will pardon the boldness And pitty the Distressis of a poor disconsolate Widdow left alone with three small Children And have nothing to Support my self and them But my own labour. The inhuman phizition That attended my husband in his Sickness Has siezed my furniture and will expose it for sail Unless I Can procure money enough to defray His Charges. Hear I am a lone woman not A relative to apploy to in my distress and what Method to take to save what littel property I have Got I know not. I therefore take the boldness to seek for mercy at your hands hoping your Honner will pitty my aflictions and send me A Small Sum of money to relieve my present Distress. And I hope the Supream givern of all things will reward you for the kindness you will

---

* The Western Market was located on the north side of Pennsylvania Avenue between Twentieth and Twenty-first streets, N.W. Bryan, *A History of the National Capital* I:486–87.

Do me and my fervent prayrs Shall be raisd to heavin Continuly for your long life and Prosperity.

Your Honnrs Humble Servt.

SALLY PALMER

The economic depression which struck seaport towns when the Jefferson administration imposed an embargo on all shipping in 1808 was felt hardest by marginal workers such as the following widow, Eliza Penny, who found it impossible to find work as a seamstress.

Naming one's children after the founding fathers, as she did, was common at this time. The president received many letters from parents of children with the name Jefferson, but he gave these letters no particular preference over others.

Baltimore Aprile the [8th, 1808]

RESPECTED SIR

You will no Doupt think Me posest of a Deal of asureance for adressing you, but Neadcesaty has no Law and Must Plead My excuse in your Benavalent Bosom. This Coms from a Distrest and friendless Widdo. My Husband Died in Liverpool and Left Me 2 Small Children the oldest Thomas Jaffarson, 3 years, the youngest George Washington ⟨7⟩ Months. I belong to Alexandria in Virginia and Was Marid thear. Followd With My Husband to Baltimore 4 years past but has nether friends or acquaintenc and has no Way to Git My Living but My Needle and I have no imployment for that. Whare I make application I am answard the times is so hard the[y] cant aford anything to Doe. On Friday the 30 My Landlord threatens to Distress [me] for 20 Dollars rent Wich Will Leave Me nothing but My fatherless Children With out bed or shelter. To God and you I look for Succur.

Father of My Country let Me intreat your Charity for My Children. I Beg I have nothing to offer in Return but the thanks and prars of a Grateful Hart. Sumthing bids Me Hope this Will not go unansward.

Sir your Most obident and Humble Sarvant

ELIZA W PENNY, French S[t]reet Old Town

One woman to whom Jefferson did send money was Lydia Broadnax, the free, black housekeeper of his law teacher and lifelong friend, George Wythe, who lived in Richmond, Virginia. The death of Wythe in 1806 caused a sensation, for Broadnax, Wythe, and a free mulatto boy, Michael Brown, who lived with Wythe and was his student, were all poisoned with arsenic. Wythe and the fifteen-year-old boy died lingering, painful deaths, but Broadnax survived. George Sweeney, Wythe's grandnephew, was accused of the murder. He was supposedly upset by Wythe's will, which left much of his estate to Broadnax and Brown. Although arsenic was found in Sweeney's room and there was a strong case against him, he was acquitted, reputedly because much of the evidence was from blacks and they could not testify against whites under Virginia law.[8]

Jefferson sent Broadnax fifty dollars, but not directly. He instructed his Virginia agent—a cousin, George Jefferson—to forward the money for him. "I have received a letter," he wrote, "from Lydia Broadnax, the freed woman of my deceased friend Mr Wythe, stating that she is in considerable embarrassment for the daily necessaries of life, & asking some charity. I cannot from here make any remittance, but will thank you to inform her that you are authorized to pay her 50. D. out of the money your are to receive from me."[9]

Jefferson was careful about writing directly to women during his presidency for fear the mail would be opened enroute and his privacy compromised. This was particularly true in a sensitive case like the Wythe murder with its unanswered questions about why he would leave much of his estate to a black woman and a mulatto boy. If Jefferson gave money to a woman, it was likely to be through an intermediary, as he did with Broadnax.

Her letter indicates that she was a woman with some education.

Richmond 9 April 1807.

SIR,

I beg leave to trouble you with these lines, hoping you will lay such favorable construction as the nature of my distressed situation shall appear & at present require.

You must know Sir, that since the death of my dear old Master (Judge Wythe) I have already labored under many tedious difficulties, and what is more unfortunate my eyesight has almost failed me. I believe it is owing to the dreadful complaint the whole family was afflicted with at the decease of my poor Master—supposed to be the effect of poison. It is true I have a tolerable, comfortable house to live in, but being almost intirely deprived of my eyesight, together with old age and infirmness of health I find it extremely difficult in procuring merely the daily necessaries of life—and without some assistance I am fearful I shall sink under the burden. This being my situation I am compelled to resort to this crisis—from the old and intimate acquaintance, and knowing your benevolence do now appeal to you for some charitable aid, which I have no doubt your generous hands will not refuse when considering my embarrassed circumstances. And be well assured that nothing but this, and this alone serves me with fortitude to make my supplications known to you. If this should meet your approbation & such charity as shall think proper to bestow to me, you will please to inclose in a letter directed to me by the Mail to this City—and the favor will ever be remembered by

Your Obt. and humble Servant
LYDIA BROADNAX

One of the more self-consciously pathetic letters Jefferson ever received came from a seventeen-year-old Baltimore girl. He may have found appeals such as this difficult to evaluate. Is the young woman manipulative and melodramatic, wallowing in self-pity, or is her letter the impulsive outpouring of an innocent teenager, written in the fevered prose of the sentimental fiction she read?

Baltimore Novemb. 4 1804

SIR

A Poor and distressed girl now addresses you. I give you no title fearing to expose my ignorance, an least I should offend you by thinking it would be pleasing. I have a Father who by an unfortunate surcumstance is ruined. He was security for a man who was thaught of unblemished charector who has some time since fleed and now my Dear father has nerther house nor home but who he is depending for.

Last night I plaid on the pianoforte for the last time and the first place I came to was to your march.* This Sir is the reason why I address myself to you. My father had just before told me that he intended to leave this place for ever. I have yet one blessing while my daughter remains. I smiled and told him that with him I should always be happy and I shall. Next week I leave the spot where I was born never perhaps to see it more. I ask some little assistance to seporte My good

* "The Jefferson March" is one of a number of songs written in Jefferson's honor during his presidency. Helen Cripe, *Thomas Jefferson and Music,* (Charlottesville: University Press of Virginia, 1974), 80.

and aged father on our journe[y]. If you can spare a small triffle of money it will be the means of a poor girl seporting her father in his old age. Was we to stay hear I coud mantane myself by my wourk but my father will not [stay] at a place he once was independent to [be] berdinsom, he thinks, to them that [k]now him. Oh sir it is hear[d] to think of they days that is past. I was then carressed and f[l]attered, but since this misfortune I am looked at and not recolected.

Forgive me for blistering the pappe[r] with my tears for I can say with truth in the happist moment of my life I never felt so truly bleast as when I reconcile my father to his fate. He ast me to tell him candidly if my composure was not fained. I told him that I always wish for a oppetunity to show him fortitude (and I exnoledg this a severe Stroke) but what daughter would I change with? I could not close my eys last night to think of our journey and the season of the year that I fear for My[self].

I rouse with the daun and write to you least we should be gone before aney asistance comes to hand. May My blessings ever attend you is the prear of [your] most unfortunate girl.

EMILIA JERVIS

Direct to Me Baltimore
This day I have entred my seventhen year and I must meet my father with a smile for he little nous how I have spent the Morning.

One occupation that an increasing number of educated women of this period pursued was teaching. Enterprising women opened academies and seminaries for the daughters of affluent families. Louisa Keets's Ladies Seminary in Annapolis, Maryland, offered a typical program of study for such schools: "English and French languages, arithmetic, geography, plain and ornamental needle work, music and drawing."[10] Mrs. Keets wrote Jefferson a desperate letter when her well-planned life suddenly fell apart. She was six months pregnant; she had lost all of her money, and she must travel 600 miles over bad roads to Kentucky, and arrive there before the birth of her baby. She has been an independent woman, apparently supporting her husband, and she is now too proud to ask for money from those she has lived with as an equal. She can, however, ask for help from the nation's patriarch.

Annapolis July 16th 1806

The hope which is kindled from the very ashes of despair alone emboldens me to address you. You to whom Nations bow, to whom all look Up, I from desperation and fearless of exposure confidently write. I own I feel there is something like madness in it, a degree of madness which my situation alone can plead for pardon. Let me not however add to the offence by a long unmeaning preface.

Tho' not a native of America I have lived in it 17 years and altho' in a state of subordination, in that independance this happy country affords to the industrious. I have during that time had the daughters of the most respectable citizens of Maryland under my tuition. My efforts have been rewarded by the approbation of their parents, my emoluments sufficient to give me bread. I have been for some time solicited to go to Kentucky. Attached to many here, I could not consent 'till some misfortunes in my husbands family which have involved us also, joined to the depreciation of this City, determined me. The Hon[orable] Mr. Bedenger undertook to have an academy in readiness for me and I announced my intentions of removing this autumn; every thing wore the smiling face, does it not, of hope.* I beleved we possessed sufficient here to pay all demands and to enable us to go with

* This is probably George M. Bedinger (1756–1843), a member of the Kentucky legislature in 1792, the Kentucky Senate in 1800 and 1801, and a Kentucky Congressman from 1803 to 1807.

comfort our long journey. I have given up the academy which has been conducted under my name the last 3 years in the City. The recommendatory letters the most respectable inhabitants enabled to send forward last month were the truest compensation for my exertions here, and I may truly say I was 'till this last few days HAPPY.

Behold the reverse; a certainty of the irreparable loss of 340$ has plunged me into despair. I am almost incapable of reflection. I am miserable without a prospect of relief; from Mr. Keets' family nothing can be expected. I am alone without connections myself, too far from Mr. Bedenger to receive releif in time, for to add to the tale of woe, I expect confinement in October.

I therefore must set off in the first week of Sep. or my life must answer it, without a dollar to prepare for a journey of 600 miles in a situation which precludes all possibility of daring those hardships which in health I should not regard. What can I do? The probability is, that by applying to those who have been my patrons here I might obtain a sufficient supply, but there is distruction in the idea. My intercourse with the world teaches me how few there are who, while they releve indigence, can respect that misery which no prudence could have prevented, no foresight have avoided.

I have to ask assistance; I could not beg of those with whom I have lived in equality, but I can of you, whose virtues are the brightest ornament of your exalted station, solicit releif. 'Tis true I have no security to offer you, consequently if you consider my story as worth assistance you must risk the return. There is another being whose benevolence is the bright distinction of his name, I shall also apply to but his power is confined. My suit appears stretched to you for an answer on which depends little less than life or death. To be enabled to support my family by my own industry is the summit of my desires. I ask no more, but that is now entirely out of my power in my present situation. . . .

Should you condescend to notice me, a line addressed to me at this City will find the wretched suppliant.

LOUISA C. KEETS

Mrs. Keets's story had a happy ending. She managed to find money to travel to Frankfort, Kentucky, where, I would like to think, she gave birth to a healthy baby. She opened a Domestic Academy for young ladies and named the site of her new school "Home-at-Last".*

MARIE RIVARDI was a much more successful educational entrepreneur. She and her husband for a time operated two schools for girls, one in New Orleans in the summer and another in Philadelphia during the winter months.[11] When she wrote to Jefferson in 1807, Mrs. Rivardi's Seminary in Philadelphia was such a successful local institution that she hoped to gain national support for it from the federal government, with the president's endorsement. Her reference to Jefferson as the "first scientific and literary character in the United States" was no doubt meant to be flattering, but it also reflected his reputation among educated Americans as a philosopher, scientist, and patron of the arts.

She included with her letter an announcement for the school (see page 160). It illustrates the kind of education available to young women whose families could afford the tuition.

---

* Advertisement in the Frankfort, Kentucky, *Palladium,* 1 September 1810. Presumably her school was successful, for she advertised that she was adding a full-time music teacher to her staff.

Philadelphia January 6th 1807

SIR

As to the natural patron of the sciences & liberal arts in the country over which you preside; as to one who would be such, even if his high station did not add the weight of official, to that of personal influence, I take the liberty of presenting to you the plan of an Institution, which has, I hope, distinguished itself already during several years & is still susceptible of being considerably extended & improved. This success I am not vain enough to ascribe to my exertions alone, but also to those able teachers whose assistance I have been fortunate enough to obtain, to the improvements of the pupils & to the kind advice & influence of those gentlemen who allow me to consider them as the particular friends of the Establishment. All these circumstances induce me to hope, especially as Governor McKean is among the patrons of the Seminary, that the Legislature will encourage my efforts, by providing a building for the use of the Establishment & indeed they have at this moment under their consideration, a bill to that effect.*

As of upwards of 60 young ladies, which I have at present under my care the greatest number are from the different states of the Union and from foreign countries, I may perhaps consider this more as a national, than as a local Establishment. I may profess at least that it is my ambition to render it such. This laudable aim will I hope secure me the support of the first Magistrate who at the same time is the first scientific & literary character of the United States.

I have the honor to be with the highest respect Sir Your Excellency's

most obedient & most humble Servant
MARIA RIVARDI

---

* Thomas McKean (1734–1817), Governor of Pennsylvania, 1800–1808.

Jefferson's failure to respond to Mrs. Rivardi's letter may have had something to do with her husband, who had applied for a position as a coastal surveyor. About Major Rivardi, he wrote, ". . . there is something suspecting his extravagance in the waste of public money. . . ." Rivardi did not get an appointment.[12]

The appeal of the following youthful writer was direct; she wanted a Valentine gift from the president. Her reference to "making So free with your Servant man" suggests that she attempted to see Jefferson and possibly engaged in some banter with his secretary or one of the servants.

George Town, March 14th 1802

SIR

I took the liberty to Send you a valintine by poste the 14th of Febr. 1802, and I have ben waitng for a answer but never [received] none which I have taken the opertunity to informe you where to Send the present, as you know not where I lived and I hope that you will not take it as amiss for my making So free with your Servant man—as I am but a poor Girl but honest and has nothing to Suport me but my hands whiich I hope your honour will not be again[st] giving me a present by Post or any way that you think proper.

I remain your humble Servant
MISS SUSANNAH SANTORAN
at the Corner of High and Bridg Street
with Miss MacDougal

Not all of Jefferson's women correspondents asked favors of him. Elize Winn's letter, within the modest limits of her writing skills, was an outburst of rapturous praise for the

president. It was accompanied by a gift, for which Jefferson
sent a note of thanks.

Lou[i]sville, Ky. Feby 20th 1803

Thomas Jefferson, Presedt. of the U.S.

HAIL

Father of the nations, our emperor, the man we love.
Ker[e]ct heaven if I said more; twere scarce a sin. You are all
thats good and god like. In the full vintage of thy flowing
honours I sat still And saw it presst by other hands. Fortune
came smileing to thy youth; an[d] woo[e]d it, and purple
greatness, met thy Ripend years.

When first you Cam [the] Empire was borne on tides of
people. To thy triumph the wish of nations and the willing
world recievd as the pledge of futer peace.

O peace sweet union of States what else but thou gives
strength and glory to a people. Me think again I see those
gentle days renewed that blessd our isle. I see our plains
unbounded waveing with the gifts of harvest, Our seas with
Commerce Throng, our busey ports with Cheerful toil.

Our nymphs and shepherds sporting in each vale inspire
New Song and wake the pastoral reed. Come my sons, I long
To see this prince of whom the world speaks largely well,
whose name Ile teach you to lisp, whose fortunes You shall
follow.

His cause thy nervous arms shall defend and may those
wings that sprede from shore to shore Vouchsaf to shelter
me and my little familey. And long may he live to rule America. O may he be blessd as he deserves is the prayers of his
most Humble and obedient Servt.

Except as a pledge of my love and ready obedience a few
peccans. They were sent to me by a French lady from St.
Vincenes [Vincennes, Indiana Territory]. I never opend them

but Send them On to you with my preyers and beg you may recieve Them. I am Dear Sir your ever faithful Servt

ELIZE WINN

She no doubt intended the pecans to be eaten, but for Jefferson they were far more valuable as seeds. He frequently urged the planting of pecan trees, and shipped nuts to agricultural correspondents in this country and Europe. He sent the following reply to Elize Winn:

Monticello. March 21. 1803.

Th: Jefferson returns his thanks to Mrs. Winn for the Peccan nuts she was so kind as to send him; which being received here, and in the season for planting, he has immediately committed to the earth. He makes his acknolegements also for the flattering terms in which she is pleased to speak of his political conduct; terms far beyond it's actual merit. He sincerely desires to direct the affairs of his country to the best advantage of all; and asks for it no reward but the approbation of his fellow citizens. He receives it therefore on this, as on every other occasion, with a just sensibility; & prays her to accept his respectful salutations and best wishes.*

---

* When Jefferson wrote of himself in the third person, as here, he did not add his signature. Because all letters were handwritten, his name in the text was his signature.

5

Debt and Justice

"Wretched in the extreme"

THE numerous unsolicited appeals for cash that Jefferson received were a reflection of both the desperation and the optimism of the citizens of the early republic. In an age of debtor's jail and limited bankruptcy laws, insolvency was a real fear for the small businessman, mechanic, and farmer. Currency was scarce, and a subsistence living was the plight of many Americans. Shay's rebellion and the Whiskey Rebellion had dramatized the often desperate condition of farmers who were victims of an economy and a tax system that placed them at constant risk of financial ruin—the loss of farm and possessions, and ultimately debtor's prison. A business decline, bad health, or poor weather could destroy a lifetime's work.

Coupled with this fear of insolvency was an optimistic conviction that conditions would improve—that a loan, or better yet a gift, would turn things around. When creditors, friends, or family failed to produce this loan, many turned as a last hope to the nation's paterfamilias, whose princely annual salary of $25,000 was well known. If the urgency of need could somehow be communicated, bank bills would magically appear by return mail, tucked into a presidential letter. After all, Jefferson had the reputation of being a charitable man; the catalogue of his attainments which appeared regularly in the Republican press often included the promising appellation "philanthropist."

His charity, however, was based on a principle he termed "the law of usefulness." He explained it in replying to an appeal for a donation to a religious mission in the East Indies:

> ... I deem it the duty of every man to devote a certain proportion of his income for charitable purposes, & that it is his further duty to see it so applied as to do the most good of which it is capable. This I believe to be best ensured by keeping within the circle of his own enquiry & information the objects of distress to whose relief his contributions shall be applied. ... However disposed the mind may feel to unlimited good, our means having limits we are necessarily circumscribed by them. They are too narrow to relieve even the distresses under our own eye; & to desert these for others which we neither see nor know, is to omit doing a certain good for one which is uncertain. I know indeed there have been splendid associations for effecting benevolent purposes in remote regions of the earth, but no experience of their effect has proved that more good would not have been done by the same means employed nearer home. In explaining however my own motives of action, I must not be understood as impeaching those of others. Their views are those of an expanded liberality; mine may be too much restrained by the law of usefulness, but it is a law to me. ...[1]

He was, therefore, selective about donations, giving them where he thought they would produce visible results. By this measure, most of the unsolicited requests for charity from strangers failed to meet his standard of "doing a certain good for one that is uncertain."

PAUL BROWN of Paxton, Massachusetts, launched his appeal for money on a heavy sea of malapropisms. His letter is an extreme example of the elevated rhetoric attempted by many of Jefferson's working-class correspondents. They are convinced that not only must all codes of etiquette and rules of decorum be followed when writing to a person of rank, but all the furnishings in one's educational establishment are to be displayed. Like Bottom in *A Midsummer Night's Dream,* Brown obviously believed that the chief magistrate's resistance could be crushed by the sheer weight of language. Brown never mentions what the money is needed for, but, like many of Jefferson's suppliants, he is quite specific about how it is to be sent through the mail. When he received no response to this letter, he mailed a virtual duplicate of it five months later, but this too went unanswered.

Paxton [Mass.] Jan. 27. 1806

Being in very straiten'd & sometimes distressing Circumstances, after being denied & evaded, legally, by more immediate, a man betakes to implant the Commisserations of one celebrated for his Benevolence, tho' in a public Station, & judicious Beneficence in public transactions, even for a private Benefit, in a peculiar sort of Exigence. I request you to transmit (as early as may be after receiving this) 250 or 300 Dollars, in a single light bank Bill (if conveniently impetrable) enclosed in a Letter directed by the mail, to the subscriber of this at Paxton Massachusetts, to be loaded at Leicester Post Office.

I have no Accomplices to pervert any such Fortune, no Participators in this Onset; no Friends; no Neighbours, tost by the bleak blast of Poverty which Chance shouted with sundering sweep to the sympathetic Bands of Thousands: Chance, that governs the possession [of] Lots of mortal men even in a Land of Equality, Liberty, & Justice.

Your Excellency need not be apprehensive of an Iteration

of this sort of Request. If you be a Patron of useful Science, & benevolent Purposes, fail not to transmit this. I will pledge myself that it shall not be known to others, if your excellency's self shal prefer that Concealment. One trembling on the verge of a long & laborious Life hurrying out the glimmering taper by harrassing toils & Cares to which his is unequal necessitated; seperated by the slightest Partition from public Maintenance, is very rare in this Country (with gratitude to our Patriot, be it observed) yet there are some. . . .

The Father of his Country, the Cherisher of national Liberty, the mild Pilot of a Nation of Freemen in perilous Compasses, will extend even into Obscurity the fostering hand of Benignity over the stifled seeds of usefulness, & will encourage the Arts & Sciences, but beyond all others Humanity. Thou shalt dry up the tears of trampl'd Despondancy struggling with virtuous Speculations, & cause the Fingers of those who languish in Indigence to commove the grateful Cymbals of thy honour.

I am with Reverence, your Excellency's obedient

humble Servant
PAUL BROWN

Like the previous writer, William Dunn uses the persuasive strategies common to many of Jefferson's correspondents. His epic diction ("my troubled mind . . . is like the surges of the Sea tosed to and fro when wind is combatting the waves . . .") is amusing to twentieth-century readers, but it was merely a bombastic version of the accepted rhetorical style of the period. In what has been described as an "eighteen-century revolution," writers were taught by rhetoricians such as John Ward and Hugh Blair that persuasion was achieved more by affecting the passions with theatrical language than by lean, abstract logic.[2] The letters of many of Jefferson's minimally schooled correspondents show that these ideas had filtered down to the laboring classes.

Dunn, like Paul Brown asked for $300, but he did not further his cause by commenting that this small sum would never be missed by Jefferson, for it came at a time when the president's own debts were increasing dangerously. Dunn wrote three times, each letter roughly a duplicate of the others. Jefferson received all of them, including the first one, mentioned here, which Dunn assumed had gone astray. Dunn's fear of debtor's prison seems to be equaled by his concern for his public humiliation at becoming insolvent. (There was also the practical consideration that a debtor lost everything he owned but the clothes on his back and a bed to sleep in.) His mention of the "vindictive passions of some men" suggests that he may have been unpopular with his neighbors. One of those neighbors was Thomas Jefferson, who owned a large plantation and house at Poplar Forest, in Bedford County, Virginia.

Liberty, Bedford County Va. May the 27, 1807.

HONORED SIR

I hope you will read the following lines with Sympithy and answer the petitioners request. I wrote a letter a bout seven weeks ago and sent it to Washington. I understood directly after I had sent it you had gone to Monticello and whether you ever got it I no not. I received no answer. My present case is desparet and how to extricate my self I no not.

I am a poor man and descended from poor parrents and I have heretofore endeavoured to keep up as good a character as my circumstances would permit: but my case is altered; fortune is frown upon me. Sickness and affliction has reduced me to this deplorable condition. I am enthrald in debt and I want relief and with out it my case will be wo[r]se than it is now. Oh merciful benefactor have compassion on me and deliver me; three hundred dollars would pay all my debts and enable me to follow my business. If you would be so merciful lend me that sum which I hope to God you will. I will return it to you in two or three years. I expect every day to be plundged in to a gloomy prison there to remain at the will of a merciless creditor or come out by the ignominious oath of insolvency. I hate to fly my country. I wish to pay all my debts. I hate to meet a man with a pair of saddle bags for fear that it is the sherif that is just agoing to take me and put me in jail and have no chance of bail.

You wonder [why] the people will not indulge me knowing my situation. But Dear Sir when the vindictive passions of some men are raised they will be gratified if it should be for ever the confinement of their victim and their tongues with malignant darts will for ever stab his character with infamy. You may Sir judge I have conducted my self so bad that I am unworthy of your notice but I hope to God that you will not censure me so hard for you are my only dep⟨endence⟩ of mercy. If you turn a deaf ear to my petition I am undone and nothing remains for me but the gloomy prison and the bitter imprecations of my Creditors which will bla⟨cken⟩ my character for ever. That small sum you scarcely would miss out of your coffers would relieve my distresses and alleviate my troubled mind which at this time is like the surges of the Sea tosed to and fro when the wind is combatting the waves and make them roll and roar with impetuous fury.

You may allow Sir that I have formed ⟨this⟩ Story in order to deceive you to satisfy my own gratification. Oh do put the most favourable constructions on my letter. Thoughts of your censuring of me fills my Soul with horrer and dismay. I intend the honest thing. If ever truth was written it is now—yes unsullied truth. I end here. I be⟨lieve⟩ I will end my petition hoping and trusting to God that I shall receive a kind answer in short time from your humble petitioner.

WILLIAM DUNN

After Jefferson retired from the presidency, Dunn wrote once more asking for money, but this time proposing that he come to Jefferson's Poplar Forest house in Bedford County for an interview: "Take a view of both of our Situations. You Sir are basking in the Sun Shine of Fortune and roling in all the pleasures this World can afford and I in the lowest depth of humility Sighing under the yoke of Malignant Predators and groaning under the oppression of poverty. I hope that you will not expose me to the world." His letter was ill timed, for Jefferson was struggling to meet the heavy debt he had incurred as president. Jefferson never responded to Dunn.[3]

The writer of the following letter appears to be an industrious, enterprising farmer who faces bankruptcy through no fault of his own, but one wonders whether he ever really expected the president of the United States to place a thousand dollars in a letter and mail it to a total stranger. Like many of Jefferson's correspondents, he believes he is the only person unknown to the president who ever asked him for money.

Moretown Vermont June 24th 1803

Dear Sir—

Doubtless you will think it Strange to Receive A letter from one you never herd of nor Saw in the world & More so when you come to see what Subject it is on. I am A man that was bred up A farmer in Vermont. Haveing A mind to Settle in the world I Moved in to A new town with About five hundred dollars which I had Acumilated by my own Industree. The town being Very new & the want of Mills was Very much felt in this place, I determined to undertake to Buil[d] if noboddy Else would. Acordingly in the Spring 98 I proceded on the business & by the first of November following I had Arected A Saw and grist mill on what is cauled Mad River. On the 28th day of that same Month Novb.

there Came the Largest flood Ever known by the oldest man on the River. The water was 24 feet Rite up & Caried Both of my mills Away before I had the Satisfaction of Injoying them one Month & Landed me About five hundred dollars bad.

Far from being disscurorged I Resolved to try to Extend by Credit & Rebuild. Acordingly the next Spring I profesd my determination, Acordingly Rebuilt Both By the forth of the next October and built them So Stout that Water Could not Inundate them, in which posision I have Bin Ever Since. But the grate Expence Incurd by Building plunged me into debt About 2 thousand dollars, for which I had to Mortgage the mills & Land I owned in this town, & have mantaned my family & Lesoned the demand to 1 thousand dollars. The Mortgage now being Run out the man Sese fit to Eject me off the premisis thinking to get the propety that is worth 25 hundred dollars for ten hundred. The time that I must geve them up will be the first of March next which Must unadvoidly take place unless Some boddy interferes in my behalf.

Having always herd that you was A man that was posesed of Real benevolence, Knowing that one thousand dollars never could make A blank in your property or frustate your happiness in the Lest, I Must Come forred in this way to Requst 10 or twelve hundred dollars of you. I am Confident when you Com to Red these & Consider that Sum Will Be mene of Makeing A man of business of me & Make So Smale A blank in your property you will not hisetate to Send me the Money & Point out whether you will Make A present of it to me or whether I must pay you at Some futer day, Either of which I shall happily Comply with. It has Every be Reported in this Country that you are A man of Charity and had Extended the Arme of Charity far beyond your predesesors in office.

With high consideration I Subscribe my Selfe—

Your Friend & humble Servent
CEPHAS CARPENTER

You will Be plesed to put the bills in to A letter Aderest it to the Subscriber here of at Moretown in Chittendown County to be Left at the post office at Waterbury in Said County Where I shall be likely to get the Money Sone. You will not hissetate to Send the Money as this is Stated Acording to Real fact & Honnesty & If you dont Send the Money I might unadvoidly be Come A bankrupt. If you hisetate in the Lest About the honesty of these be plesed to wright me whether I Can have the Mony If I Come down their.

C CARPENTER

Jefferson's correspondents assessed him accurately; he was a charitable man. His memorandum books show that in the first year of his presidency, for example, he gave nearly a thousand dollars in charity. The next year his charitable contributions were a third more.[4] By the time he was about to leave the presidency, however, and the full extent of his own debts was realized (he was some twenty thousand dollars more in arrears than he had been aware of), his attitude toward solicitations for money hardened. A month before his return to Monticello after eight years in office, for example, he received a pathetic appeal from Ezekiel Pitman, who had been a blacksmith at the Navy Yard in Washington: "untill October last, since which time, my health has been too much impaired, to conduct business any longer. I am also now, far advanced in age, so that I cannot work." He wanted enough money to "convey me home to my family, whom I have left seven hundred miles behind me." He was "destitute of every necessary in life, having not *been able to* work this winter, and am at this present time, owing for board and lodging, and no means to defray it. I inavitably must perish, unless I can have some immediate assistance, being an old *Man* and a great way from home."[5]

Jefferson endorsed the letter and added a single comment: "begging." He was to use this word repeatedly on letters soliciting him for money in the final year of his presidency.

JEFFERSON received numerous letters from the nation's jails. He was no sooner in office than he was confronted with a series of petitions from prisoners requesting their freedom. These appeals forced him to confront the flaws of the justice and penal systems of the early American republic. Justice was seldom swift; punishment was often a loose fit for the crime, and jails were not designed for the claustrophobic.

Many of the appeals Jefferson received were from men imprisoned for trivial debts. The reason the president of the United States was forced to deal with petty cases such as these, seemingly the venue of a lower court judge, was the constitutional right of every citizen to petition the government—and the president's ability to grant pardons. For many citizens, the right to petition meant a direct appeal to the president for a pardon from a jail sentence. Throughout his two terms, Jefferson received requests from individuals for a variety of executive favors, but none were more urgent than those asking for freedom from debtor's prison.

The rapid descent from debt to prison was demonstrated to Jefferson first hand by a young man whose family he was acquainted with. Samuel Quarrier wrote to the president on February 2, 1802, announcing that he had come to Washington hoping for an army appointment, had failed to receive one, and he was now stranded, broke, and needed money "to permit me to leave this place" and return to his father's home in Richmond, Virginia. Jefferson knew and had corresponded with Quarrier's father, a prominent Richmond coach maker, and also knew that he had become something of a laughingstock in Richmond two years earlier by firing his pistol into his own foot while fighting a duel.[6] Jefferson promptly sent young Quarrier the $25 fare, undoubtedly as a courtesy to his family.

Quarrier immediately addressed another letter to the president. He thanked him for the $25, which was indeed enough for the stagecoach fare to Richmond, but he needed a "further extention of your philantropic aid"—another $60 to pay his debts in Washington.

City of Washington Gail.
February 10th, 1802.

Thomas Jefferson Esqr. President of the U States
Sir.

I hope my unfortunate situation will pardon, & excuse my intrud[ing] on you the contents of this letter, after the reception my last one meet with. From that transaction you must think me void of delicasy, of feeling, for to importune on a like subject, or extreemly implicated in distress. The latter sory am I to say is but too much the case. Distress I now feele which exsperience never yet taught me. In theory only I knew what I know too well in practice, from the short residence I've already had. Permit me to informe you of my melancholy situation.

Yesterday I was arested, and conducted to Prison, for the sum of 41 Dollars, I was ushered into the debtors appartment (a room about twelve feet square) where I found a parcel of Creaturs in the form of men, they were in the full tide of disipation—Drinking, swearing, gaming, with every other vice that Depravity could invent. Nature was at lenth exausted in the Vortext of intoxication, they then strewed themselves on the floor, where sleep temporarily relieved them from theire misery, if such thay felt.

The chance offered for me to adress you, I embraced it. I took up the pen to solicit your friendly benevolence, thinking when you were acquainted with it, you might be induced to relieve me from What I suffer. I declare Sir, you'r the last one I should presume to think of troubleing upon an occasion like this, if I'd any one else to apply to. Its but too melancholy a truth I have not.

Heere I am close confined, in *Prison,* without one single cent, without cloths except those on my back, & whats worse the Loss of which is dearer to me than existance *Liberty.* As Cato says A day, an hour, of Virtuouse liberty is worth A hole eternity of Bondage.* Language is poor to express to you my feelings on this unhappy business. I feele the most heart felt anguish, it is indeed a revers of fortune I but little expected. Never did I think my *Father* would have deserted me in this maner, to Leave me to perish to starve in a Comon *Prison.* Oh God exstend they mercie to me thy unfortunate creature.

Pardon those exspressions which are the affects of a heart that feeles. You'r high, & respectable station in life ought to prevent my intrudeing myselfe, again on you. (Exclusive of the reception I meet with by letter) your knowledg of me does not sanction my taking a liberty of a pecuniary nature in any respect—except what your Kindness may dictate. Was there any other sourse that I could apply I never would to you. On a perusal of this I hope, & trust you'll relieve, & help the unfortunate son of Alexander Quarrier. If I'me so fortunate as to feele again your benevolent aid I shall immediately return to my Father where I shall apply to business, as soone as possible never again to leave it for mere speculative fansies. What I now suffer can never be erased from my memory, nor ever thought of without a Sight.

Be pleased to inform me by the Bearer of this the result of this my humble Letter. I beg, & request if theres any thing in this Letter that may not be proper, it will be overloocked

* "A Day, an hour of virtuous liberty
Is worth a whole eternity of bondage,"
Joseph Addison, *The Tragedy of Cato,* act 2, sc. 4.

by you as it must arise from ignorance, & inability, & not from a wish or Voluntary inovation from me.

> May god grant you every
> blessing that this life can
> give, is the most fervent
> Prayer of the Miserable
>   SAML. QUARRIER

Three days later, Quarrier wrote again, reporting that "this ignominious imprisonment unmans the heart, & depresses the Soul."

The president, however, did not respond again to the troublesome prodigal. On March 29, 1802, seven weeks later, Quarrier was still in jail for a debt of $11.25, "and also for want of bail."[7] By April 3, he was out, writing once again, informing the president that his father had taken a fall, was in a "weak & low state," and that it was necessary that he "repair with all possible speede to aleviate & to assist all that a fond & affectionate son could the Sufferings of his father." It is true that his father's conduct "has been extreemly harsh," but he can "never loose sight of his being my Father. . . ." Would Jefferson send him enough money to get back to Richmond?

Five days later, he wrote a two-page letter imploring Jefferson once again to lend him the fare to Richmond. "It's my intention to profit from my past imprudent & misfortunate actions by a steady assidious, & industrious exercise of the first business I can procure an occupation in."[8] But no record exists that Jefferson gave any more money to young Quarrier.

QUARRIER'S plight illustrated an injustice that had been retained virtually intact from British common law—imprisonment for debt. All of the American states had incorporated English creditor-debtor laws into their statutes, and they were not changed until well into the nineteenth century. Although creditor-debtor laws varied from state to state, they uniformly gave creditors who had obtained a legal judgment the right to imprison a debtor until the amount owed was paid. The size of the debt had nothing to do with the penalty; a man could be jailed indefinitely for owing a few dollars, and many were.

In an attempt to deal with the injustices of jailing impoverished people for debt, insolvency laws were passed to allow a debtor to obtain freedom by declaring himself destitute. After his property was sold, and the proceeds awarded to his creditors, he was released from prison. Declaring insolvency gave relief especially to urban tradesmen whose only economic resources were the skills they were prevented from practicing while they were in jail. Farmers in debt, on the other hand, could continue to have their land worked by family members and earn money while in jail. It was often in a farmer's interest, therefore, to remain in jail rather than declare insolvency and have his farm and possessions sold at auction prices. This was also true of merchants who owned real estate and merchandise that was worth more than their debts.[9]

Jefferson was seemingly disturbed by the petitions and letters he received from debtor's prison, for he requested information about the number of prisoners being held in the Washington jail, their living conditions, and their legal status. On March 29, 1802, he obtained from the "Marshal of Prisoners" a list of twenty-one men in jail, five of them for debts of $1.68, $1.75, $3.33, $3.62, and $3.78. The greatest amount owed was $26.10. He also received the "Dimentions of Jail in Washington City":

Debtors room lower floor—10 F. by 14 F.
D[itt]o Do upper Do—8. by 9.

Criminal's room upper floor—9. by 12.
Do   Do lower Do—5. by 7.

In these four small rooms, twenty-two debtors and "Fourteen Criminals & Runaways" were housed. The runaways were slaves.[10]

A week later, Jefferson received the following legal opinion from John Mason, federal attorney for the District of Columbia. It demonstrated how an insignificant debt could escalate while the debtor was in prison by the addition of "poundage"—a commission received by the marshal on all debts and costs involved in the case.

29th March 1802

If a Man be committed to Jail for Debt upon a Ca. Sa. [Capias ad satisfaciendum—imprisonment of a defendant until a plaintiff's claim is satisfied] he can not demand a discharge of the Marshall upon the payment of the Debt and costs of suit. He must also pay the Marshall his poundage fees upon the amount of the Debt & Costs for which he was committed and also the fees due by law for his imprisonment before he can of right demand his discharge. . . .

N.B. If a man be released under the insolvent act it discharges him from the sheriffs demands as well as all others—

JOHN T. MASON

Daniel C. Brent, marshal of the District of Columbia, broke down the costs involved for a debt of one dollar and concluded that "the Costs alone upon a Debt of one dollar may amount to $4.03 cents. . . . Besides for every day the Debtor is in Jail he is chargeable with twenty Cents per day."[11]

An inability to pay fines and court costs could result in an indefinite prison sentence. This is illustrated in the case of a carpenter, Charles Houseman, who petitioned the president for release from jail. Jefferson sent the petition to a Washington judge, William Cranch, for more information on the case. Cranch's reply included an appeal for leniency, but it also incidentally revealed the severe punishments inflicted for minor offenses during this period.

City of Washington Decr. 19th. 1801.

To the President of the United States

SIR,

In consequence of a note at the bottom of a petition to you in behalf of Charles Houseman, I have the honour to state, that he was indicted at June term last for stealing plank, and Carpenters' tools from three several persons. It appear'd in evidence that the articles were found in his possession, but were of little value. He was found guilty on each indictment, and sentenced to be burnt in the hand, whip'd a certain number of stripes, and to pay four fold the value of the articles stolen.*

The corporal part of his punishment was inflicted, and he was thereupon discharged from the custody of the Marshall by order of the Court, who were inform'd that it was not in his power to pay the fine. A Capias was afterwards issued, as I believe, to compel him to pay the fine and costs, upon which he was arrested and not being able to satisfy them, he has remain'd in custody ever since.

I do not recollect whether any evidence was offer'd as to his character, at the trial, or any other circumstances, except his inability to discharge the fine & Costs, which would entitle his case to peculiar regard from the Executive, but I hope I shall not be deem'd officious in saying that there seems to

---

*The Washington *National Intelligencer* reported on 8 July 1801 that the Circuit Court for the District of Columbia tried Houseman, found him guilty on three charges, and that he was "publicly whipped and burnt in the hand. . . ."

be no probability that the United States, or the district of Columbia, will be benefited by his further imprisonment.

> I have the honour, to be, Sir,
> with great respect, your obdt. servt.
> MR. CRANCH

More then three months later, on March 29, 1802, Houseman was still in jail, but not for too much longer.[12] The Washington *National Intelligencer* reported on June 21, 1802, that a fifty-dollar reward was being offered for the return of prisoners who had escaped from the Washington jail on the night of June 6, 1802. One of the escaped prisoners was "Charles Houseman, a Dutchman, is about 50 years of age, 5 feet 6 or seven inches high, has a number of scars on his back and is a lusty fellow." There is no report that he was ever captured.

JESSE CARPENTER, a farmer, wrote Jefferson from the Washington jail where he was being held for his "appearance at June Cort" for debt. He had only fifteen shillings to his name, he had a sick wife and eight small children at home, and worst of all, he was "not fit for to be seen By my fellow mortals for I fetcht But one suit from home with me."[13] A few days later, he wrote again.

[Received 31 March 1808]

MR THOMAS JEFFERSON MOST REVERANT SIR
  I Rote to you for asistance Not for Relesement for I No in asivel [I know in a civil] Cases you Can do Nothing. But as I am at distant from home and fetched without money or Close I applyd to you for ade and asistanc. If it only plses your Honnour to Gave me only apair of overhauls and shirt

"Thomas Jefferson
You are the danedest fool that God put life into, God dam you"
This is one of a number of abusive notes Jefferson received.

THY DESTRUCTION IS NEAR AL. HAND THOMAS.
THE, RETRIBUTIVE, SWORD is SUSPENDED OVER. THY
HEAD, BY A SLENDER THREAD. BEWARE

Jefferson received assassination threats
as well as crank warnings such as this
one. He ignored all of them.

Burbon
Kentucky
Paris
14th, July
1805
1805

Eternity!

When Death Brings us there,
who will be on the Safe Side,
the Christian, or he that denies the
Christian religion, —

—— William Martin

Federalist claims that Jefferson was an atheist prompted this note. He believed in the humanity, but not the divinity, of Christ and admitted to being a Unitarian in his later years.

"Friend Thomas
If Thou Should Live 3 Months after leaving Thy office, (which permit me to
Doubt) Thou Wilt Thank me for My Communications
Thy Friend
Exchuse this as wrote in the Dark."

Phonetic spelling and no punctuation made letters such as this one from a Philadelphia seaman difficult to read. He complains of the hardships caused by the embargo. See page 31.

A Statement of the Rules and Regulations observed in Mrs. Rivardi's Seminary, South Second the corner of Union Street.

THE Establishment, as far as relates to all the different studies, is under the care and direction of Mr. Rivardi. In each department the Young Ladies are divided in a certain number of classes and promoted from one to the other, according to their progress. Mrs. Rivardi devotes her whole time and attention to the benefit and improvement of her pupils; she is assisted by several English and French Ladies who reside with her, and in every room, where lessons are given, a governess is always present to see that the necessary order and silence are kept. It is the chief object of Mrs. R. in order to secure and accelerate the progress of her pupils, to excite a spirit of emulation without giving rise to envy or jealousy, by this means the heart and the mind are equally cultivated and improved. The masters attend punctually both summer and winter. In June Mrs. R. removes to a healthy and eligible country residence, and returns to the city whenever the season renders it proper. Every first Tuesday in each month (January excepted) the Young Ladies are examined in the several branches of their education; their writing, drawing, and works exhibited, and all their parents or guardians admitted. Certificates, on those days, are conferred on the best scholars in each department, and on the first examination in May, those who produce most certificates, are presented with premiums expressive of the satisfaction arising from their good conduct and application. One afternoon in every week is particularly dedicated to Epistolary Style. The Young Ladies are obliged on that day, to write to their parents or relations; the letters are presented to Mrs. R. for inspection, and the errors pointed out, but the Young Ladies are not permitted to copy their productions; every letter is sent in its original state, in order to shew the real progress of those who composed them. The scholars of the First Class also write once a week, on subjects proposed to them by Mr. R. those subjects generally relate to morality, history, or geography. And morning and evening the whole Seminary unite in prayer and thanksgiving to the Almighty.

Every Sunday (if the weather allows it) all the Young Ladies attend divine service, Mrs. R. considering it one of her first duties to preserve her pupils in the religious tenets which they profess; a catholic governess conducts the Young Ladies of that religion, an Episcopalian the Episcopalians, a Presbyterian the Presbyterians, &c. to their respective places of worship. Whenever circumstances prevent their leaving the house, the Young Ladies read a sermon in Mrs. R.'s presence, and in the evening all those who have made sufficient progress in music, join in performing sacred harmony; a selection of which has lately been published at Mrs. R.'s particular request, by Messrs. Carr & Schetky.

This prospectus for Mrs. Rivardi's Seminary for Young Ladies is typical of the kind of education available to women in the early nineteenth century.
See page 133.

To the President of the United States of America.

The Petition of Richard Quince Hoskins of Boston, in the County of Suffolk, and Commonwealth of Massachusetts Humbly sheweth.

That your petitioner was tried at the Circuit Court of this District in June term 1805, on a charge of embezzling and secreting a letter from the Post Office in said Boston, and found guilty of the same; but owing to an action in arrest of judgment filed by the Council of your petitioner, which action was unknown to him, till last December, the sentence was postponed for further consideration until October term, a lapse of four and an half months.

Your petitioner, begs leave, further to state to your Excellency, that since the first finding of the Indictment against him, he has already suffered Fifty months Imprisonment, your petitioner, therefore humbly prays, that your excellency would be pleased to look in tenderness upon his calamitous situation, and extend to him your pardon.

And as in duty bound, will ever pray.

Richard Quince Hoskins

Charlestown Prison.
Aug. 14. 1808.

31880

This petition for a pardon by a convicted embezzler is an example of fine calligraphic handwriting by some of Jefferson's correspondents. See page 183.

Mr. President
if you know
what is good
for your future
welfare you
will take off
the embargo
that is now
such a check
upon the amer-
ican Commerce
and lay it upon
some thing
else or
if you could
lay it upon
the hot weather
it would add
more to your
credet I pray
your are a
friend to france
but not to G.
Britain which
I am sorry
to inform you
of I am in hopes
you will put
our affairs in
a good training
I bid you a
due for the
present and
trust 31638

Letters to the president came in all shapes and sizes. This one was written on both sides of a 1½-by-9-inch piece of paper. See page 19.

Copies of Jefferson's letters made with a copying press, such as this one, were frequently smudged. See page 276.

Sir

Washington Mar. 4. 05

Your letter of the 1st. instant informing me of your discovery of a method of converting iron into steel, is recieved. however desirable & useful improvements in the arts are to every nation, yet ours, by their constitution, has allowed no particular encouragement to be given but a patent securing for 14. years the exclusive benefit of his invention to the inventor,

To this I must add that, convinced that all manufactures carried on on private account are so much more economically conducted than by the public, that whatsoever can be found at market can be cheaper bought there than manufactured by the public, we undertake no manufactures of any thing which can be got at market. small arms are the only exception to this rule, consequently there can be no opportunity of employing you for the public in the enterprise you suppose of converting iron into steel. accept my salutations & wishes for the success of your discovery in some other way.

Th: Jefferson

Mr. Saml Marsh.

Copies of letters made with the polygraph, such as this one, were virtual duplicates of the original. This letter states a typical Jeffersonian position on the limited role of government in commerce.

OPPOSITE. Jefferson's correspondents frequently accompanied their descriptions of inventions with illustrations, such as this sketch of a steam-powered boat propelled by a jet of water. See page 249.

Page 5

a thing may not be lost to our Country and especia
for the new acquired Territory I trust after examine
the plan if you have a good experience of the thing you
will not fail to incourage the accomplishment of
I now procede to describe the principle which I th
as by giveing you the outlines of the form in whic
I tryed the experiment as in the figure below whe
is a section of the Boat with a large but short l
ing pump A B C D is the Boat at C is the Bo
or chamber of a common lifting Pump with
diaphram and valves, the lower valve shutts on th
bottom of the Boat, as in figure at B is a vessel
receive the water from the pump at C which is
changes by a pipe or tube going from the bottom
the vessel B, to the stern or hinder part of the B
at A it will now be easy to understand the effect
water must pass from this position as it is founde
on the natural pressure of fluids, which at an
equal depth below the surface of the fluid pr
is every way equally, and so presses an eq
quantity of the surface of the vessel at equal
depth, with equal force, in every direction ind
ently; and now if the passage from B to C wcase
at B and the water standing to the hight C thi
there would be no power to move the Boat be
of equal pressure on every side let the form
as it may, but by takeing away part of the
surface of the vessel on one side the equilib

or equal pressure is destroyd, and the differ
of pressure is left on the side of the opening i
exact proportion to the size of the aperture and
hight of the fluid above it, or in other word
force is exactly expressed by the weight of a col
of water whose base is the size of the aperture
and hight that of the fluid above it, and what
this column weighs is the exact force by which
Boat is pressed forward, the power to be
applyed is to work the pump to supply the
said Bason up a suiteable hight of the
there is one thing peculiar to this application
of the power applyed in this way, and that is the Boa
with respect to the judging the power
may be competent to the effect or at rest, the
the pressure being the same wheather the Bo
moves fast or slow or not or wheather it
move with or against the current whic

as I have No Remedy but to Crave asistance from some person. I am sued for det that I Never Contracted; for this Reason I wer so onperpared. I am apore man; also I have awife
and Eight small Children. Also I have Rote home to them
but thar is None of the[m] able to Come and fetch me Close
in time. The Nabours are all prepairing for a Crop; thay are
None at liberty at this season. Now if it plse your honour to
Gave me some asistance I am very durty. Now this is the 11
day I am from home for which I wod been home again Friday. Now if it may plese your honnour to Conside[r] my
Case and do some thing for me as I am Now are in distress
I shall Return you tenthousant thanks as I am Now in th[is]
perdicament.

   I am your umble servant

                                                    JESSE CARPENTER

The distance I am from is from the mouth of the south Branch.*
My oldes son are twelve years old. You may Judge the way
I am fix.

Richard Fenwick, also with a large family, was jailed after
he was imprudent enough to interfere in a domestic quarrel
between a husband and wife. The wife took him to court and
he was fined. Now he was in jail until he could be released
under the insolvency laws. His unpaid fine was seven dollars.
Fenwick had his own wife deliver a letter to Jefferson, and
she apparently had no difficulty seeing him.

---

*He apparently refers to the Potomac; in his first letter he states that his home is 120
miles from Washington.

[Received 30 March 1802]

Thomas Jefferson Esqr. President of the United States—
Sir

... From casualities insidental to human nature I'me unfortunately the residenter of A prison, and the Father of a large helpless family. Portray to yourself A person in imprisonment, a wife & six small children to exist with barely the means of doing it. It's a situation that a moments reflection must pronounce Wretched in the extreme. Fifteen days have I been imprisoned & thirty five more I have to remain, when I shall be exonerated from confinement by the Statute for the relief of insolvent debtors. Under those considerations I humbly request you'r interference in behalfe of me in a transaction I was unintentionaly & unmeaningly implicated with.

Tranciently passing by the doore of a Mr. Sawyer, himselfe & wife where in the act of brutally belabouring one & other. I steped in to seperate them &c. Some time since the wife presented me, the present court have thought proper to fine me which fine & the costs accrueing from the presentment I'me not able to discharge. From that, as it being an action where the State is prosecutor I cannot be emancipated from Jail, by the act of Insolvency when the time arives for that purpose.

Therefor I hope and trust you'll be pleased to take my Condition into consideration & to exert you'r benevolent humanity in my behalfe so that it may be no impediment to my being again restored to *Liberty,* & my unhappy Family. My wife whoes the bearer of this will give you any particulars you may please to desire on this truely disagreeable & unpleasant business.

Relying on your Known excellence of heart & understanding, I request you'r forgiveness for this trouble & innovation. With wishing you every blessing that this transitory life affords I'me the unfortunate—

RICHD. FENWICK—

Philip Mayer also sent his wife to deliver a letter to Jefferson. His story would have been a common tale of aristocratic tyranny in the old world; in the new American democracy, power and affluence could achieve the same results.

Washington City March 19th 1802

Thomas Jefferson President of the United States

Sʀ,

The humble *petition* of the subscriber I hope will not be thought improper. I am a poor *unfortunate* Man *imprisoned* and overcome by the Iron hand of A man of fortune. It may be said I'me not imprisoned by him but may truely date all my present misfortunes through him. The person of whom I'me speaking is a residenter of Georgetown; his name is John Therlkeld. He has injured me by taken the most unwarantabl liberties with my wife. He first tried all that art and seduction could invent to seduce her from *morality,* & the mariage bed. Finding that would not answer his *unmanly* ends—I blush to say it, he brought in force to his aid to accomplish an end that depravity itselfe must shrink at.

One evening knowing my absence from my family, he came to my dwelling, & renued his former conduct towards my wife with a brutality unprecedented amongst Civilized society. In this *unprotected* state he commited acts that would be unnecesary & indelicate for me to repeat. After my return I applied to the Law for redress. Sory am I to say poverty was too powerful [an] opponent against me. I *applied* to a Lawyer but with no affect for I'd no money to fee him to prosecute the cause. Not content with commiting his outrages on my wife, he sought every means in his power to prevent my futur peace. He went to Fredricksburg, & Baltimore for the purpose of urgeing my Creditors to means which would have never been complied with but from the most vile misrepresentations he made use of, to destroy my reputation. Those he could not bring over, he purchased for the intire intention of ruining me intoto, by throwing me in Prison. In consequence of which I was arested & am now suffering the most rigorous confinement. Bail I could have procured but for the *powerful* preponderance of his influence by the means of his riches. In short every infamous subterfuge he stooped to, to destroy me & my unhappy family.

My wife, & three small children are now exsperiencing all the *misery* that *poverty* & it's attendants can entail or stamp on it's unfortunate votaries. Situated as I am, I cannot receive that Justice which the Laws hath pointed out to every individual. The condition I'me in is a scene of the most poignat distress. Laying in Jail my wife & family perishing by the harshe hand of hunger except what the inhospitable service Charity bestowes.

I hope & trust you'll excuse, & pardon this liberty which I've taken. It arises from several reasons, first, & principal one is, at present you'r not only the illustrious President of the U States, but the supreme Magistrate of this Territory. As such I'me sure of not meeting with a repulse but in every respect the reverse. Seconly I address you, from *you'r* long tried Justice, magnanimity & Virtue—& lastly you'r benevolence & philantropic generosity was never refused to the hand of suffering distress & inocence.

If you should think proper to receive any further Information on this disagreeable & unhappy business my Wife who's the bearer of this will give it you. If you will please to interfeer so far as Justice is wanting it's all that the unfortunate Writer wishes to receive from you. That this may meet you'r approbation is the fond prayer of respected Sir the forlorn,

PHILIP MAYER

NB An answer by the bearer of this is humbly solicited by PM.

Mayer's letter, and any corroborating information that may have been offered personally by his wife, presented Jefferson with a delicate problem, for he knew the man Mayer accused of sexually abusing his wife. John Threlkeld was a wealthy landowner in the Georgetown area, and Jefferson reportedly made a gift of some pecan trees to him when Threlkeld married. During and after his presidency, Jefferson also exchanged horticultural specimens with Threlkeld.[14]

Whether this acquaintance with Threlkeld influenced Jefferson's decision in Mayer's case is unknown, but Mayer's accusations did not prevent him, in 1807, from appointing Threlkeld justice of the peace for Washington County.[15]

Normally, Jefferson did not simply ignore appeals such as Mayer's, as he did most of the unsolicited requests he received for money, jobs, or favors. The way he routinely handled them is indicated by a letter he wrote to George Blake, the federal attorney for Massachusetts.

George Blake esq.
Washington Mar. 12. 05.

SIR

I inclose an application for pardon from a person of the name of John Southark, who says he is now in Boston jail under sentence for forgery, having been confined there already 22. months and having still 14. to remain, & a sum to be paid. Considering the judges who sit in a cause, & the attorney who tries it as possessed of those circumstances which may decide whether any & what mitigation of sentence may be admitted in conformity with the objects of the constitution in confiding power of pardon to the Executive, I have usually referred these applications to them & asked their opinion. Will you be so good as to make this request of them in the present case, & at the same time to favor me with your own opinion. Accept my salutations & assurances of great respect.

TH: JEFFERSON

Blake replied that "the Culprit has not the least pretence of claim to a mitigation of his sentence. The fraud of which he is convict[ed] was in itself of a flagrant character; besides which it appeared in the trial, to have been but an item in a series of transactions of a similar nature in which the Defendant had long been concerned."[16]

There are not many records of Jefferson's releasing prisoners from jail by executive order. When the prisoner wrote to thank the president his release was recorded in Jefferson's correspondence. On October 10, 1802, for example, Joseph Parsons wrote Jefferson a note stating that he and his wife were confined in the city jail for nonpayment of a doctor's bill. In two days, he was free, writing a thank-you note:

Washington City October the 12th 1802

Your Excellency was pleased to endevered to take notice of my unfortunate situation and release me from Prison. I now take the earliest opportunity to render you my humble and warmest acknoledgments for your humane and generous interference in my favour. That you may live long and enjoy all the happiness this life can bestow will be the constant prayer of your Excellencys—

Most Obedient and much Obliged
Humble Sevt.
JOSEPH PARSONS*

Jonathan Faw, like Samuel Quarrier, had a serious oedipal conflict, but unlike Quarrier, whose father merely refused to

*Six days after sending this letter, Parsons wrote again, stating that because of his injury, he was unable to work as a seaman. He wanted a "small post" to "afford some relief at least for the present, till A return of my health and Strength." (18 October 1802, DLC) In the meantime, Jefferson had sent thirty dollars to Parsons through marshal Daniel C. Brent. "Gave D. C. Brent ord. on Barnes 30. D. charity to Parsons." Bear and Stanton, *Jefferson's Memorandum Books,* 11 October 1802.

bail his son out of jail, Faw's father, a justice of the peace, actually had his son imprisoned. Faw, who was educated, and a writer of some skill, penned a twelve-page letter describing in detail the hostilities between father and son. He prefaced his story with five pages of learned discourse on republicanism and liberty, apparently to demonstrate his talent as a political journalist, then proceeded with a life history that helped explain his father's wrath:

Washington Jail Oct. 22nd. 1803

HIS EXCELLENCY THOS. JEFFERSON ESQR.

... I am a man aged 30 years, & brought up to the service of the Law, under L. Martin whom you very well know. Possessed of a mind active, ardent, and a sensibility almost morbid, I have been nursed in the lap of prosperity; and until within the last year of my life have never exerted the powers of mind which I possess. Want of Fortitude, (not active courage) has hitherto been the great defect in my character, and the prime cause of my misfortunes. Ardent & restless as I before observed, never in a medium, I have alternately experienced the solid pleasures of severe study, and the miseries of excessive dissipation. The sensibility of my mind, aided by a very vivid imagination, magnified unexpected inconveniences & a failure of prospects, into evil incurable; and despair & drinking was the consequence, which was quickly succeeded by a fit of intense study, for 3 or 4 months by way of atonement. I speak of the last two years of my Life; the Seven immediately preceeding, were spent in professional pursuits, the requisition of science, and the deceitful pleasures of dissipation. A stranger to apathy, I have lived in a continued storm, & have been very happy and very miserable.

I have lived for a number of years upon very uneasy terms, with Abraham Faw, one of the Justices of the peace appointed by yourself, and who says he is my Father. About seven weeks ago, he desired me for ever, to quit his roof and protection; which I cheerfully complied with. . . .

In order to procure what I think an honourable subsistence, I intended to have had recourse to the labours of my pen. As I am no very great favourite of the *Muse* the Field of Politics, though much beaten, presented to my mind a flattering prospect. For I entertain no very exalted opinion, of the newpaper and pamphlet writers of America, *federal* or democratic, either with respect to their style or their matter. I remained in this state for the space of a Week when Mr. Faw requested me to become again a resident in his House, which I refused; upon which, as a Justice of the peace, he wrote the following commitment viz.

Alexander County St.

Whereas Jonathan Faw is going at large about the Town, insulting and abusing the Citizens contrary to Law & he being adjudged to find security for his good behaviour which he has failed to do You are therefore required to receive him into your custody & jail and him keep until such security be given, or otherwise discharged according to Law. Given under my hand and Seal this 15th September 1803. Capt. James Campbell Signed A: Faw (seal)

Now sir this commitment and the proceedings theron, *are* I will venture to pronounce *unprecedented* in the Annals of Tyranny under the form of Law. The Commitment is the first notification I had of the kind intentions of Mr. Faw; there never was a complaint to my knowledge, made to him, there was not a human being in Alexandria who could have made any complaint, as I had given just cause of offence to none. The Commitment itself does not state any complaint made against me, of my having violated, or that there was just ground to suspect I would violate, any, even the most minute Laws of my Country. It states indeed some nonsense about *insults* &c, which even if true, *(as it is the reverse),* he as a Justice of the Peace had nothing to do with: for insults offered

by one *free white* individual to another, I have always understood to be cognizable in a Court of honour, *injuries or the
reasonable probability of their commission* before the civil Magistrate.

But to proceed. There never was a warrant either issued
or served upon me, I was never, brought before him, or any
other Magistrate, I was never adjudged to give any security,
(because he very well knew that I could easily have procured
the most respectable characters in Alexa[ndria] to have bound
themselves for me. *The trial, the judg[ment], the failure to comply
with it* on my part, I solemnly declare, never existed any where
except in the prolific fancy of Mr. Faw; and the commitment
aforesaid, the first the only proceeding on his part, was at
once put to the hands of a Constable, with directions to
apprehend me wherever I might be found, and carry me to
Prison.

In pursuance of which, on the Day mentioned therein, about
four O Clock p m, as I was peaceably and orderly conversing
with some Gentlemen at the upper end of King Street, I was
accosted by the officer and desired to walk to jail. As much
astonished, as if I had been requested to walk to Arcassia, I
demanded to know, to what authority I was indebted for his
polite attention, when he produced the Commitment.* Enraged
at the villainy, as well as the illegality of the proceedure, I
told him nothing but the exertion of superior physical power,
could procure a compliance on my part. Consequently he
summoned the *Posse Comitatus.*** The Gentlemen who were
present refused to participate in the infamous transaction; and
I should have escaped the clutches of petty despotism, had it
not been for the interference of a poor wretch, one of the
lowest among the very dregs of Society. With his assistance,
I was forcibly dragged through the streets like the vilest

---

* "Arcassia," apparently from Arcas, ancestor of the Arcadians, hence Arcadia.
** *Posse comitatus,* "the body of men above the age of fifteen in a country . . . whom the
sheriff may summon or 'raise' to repress a riot or for other purposes. . . ." *Oxford English
Dictionary*

malefactor, and confined in a prison for the space of three weeks, in which under existing circumstances, I declare I should have thought myself a monster of inhumanity, to have shut up the most execrable villain, that ever disgraced the world. For you will be pleased to observe, that the Jail I speak of, *is the very same,* in which on account of the prevailing epidemick, Doctr. Dick the health officer of Alexandria, had previously declared, that it was impossible for any human being to exist for any length of time; and from *which* the humane interference of the Judge, *had* (to the knowledge of Mr. Faw) before my confinement, *removed* every prisoner. . . .*

And how much is the dye of this transaction deepened, when I consider, that the very day after he had thus placed me in the center of contagion, he removed himself with his family, from the most healthy part of Alexandria to Frederick Town, in order to escape the prevailing disease? That Family consists of one brother, & two sisters by my Fathers side, and their mother his *present* wife. . . .**

After remaining as I before observed, three weeks in the Jail of Alexandria, I was on the eighth Day of this month, in consequence of an order from Judge Cranch, *removed* to the jail of this City, where altho the humanity of the Marshal sometimes permits me to walk about on my *parol,* I am still in Law a prisoner.[17] I do not know that you have any constitutional power to interfere in my case; the best method of obtaining a release *is,* to be discharged by a Judge on a *Habeas Corpus* and with respect to obtaining a Redress for the injury I have sustained, the Laws of my Country afford me the Action of *False Imprisonment.* . . .

I rely for my justification for the whole of this letter, on your liberality and nobleness of mind, which will not permit

---

*A yellow-fever epidemic took numerous lives in Alexandria; Jefferson contributed one hundred dollars for sick relief. Bear and Stanton, *Jefferson's Memorandum Books,* 29 September 1803.

**This information suggests that Faw's difficulties with his father may have resulted in part from his being displaced in his father's affections by a stepmother and her three children.

Truth to depend upon time, place, or accident; and upon the maxim *"Homo sum et nihil humanum alienum a me puto,"* by which I believe you to have been always actuated, and which you must have used before I was born.*

Accept my poor wishes for your health and prosperity, and permit me to subscribe myself, with sentiments of very great respect

Yr obedt. servt
JONA. FAW

This was a letter that Jefferson answered. His reply was tactful, but it placed blame on both father and son, the father for overstepping his legal authority, and the son for voluntarily failing to obtain a habeas corpus—presumably to punish his father by endangering his own life in a pestilent jail.

Mr. Jona. Faw.
Washington Oct. 25. 03.

SIR

The case, which is the subject of the letter you favoured me yesterday, was so perfectly understood by yourself, what the law is, & what the remedy, and that that remedy, the Habeus corpus is always within your own reach, that no information respecting it seems necessary from me, or to be required. Indeed it appears altogether a family misunderstanding in which the exercise of paternal & legal authorities have perhaps been improperly blended, & that the submission on your part is voluntary and regretful. It is impossible for a stranger to judge between parties whose relations & close feelings constitute the whole difficulty of the case. And altho' I should certainly interpose in any case of illegal & involuntary confinement communicated to me, yet it would

---

* *"Homo sum; humani nihil a me alienum puto"*: I am a man; nothing human is foreign to me. Terence, *Heuton Timorous menos,* 1. 77.

not be till a Habeus corpus had been refused or an inability to apply for it made known to me. In the present case I suppose neither of these alternatives to exist, and I persuade myself that the parties will find in their affections a remedy & reconciliation. Accept my wishes that this may soon take place.

TH: JEFFERSON

Another young man, George Todd, also had an irate father dispatch him to jail, but in this case it was not his own father. Running off with a man's underage daughter, he discovered, could bring serious consequences.

Richmond 8th Nov. 1805.

His Excellency Thomas Jefferson Esq.

HON'D SIR

It is with extreme regret that I am compelled to trouble you with a narrative of my miserable situation, for being deprived [of] the enjoyment of my liberty which is more dear to me than life itself, for a charge of Misdemeanor for—taking a young woman under the age of sixteen Out of and from the possession of her father, though proved to be upwards of fifteen years of age, for which charge I was on Friday the 6th of September last sentenced by a jury of twelve men to undergo a confinement in the Common gaol by the space of eighteen months. I am good Sir in hopes you will pardon the liberty I take in addressing my feeble words to you for a restoration of my lost liberty. As my unhappy situation not only calls upon your humanity but of your compassion also; for being a young man in the bloom and vigor of life scarcely as yet one and twenty years of age and having a venerable mother whose tears perhaps at this present moment are trickling down her withered cheeks; besides an affectionate father who is now and has been for these thirty years past a reputable citizen of this town, for the consolation of my distressed friends and relations as well as for the restoration of my own liberty, I most earnestly supplicate you Sir for a pardon. . . .

I am your Excellencys Most Obt

> Humble Servant
> GEORGE RICHARDSON TODD

The following letter is not easily deciphered because the narrative is so disjointed. A young sailor seemingly went to a brothel, was involved in a gambling game and won, but was then accused of theft and subsequently imprisoned. He wants to be released from jail to serve in the U.S. Navy.

Norfolk Jail, March 12, 1807

HIS EXCELLENCY THO. JEFFERSON P. U.S.

Respected Sir, pardon me for Writing a few lines To a Gentleman of yr. repute and high Estimation But emmergentcy compels me to inform you of my Misfortune in this place. Having no friend and an entire Stranger makes me Address you Sir with a few lines which I hope will be Pardoned.

I am Sir a True Born American likewise would loose the last drop of blood in behalf of my Country at any Time when call'd upon. On the 20 of Jany. theare was a acquasation brought against me So Strange and absurd in Every sence of the word that Sir, it would put almost any One to clear Themselves of the charge. I happened with 2 young men in one of those houses of Low fame and theare was a Equality play Exhibited.* I happen'd to be Successful and Won, a Cruel Banditry. One Said they lost a Small Pocket Book with 50 dolrs. and the money must be Theares. No one Saw me take

---

*The term "Equality play" has not been found in any of the standard reference works on gambling or gaming.

any thing; I was Search'd nothing found with me belonging to them—neither in my trunk nor no wheare.

I always Bought hard for what I Got and Gentleman of Rank was fond of my company. My father and mother are both dead and I have a recommendation Throughout the Globe. I serv'd my time with Valentine Reintzel, Sadler, George Town Joining the city.* My constitution no ways impaired, I will Enter on Board the Chesapeak or any vessel of the navy. Usualy Your order Sir is Sufficient and I am at Your command. Sign'd a

True Republican and a Distress'd Young Fellow

in a Strange place

THOMAS M. FERRALL

. . . My attorney Mr. Rob. B. Taylor Says theare is no proof; he will get me of[f] but I suffer in Jail. Sir none but people of the Worst caracters against me and will Swear any thing which can be prov'd.

The following correspondent, Edon Marchant, received what seems an unusually harsh sentence for the equivalent in his day of refusing to move out of the passing lane of a highway. He was undoubtedly prosecuted, as he claimed, as an example to other drivers to yield the road to the mail stage, but his case also reveals the deplorable condition of roads in the nation's federal period. On a major turnpike, it was often impossible for one vehicle to pass another on narrow, muddy, rutted roadbeds. Marchant was, however, stubborn in his refusal to allow the stage to pass immediately, and it cost him dearly. His case also demonstrated once again how jail costs could mount disastrously for prisoners.

His letter was accompanied by a note from the jailer, John H. Bentley, certifying that the facts of his sentencing and imprisonment were correct.

*Ferrall had been a saddler's apprentice.

Baltimore Jail, 23d. March, 1808.

To Thomas Jefferson Esquire,
President of the United States

Sir,

I could write my remonstrance with more confidence if I thought that, amidst the loud calls of publick, official duties, which now peculiarly demand your attention and claim your allmost ceaseless care, the tale of individual private misery, could reach your ear. And, did I not recollect, that your philanthropic disposition induces you (as well as a regard for administering Justice in misery) to relieve distress, *when not produced by flagrant crime*—I would yet be silent.

I will in a few words Submit a true Statement of facts to your excellency: In the month of December last, I undertook to drive a waggon loaded with flour and leather, from Berkley County in the State of Virginia to this City. On the 29th. day of that Month, I was driving along, without accident on the Fredrick Turnpike, near Ellicots Mills, when the mail Stage drove up. I was *ordered* to clear my waggon out of the driver's way and as it was done in a tone of menace, I do confess (for I will let you know the *worst* features of my case) I did not immediately obey him, but at length finding it to be the stage which carried the newspapers, letters &c. which *I did not know at first,* I turned my Horses aside for it. At the *utmost,* he could not have been detained above *six* or *eight minutes.* How was I surprised, when for this slight offense, I was, on the 31st. day of the same month arrested in Baltimore, and carried before his Honour Judge Chase, who immediately commited me to Prison.* As I was taken by surprise, I had no time to reflect; nor could I, being an utter stranger to this City, have found bail. It was with much difficulty I found a Waggoner, who agreed for an exorbitant Sum to convey the waggon and team back again to Berckley, where I fear my Father, Mother

---

*Samuel Chase, justice of the Supreme Court.

and Friends are obliged to hang down their heads, from malicious reports, that I am in Gaol for some henious transgression.

I ought here to acquaint your Honour, that the charges in the commitment are as follows: "for that he did knowingly and willingly obstruct the Driver of the Mail Stage on the Fredrick Town Turnpike road." Yet, the driver confessed at the same time that he sued *me* to make me an example to others. The hardships of a man *closely* confined in an unsavory and crowded appartment, especially me, who had always been accustomed to an out-of-door business, you may readily conceive. I have been near three months in it, and *all my money is gone:* for I found it impossible to live on the Jail allowance alone. The court will not commence till the month of *May* next, and then I could only state the very same things I have done to your excellency, which however the driver of the Mail Stage cannot deny.

Now, Sir, I humbly submit it to your excellency, Wheather, for so small an offence, I have not been already Sufficiently punished? And, should it please you, to direct the district Attorney Mr. Stevens, to set me free by some means or other; *if, upon examination he find my story to be true,* your excellency will act as *mercifully* as *justly* for, Should I be fined or confined, at the court for this offence, I can not extricate myself in either case, after the sentence is complied with, as the Jail fees claimed here are enormous; and the Sheriff has a custom of *selling convicted persons for them!*

If I am so fortunate as to obtain your excellency's consent to my release from this hateful and irksome situation, I pledge myself by every particle of spirit and feeling that animates my frame, to show myself *(if war ensue,)* not unworthy of your excellency's bounty.

I remain your hble. Servt.
EDON MARCHANT.

The following formal petition on behalf of James Carroll was signed by forty-three men. That this many white men would object to the imprisonment of another white man for beating two black men is not surprising for this time and place. Jefferson characteristically requested an opinion from the official involved in the case, in this instance, John T. Mason, attorney for the District of Columbia. Under the endorsement on the petition Jefferson wrote: "rejected on the recommendation of J.T.M." It was an appropriate decision for the man whose ringing declaration, "all men are created equal," had become one of the anthems of the new American republic.

[Received 10 July 1802]

To THE PRESIDENT OF THE UNITED STATES

The Petition of James Carroll of the City of Washington, Blacksmith; most humbly Sheweth,

That at a Circuit Court of the District of Columbia, begun and held in the City of Washington on the fourth Monday of June last, your Petitioner was fined at the suit of the United States in the sum of Twenty dollars and costs of suit for an assault and battery on the body of John Veach, a black man, and in the sum of Twenty dollars and costs of suit, for an assault and battery on the body of Daniel McGinnis, a black man; for non payment whereof, he is now confined in Washington County prison.

That the motive which urged him to these breaches of the Law, arose from those black men's having previously beat and abused his employer John Galloway, a white man, with whom your Petitioner then wrought at his trade.

That his reputation has not been sullied by any other charges, than those for which he is fined, and he trusts that the certificate hereto annexed, attested by persons who have a knowledge of him, and his humility and affliction, will induce the exercise of the prerogative of Mercy in his favor. He

therefore most humbly implores you to remit the fines aforesaid; and thereby enable him to apply his labor to the discharge of the costs accruing thereon.

And he is in duty bound will pray &c.

We whose names are hereunto annexed knowing the Petitioner James Carroll to be a sober, honest and industrious
man, and believing the facts stated by him to be true; do
recommend him as a proper object for having the fines alluded
to in his Petition remitted him.

[Signed by forty-three men]

Jefferson did take action, however, in the case of Richard
Hoskins, formerly chief clerk in the Boston Post Office, whose
constitutional right to swift justice was blatantly infringed.

Charlestown Prison, Augt. 14. 1808.

To the President of the United States of America

The Petition of Richard Quince Hoskins of Boston, in the
County of Suffolk, and Commonwealth of Massachusetts,
Humbly sheweth:

That your petitioner was tried at the Circuit Court of this
District in June term 1805, on a charge of embezzling, and
secreting a letter from the Post Office in said Boston, and
found guilty of the same, but owing to an action in arrest of
judgment, filed by the Council of your Petitioner, which action
was unknown to him, til last December, the sentence was
postponed for further consideration until October term, a lapse
of four and an half months.*

Your petitioner, begs leave, further to state to your Excellency, that since the first finding of the Indictment against
him, he has already suffered Fifty months imprisonment. Your
petitioner, therefore humbly prays, that your Excellency would

---

*Unknown to Hoskins, his lawyer filed a motion to have his sentence postponed, caus-
ing a further delay in his sentencing.

be pleased to look in tenderness upon his calamitous situation, and extend to him your pardon.

And as in duty bound, will ever pray

RICHARD QUINCE HOSKINS

Boston Augt. 28. 1808.

To the President of the United States
SIR

Permit me the liberty to return to you, my sincere thanks, for your generosity in restoreing me to my family, friends, and liberty, which took place yesterday afternoon. Rest assured, Sir, that the favor is not thrown away upon an unworthy object, but granted to one who will ever endeavour to merit it.

With Sincere Respect and Esteem
I remain Sir,
your most humle. Servt.

RICHARD QUINCE HOSKINS

The following pair of letters from husband and wife are a contrast in styles. The husband was a Bristol, Rhode Island, sea captain who was convicted of illegally engaging in the slave trade and fined $14,000. The British had captured his ship and confiscated both the vessel and the slaves. He had lost everything, and was now destitute, he claimed, with a wife, five children, and a mother to feed. He had forwarded two petitions to Jefferson, signed by numerous Bristol citizens, asking for his release.[18] He is as complete a phonetic speller as anyone who ever wrote to Jefferson; however, his barely readable letter makes up in assertiveness what it lacks in literacy. His wife is obviously his superior in education, but she is typical of the women who wrote to Jefferson; in the paternalistic society of this period, men demanded; women pleaded. Her letter strips away all legalities and arguments— her husband's offense is never mentioned by either of them— and reduces her suit to a naked cry for help.

Bristol [R.I.]April the 28th 1803

To the President of the United States

MOST HONOURED SUR

I am the Poor and humbel Petitioner that has sent on two Petition for my Rel[ie]f and Eant heaired Eany thing from them Nor from your honour, most honoured Sur. Sur I am Poor and Eant Nothing to Suport me and my famly on. Most honorered Sur I Eant marster of Eany trade to Supoort me and my famly With. I humbly Badg that you, Sur Will Send me Sum relf. If not Sur I and my famly must Sufer in a Criston land. If I Sur Was in a furing Curnty and a Prisner With the trippooling I Should have Sum Suport from their Chif but Sur heir I am, and Eant had Eany Suport from no one and God Only Noes Wheir It is a Coming from.* Sur but grant me the Libty of going about the town to Work for my Suport for hear Sur their is Nothing hear to Suport me and my famly With in this Prisen but the bear Worls [walls]. Sur I humbelly Wish to have a few Lins from your honour to Let me No If their is Eany time Sat for my relf. This Sur Is the Secont that I have Sant to your honour and I hope Sur that I Shant have a Cashon [occasion] to Sand No mor.

I am your Most humbel Sarvent
NATHANIEL INGRAHAM

Ten days after Ingraham's letter arrived, Jefferson received an appeal from his wife, Mary Ingraham. Her letter had been

*He refers to American seamen held captive by Tripolitan pirates.

mailed five months earlier—on October 30 of the previous year—a sorry commentary on the efficiency of mail delivery in early America.

Bristol Octo. 30 1802

To the President of the United States

RESPECTED SIR,

After You have heard the Petition presented for an unhappy Man, [Nathaniel Ingraham] will you not Sir lend a favorable ear to mine? It is a Wife petitioning for the liberty—for the life of her husband, for will not his health—his life be the sacrifice of an imprisonment embittered by the painful reflection of a suffering Wife and five lovely children consign'd to poverty and distress.

We Sir have no Parent to reach forth the fostering hand, or shelter us beneath the paternal roof through the approaching inclement season. A widowed Mother alone survives to mourn the disappointment of her hopes. Of seven Sons (by a life of prudence and economy reared to manhood) two only survives. The rest have been swallowed up by the devouring seas. From my Husband she looked for comfort and support in her decline of life. Oh Sir, will You not pity her? Will You not have compassion on us all? We offer no excuse—we attempt no palliation! It is your Clemency Great Sir we entreat. Speak but the word, and my Husband will be released—restored to his usefulness—and rendered to happiness. Pardon respected Sir this tale of woe, this intrusion on your time. Reflect on the importance of the subject to a Wife to a Mother, and that it is natural to affliction to complain. You Sir who are a son, and probably a Father, will you not bring our case home to your own feelings?

Your known character for humanity and tenderness makes me hope that you will—and that I shall not plead in vain. In

that hope (Oh may it not prove illusive) I subscribe myself
Great Sir Your Most Obedient

Humble Servant
MARY INGRAHAM

Mary Ingraham's emotional plea for clemency is a striking illustration of women's willingness to sacrifice pride for the sake of a husband's well-being. Her letter won no sympathy for her husband, however; Jefferson considered him a common criminal. In a letter to Senator Christopher Ellery of Rhode Island, Jefferson noted that Ingraham was in prison after being fined $14,000 and costs "for having been the master of a vessel which brought from Africa a cargo of the natives of that country to be sold into slavery."[19] Ingraham now petitions for a pardon, wrote Jefferson,

> as does his wife also on behalf of herself her children & his mother. His situation so far as concerns himself merits no consideration, short of his wife, children & mother, suffering for want of his aid, even so also does the condition of the unhappy human beings whom he forcibly brought away from their native country, & whose wives, children & parents are suffering for want of their aid & comfort. Between these two sets of suffering beings whom his crimes have placed in that condition, we are to apportion our commiseration.

Jefferson cited similar cases under the insolvency laws and noted that there was a minimum penalty of two years imprisonment. "In his case of insolvency," he concluded, "he must remain therefore the two years in prison. . . ." He would consider a pardon, Jefferson declared, after two years, or whatever term the judge and district attorney who prosecuted the case believed would be sufficient to act "as a terror to others mediating the same crime." He relented on this judgment, however. After receiving documents on the case he wrote to David L. Barnes on February 24, 1804, "I have ordered a pardon as to whatever appurtains to the U.S. leaving the interests of the prosecutor untouched."[20] (The pardon applied only to federal offenses; any state laws violated remained unpardoned.)

Jefferson's comment on the inhumanity of breaking up African families by enslaving the husband was one of the strongest statements on this particular effect of bondage in all of his writings on slavery. In comparing the hardships suffered by Mary Ingraham and her family with the sufferings of the wives and families of the African men Ingraham transported into slavery, Jefferson insisted that the miseries of the white American family cannot be isolated from those of African families. The slave trader Ingraham would have thought it a curious message coming from a man who himself held black families in bondage at Monticello for all of his adult life.

Of all the letters Jefferson received pleading for justice, none was more outraged and demanding of retribution than the appeal of Henry Brinkerhoff of Hackensack, New Jersey. He wrote to the president in a prose as disjointed as his state of mind. He related in his letter that he had been living with a friend, Abraham Ackerman, who stole bonds worth £115, the deed to fifty acres of land, and then attempted to kill him. His demand for justice was quite specific:

Hackensack New Jersey April [18] 1801

MR JEFFERSON YOU HIGH PRESIDENT OF NORTH AMERICA
    . . . [Abraham Ackerman] Meant he than to kill Me than that time when I Lived with him be Bought A half Barrel of Rum for Me and I think that he bought the half Barrel of

Rum than Porpose to kill Me if he Could than he thought
that he would Got all My Money all and as soon as you Mr
Jeferson Receive all this My letter all from Me than I wish
that you will Quick Pas A Law for to have Abraham Acker-
mans Land all sold for his stealing My bonds and My Deed
of all My Land and Mr. Jeferson I advise you than Quick that
you Must tare all Abraham Ackerman Cloaths of all his back
all Clean all of him and Put him in the undermost Lowest
Dungions their and Chain him with three Chains of iron one
Chain over the Middle of his Neck and the other Chain Middle
over his Heart and the other Chain Middle over his breach
Band and he Must be Chained on his back and he Must have
three Crums of bread A Day but and Not A No More and
the first court he fetch up in and before the Court of People
that before the Lawyers and that high Judge of the Court and
the Grand the Grand Jury of the Court too and Mr. Jeferson
I will advise you for to do that because he is a Devil of a
theaf unupright and A unupright wrong Murderer he is Against
Me wrong unupright and than if you do that than than you
will do than upright for all My Love.

HENRY BRINKERHOFF

6

Literature

"Illustrious Sage! of man the gen'ral friend"

AS much as Thomas Jefferson was a writer of letters, he was a man of letters; his reading in language and literature was vast. He was a classicist, at home with Greek and Latin, and could read Anglo-Saxon, French, Spanish, and Italian.[1] Although his entire public career as a revolutionary, politician, and statesman was grounded on his skill as a writer, he was author of only one full-length book, *Notes on the State of Virginia,* first published in 1785. It was a work that was widely quoted during his presidency, often by the Federalist press, which used the sections on slavery and religion as targets for abuse. In spite of these attacks, the range of statistical knowledge, the skill at argument, and the forceful rhetoric of *Notes* increased Jefferson's reputation as a polymath and patron of the arts and sciences.

The work that won Jefferson the greatest admiration as a writer by laboring-class Americans, however, was the Declaration of Independence. For many, it was the only work of his they knew. It was frequently printed in newspapers during his presidency and was publicly read as part of patriotic celebrations on the Fourth of July. The soaring eloquence of the Declaration's claim that life, liberty, and the pursuit of happiness are the right of every American established Jefferson as master of the nation's most sublime prose.

Writers of every cast saw him as a kindred spirit, one who could appreciate their work, offer advice on how to improve it, or help to publicize it. During his presidency, he received numerous prose and verse manuscripts, and even more presentation copies of books and pamphlets. Most of these were sent with the hope of attaining the president's endorsement.

One of the first manuscripts he received after assuming the presidency was from a young man who wanted to use Jefferson's name to obtain subscribers for his book. Publishing by subscription was common in early America; it was the only way that unknown or little-known authors could get printers to take the risk of publishing their work. If the author could obtain enough promises of purchase to assure a profit, the publisher would print the book.

John West Butler's letter begins by proclaiming himself the equal to Homer and Shakespeare; he then throws himself on the mercy of the president as "a young man, just setting out in life" looking for some "encouragement." But he is clever in admitting that he is a Federalist and then quoting the much-repeated lines from Jefferson's first Inaugural Address: "We are all Republicans, we are all Federalists."

Annapolis, April 13th. 1801.

Sir,

Having issued proposals for printing the enclosed work, and intending shortly to commence a tour through many of the States, particularly Virginia, for the purpose of obtaining Subscribers, I have ventured to solicit the early patronage of a Character so well known, and justly respected, both on account of his high office, and the brilliant talents which have placed him in it, conscious that a name so celebrated and beloved, will not only add a pleasing lustre and respectibility to the Proposals, but insure a large increase of Subscribers to a work that is approved by, and graced with, the illustrious name of *Jefferson*. And, believe me, Sir, your name will by no means be dishonoured by patronizing the *"Abbess,"* a work, allowed by the highest judges, to bear the strongest marks of worth and genius. What better proof, Sir, can be produced or required, of the truth of this assertion, than, that it was written by the author of "Shakespeare's Papers," a work, the spirit and genius of which, have so near an alliance and close imitation of the British Homer, that the greatest literary judges and warmest admirers of the English Bard not only gave it their decided voice in favour of its originating in Shakespeare's fertile brain, but even the Reviewers, those literary dictators, passed on it a long Eulogium, and congratulated the lovers of wit, taste, and genius, on the restoration of those unlooked for, those valuable, inimitable, and long lost *"Papers"* of the immortal Shakespeare!

My esteem for your Character, and my firm belief that it is your sincere intention, to act up, in every respect, even the most minute, to that wise, virtuous, and liberal conduct, which your "Address" promises in such clear, nervous, and elegant language, can not be better shewn, than by informing you that I am a Federalist. In despite of party prejudice, and of flimsy evasions, to obtain a favour by renouncing my principles, I make this declaration, and, when I consider to whom I address it, every fear that you will treat me with neglect on that account, vanishes, as that noble sentiment immediately occurs to my mind, that *"We are all Republican, we are all Federalists,"* a sentiment well worthy of its Author as it is the vital principle of political tolerance and liberality.

Excuse me, Sir, for detaining you this long, impelled as I was by the impulse of my mind to let you know the truth, which is far superior, though in a homely garb, to falsehood decked in purple robes. The favour I ask, Sir, would be particularly grateful, as I am a young man, just setting out in life;

a situation in which a small encouragement is received with gratitude, and remembered with pleasure, and to whom, on the other hand, the frowns of Fortune or of Friends, are felt with keenness and cutting severity; as a youth, where embarking on the troubled and fluctuating ocean of the world, must ever have the innate sensibilities of his nature, wound up to a peculiar tone of delicacy, consequently the sunshine of Fortune, or the clouds of disappointment, make a strong and lasting impression on his mind. Should you grant this favour, Sir, it will ever be remembered with gratitude, but should you do more, and send me a line annexed, it would confer an obligation that the sweeping hand of time would be unable to erase from the mind of, Sir, your most grateful, sincere, and obedient humble Servant,

JOHN WEST BUTLER
Easton, [Pa.] April 22.

P.S. Should you Sir, grant my request, you will greatly oblige me, by directing it to me at Baltimore, whither I shall be at the time of your sending it, as I shall set off for that City in a few days.

I send this letter from Easton, having had it by me these ten days waiting an opportunity of coming hither, as well for the purpose of obtaining subscribers, as to request Mr. G. Duvall's opinion of the propriety of sending it; and having obtained his judgment thereon, which is flattering to my wishes, I now take the liberty of forwarding it.*

Jefferson was gracious enough to read Butler's manuscript. In returning it he wrote, "tho' a stranger to the work I have not hesitated to give this much of my personal support" because of a "desire to encourage the art of printing in this country." Rather than depend on his testimonial for its

---

* Gabriel Duvall (1752–1844), a member of Congress from Maryland and later a justice of the Supreme Court.

success, Jefferson wrote, he hoped instead that "Abbess" would succeed "from the solid circumstances of the merit of the work and . . . the patronage of the public."[2]

Butler was not successful in getting it published as a book. Indeed, there are no records of any books being published by him. "Shakespeare's Papers" may have been published in a newspaper or magazine, however, or self-published as a pamphlet. Although Butler did not become a published poet, he did become a newspaper editor. During Jefferson's presidency he changed his politics from Federalist to Republican. He briefly edited the Baltimore *Whig* in 1807, and in 1809 sent Jefferson a prospectus for a new weekly Annapolis newspaper, *The Maryland Republican*. He edited it for more than two years before disposing of it.[3]

Another request for a book subscription came from a German teacher who had written a pronunciation guide to the English language, and who hoped Jefferson's name on the subscription list would "encourage the wealthy Germans to subscribe." The author, Christian Becker, gained little by pleading poverty, for, as Jefferson wrote to John West Butler, he believed that a book should survive or perish on "the merit of the work."

Washington City the 18 of April 1807

SIR,

The Subscriber begs your Excellency, to be so kind as to subscribe your Name upon a List of Subscribers, for a Book which is to be printed by Subscription, entitled: "Every German his own Master of the English Language, or: The German's best Companion in the United States of North America; who teaches the Pronunciation of the English Vowels and Consonants by the Help of Numbers &c. To which are prefixed, new and easy Rules for the Pronunciation of the German Vowels and Consonants, whereby an Englishman may easily obtain the Knowledge of the German Language," as it will be of great Benefit to him, because your Excellency's Name will encourage the wealthy Germans to subscribe.

The Subscriber entertains the Hope, that your Excellency will not decline to subscribe; as he has met with the Loss of the Whole of his Property on the Shore of this hospitable Country—as the enclosed short and credible Certificat most plainly illustrates—and is therefore very poor, and consequently destitute of Friends, Assistance and a Livelihood; which he hopes, by the Help of divine Providence, to procure by the Publishing of this very difficult Piece of Work. The Subscriber beseeches your Excellency, to consider the deplorable Situation of a Man, who once had a confortable Livlihood; and who is now reduced, by the Hand of Providence, to the Want of almost all Necessities of Life; and that it is at present in your Excellency's Power, to restore in Part his former Situation; for which he most shuredly for ever remains

Your most grateful and respected Servant

CHRISTIAN BECKER
Teacher of the German Lan. in the State of Pennsylvania.

Jefferson did not answer the letter, but Becker succeeded in having his book published without the president's endorsement with a modified version of the title Becker had translated for Jefferson: *Ein jeder Deutscher sein eigner englischer Sprachmeister, oder; Der Deutschen bester Gesellschafter, in den Vereinigten Staaten von America; welcher die englische Sprache in Fragen und Antworten, auf eine ganz neue und sehr leichtet Art in kurzer Zeit Gründlich lehret. Eingerichtet zum Gebrauch der Schulen für Lehrende und Lernende.*[4] In fact, Becker wrote and published several other German textbooks, including a children's primer, purchased, no doubt, by wealthy German parents.

THE following letter consisted of twenty-seven pages: three large, tightly written folio sheets, and twenty-four small pages. These included an outline for a proposed book, plus a second letter. The writer, John Chamberlin, was a backwoods political philosopher, who wanted Jefferson's support for a "treatise on government" by one of "the common labouring part of the citizens." What makes Chamberlin's letter interesting is his graphic account of his life in the thinly populated north woods near Bangor, Maine.

Massachusetts / Maine / New Ohio, near Bangor*
Augt. 12th. 1805. Continued to Febry. 16. 1806.

Honorable Th. Jefferson Esq. President of the U. St.

HONOURED SIR,

... What ever disagreeable feelings it gives me, I must own that it is impossible under present circumstances, for me to proceed on such a work, without pecuniary aid, in some way to me unknown. My poverty, want of eloquence and address in speaking, and the rich monied men of my acquaintance being mostly on the opposite side, throw such mighty discouragements in my way, that I conceive it utterly unavailing for me to resort to any measures, previous to this communication.

Though without classical education, untaught in grammar, and never had leisure for large reading, yet have studied human nature, am not destitute of philanthropy—have spent much meditation on the nature of a free civil government, as well as that of religion, and on the genuine meaning of the civil constitution under which I have the happiness to live. On these I have the assurance to think I have made some improvements of late, from what has been generally con-

---

*This confusing dateline is Chamberlin's attempt to pinpoint an address for territory that was still part of the state of Massachusetts.

ceived by our polititians, and which, it may be hoped, would not be an unacceptable offering to the public. . . .

In my retired situation in the wilderness, nearly 30 miles from any post office or male-rout, or incorporated town or vilage to which we have access, and circumstanced otherwise as I am—have had no convenient opertunity for advice or assistance, respecting these outlines.

I have never wrote any thing for the press excepting a little for newspapers. What ever I have written in divers newspapers hath uniformly been in favour of the freedom and sovereignty of the people. . . .

I am both a farmer & mechanic, and should I make a publication I might be under one or both of these characters; but unless it would be thought that my name would be useful to the work—should choos to withold it.

Since I have taken it upon me to speak to your self—cannot be wholly silent in respect to the evils we have to encounter, in this wilderness country to which I have lately emigrated, principally to produce a farm for my two young Sons. I live not far from the centre of a tract country about the size of 40 miles square, regularly laid out in townships of 6 miles square, in most of which a few settlers have got in. Our hardships are great—prospects distressing. In this whole tract there is not one post office or mail passage, or incorporated town; we are outcasts from the privilege of sufferage, and in a great measure from society. Not a meeting or a [synod] house, and but one store in the tract, and that for the most part as bad as empty. Our roads in such an unimproved state as to be poorly passible even for single pack-horses most of the year. Our poverty and want of number prevents our making them much better. Our lands are allowed to be generally good (for New England) but the Northering, and the length & hardness of our Winters makes living much harder. I am a little North of latutude 45. We are situated on the western side of Penobscot river but some of our waters fall into Kenebec. Our trade is nearly all on the former rivers out of our own tract. We depend on them for great part of our meat, and most of our clothing &c. Those traders lay a high contribution on us, in the price of goods. I think from about 30, to nearly 100 pr. cent. from the Boston prices. Our poverty obliges us to submit. Much we have to take up, on the Credit of our crops, and many of us cannot clear out at the end of the year, as our goods are charged. . . .

It is not very uncommon for us to feel the burden of a body of snow full four feet deep on a level, thro' a great part of our long & hard winters; so that from our very scatter'd situation, fewness of numbers &c—many in our families are literally imprisoned in our log houses, with only (if we may say so) the Liberty of the yard. In fact we are, nearly all of us, in a sense imprisoned, in this dark cell of the Earth, where scarce any light visits our habitations of woe, but those of the material heavens, & from our hearths (where any we have) and those of reason & reflection; these latter serve to whet the edge of our miseries, while they announce to us the desperate probability of our wearing out our remaining stay in these complicated miseries, and leaving them as a wretched legacy to our unhappy children. For having embargued our little all for this country, we cannot go back without actual beggery!

We conceive, that many people not far from us, from the fame of the goodness of our lands, in comparison to many other parts of this district, superficially frame an opinion that our circumstances will shortly be agreeable; but what is a good soil, even if it is such as will bear that character in the western parts of the union, without civil or religious *society,* without *information,* almost without *roads,* without the means of education for our *children* and almost without *hope* but in *death?*

. . . I am writing this (dear Sir) by fire light, before the break of day, when light, must be preparing to go nearly 30 miles for some necessary supplies for my family—the man by whom I sent, having gone 12 miles of the way with an ox team had to stop for badness of roads, dispose of his load of grain & return with the necessary expense of three days time tho' an active sober, and industrious man! Nearly all of us without religous instruction, or means of education for our children—the difficulty of obtaining family supplies almost insurmountable—the hope of much better times being far distant, and almost hopeless—from our poverty, fewness of numbers, very scattered situation, and discouragements to emegrations here, on account of these troubles &c, and for the hard terms of sale &c, imposed by nonresident proprietors—We are constrained to look up to your self, and to the general good as, under God, the most likely powers on Earth to reach out to us a helping hand. . . .

I must ask pardon for the bad looks of these papers, have been obliged to write most of it in the Night time, when others sleep, for want [of] leisure, in my smoky cotage. . . .

JOHN CHAMBERLIN

N.B. The writer hopes himself not mistaken in the opinion, that all communications, to & from the president, as well as the P. M. Genl. pass post-free.

Of the numerous unsolicited publications Jefferson received in the mail, one was a pamphlet on the education of the deaf and dumb. The author, Francis Green, was born in Boston, but his pamphlet, "Vox Oculis Subjecta" ["The Voice Subjected to the Eye"], was published anonymously in London in 1783. His deaf son attended Thomas Braidwood's school for the deaf and dumb in Edinburgh, and his pamphlet concerned Braidwood's methods of education.

Medford near Boston
5th November 1805.

SIR

Philanthropy, as well as Philosophy, no less than Dignity of Station, & Influence, designating the Patron of a Beneficence, and of useful Arts & Sciences in the United States, the Pamphlet "Vox Oculis Subjecta" (so long ago hastily published during a residence in England, and now circulated in this *the native Land* of *the Author,* in hopes of eventually benefiting *an unfortunate Class* of the human race, in this western Hemisphere) is herewith humbly presented accordingly.

The Number, Sir, in that unhappy predicament within this State, alone is ascertain'd to be nearly *seventy,* if not more, & it is calculated that not less than *Two hundred* exist in these United States. As, in several of the Nations of Europe, peculiar Seminaries have of late been establish'd for the special Education of such, it is hoped, that America may, also, 'ere long, by some means, partake, in future, of a similar Alleviation of human Misery.

The Liberty herein assum'd, Sir, by an obscure Recluse, is prompted by a disinterested Zeal for the *inestimable advantage* of the naturally deaf, commonly denominated the *Deaf & Dumb,* & dictated by the Sensibility, & former Experience of a Parent; Motives which it is with respectful submission presum'd will be condescendingly regarded as some *kind* of admissible apology. In that hope, together with the best wishes for every possible degree of Happiness to my Country under your Excellency's administration and with due Deference, I beg Leave to subscribe myself

Your Excellency's truly humble Servant,
FRANCIS GREEN

Jefferson responded by thanking Green for the work, adding "the subject cannot but be interesting to every philanthropist." When it was later suggested by another, however, that one of Braidwood's schools be incorporated into the new Central College, which was to become the University of Virginia, Jefferson adamantly opposed the idea. "I should not like to have it made a member of our college," he wrote. "The objects of the two institutions are fundamentally distinct. The one is science, the other mere charity. It would be gratuitously taking a boat in tow, which may impede, but cannot aid the motion of the principal institution."[5]

This seemingly callous opinion demonstrates the sharp distinction Jefferson drew between "science," the advancement of knowledge, and "charity," remedial education, and his determination that no obstacle would be placed in the way of the institution of higher learning he was founding.

JEFFERSON was perceptive in evaluating most of the manuscripts sent to him, but he was woefully wrong in the judgment expressed in the following exchange of letters with John Davis, an author-bookseller, who had dedicated one of his books to Jefferson. The manuscript Davis offered for sale, which Jefferson rejected as "uninteresting," was William Byrd's "History of the Dividing Line." It was to become one of the most significant literary documents of early eighteenth-century America.*

Baltimore, November 28, 1808.

SIR,

A friend of mine hearing that you propose to collect documents relative to the Antiquities of North America, has requested me to inform you that he empowers me to send

---

*William Byrd II of Westover (1674–1744), was a member of the ruling elite of colonial Virginia. *History of the Dividing Line* was published in 1841, his *Secret Diary,* an intimate account of his private life, not until 1941–42.

you Colonel Byrd's Manuscript Journal, should you wish it. The M.S. contains 260 p.p. and is very fairly writtin in the Colonel's own aut[o]graphy: The object of his Expedition was to determine the boundary line between North Carolina and Virginia, and to effect this, he travelled with the Commissioners through Dismal Swamp.

Should you wish this M.S. it shall be immediately sent you; the price the owner sets on it is Thirty Dollars.

I am, Sir, Your most obedient,
most humble Servant,
JOHN DAVIS

Washington Dec. 3. 08.

Th: Jefferson presents his compliments to Mr. Davis and his thanks for the offer of the MS. of Colo. Byrd's journal: but not having in contemplation to make any collection of papers on the subject supposed, he declines the proposal. Indeed he concieves that the journal must be very uninteresting, as Colo. Byrd was employed only on the lower part of the line between Virginia & N. Carolina, and of course gives a description only of the Dismal Swamp & a little to the Westward of that, which part of the country is to this day nearly in the same condition as it was then.

Although Jefferson declined to purchase the Byrd manuscript, he later became involved in a lengthy correspondence involving an abortive attempt to publish it by the American Philosophical Society.[6] He may have changed his opinion of the manuscript by then.

When Jefferson was about to leave office after his second term, he received a presentation copy of a book that created one of the most famous legends in American history. The Reverend Mason Locke Weems—Parson Weems to thousands of Americans—sent Jefferson his *Life of George Washington*, the biography that immortalized the fiction of Washington and the cherry tree: "I can't tell a lie. I did cut it with my hatchet."[7] Weems, a writer, orator, and itinerant bookseller, demonstrated in his opening eulogy to the departing president the purple prose typical of his writing style.

> Navy Yard—Doctr. Ewells.*
> Feby. 1. 1809

SIR—

The Multitude adore the rising sun—for me, I honor the steps of his departure. My thoughts return with pleasure to the fields that were bright with his beams where the Olive gladdend in her labours and the vine shook her green leaf with Joy to the fatting ray that filld her clusters with nectar. Self descending your Excellency sits in glory—and soon to rise in multiplied radiance on all the political stars that are to shine by your absence.

I beg your Excellency's acceptance of a copy of a new work—the Private Life of the man whom, you, of all others most rever'd, and whom with such peculiar felicity you styled "Columbia's First and Greatest Son."

This is the Seventh edition—10,000 copies have been sold—and some flattering things said. But if, on perusing this private Life of Washington Your Excellency shoud be pleas'd to find that I have not, like *some* of his Eulogists, set him up as a Common Hero for military *ambition* to idolize & imitate—nor an Aristocrat, like *others,* to mislead & enslave the Nation, but a pure Republican whom all our youth shoud know, that they may love & imitate his Virtues, and thereby immortalize "the *last Republic now on earth*"—I shall heartily

---

*Thomas Ewell (1785–1826), son of Jefferson's college classmate, Jesse Ewell. Through Jefferson's influence he became a surgeon at the naval hospital in Washington.

thank you [for] a line or two in favor of it—as a School book.

That from the top of your own heaven-kissing hill you may long look around with a Parents Joy on the continuing Peace, Prosperity & universal blessings of America, is the sincerest wish of your Excellency's greatly oblig'd & most affectionate friend

M. L. WEEMS

John Burk is another of Jefferson's literary correspondents whose reputation as an author survives to this day. Burk was a gifted writer—a journalist, poet, dramatist, and historian. His *History of Virginia,* published in 1805, was the best historical account of the state to that time and is still read by historians.[8] Burk came to America in 1796 after being driven from his native Ireland for revolutionary activities against the British. He wrote several historical dramas, including *Bunker Hill, or the Death of General Warren,* a success in Boston and New York, but after one of his plays failed, he returned to political journalism as editor of the Republican New York newspaper, *The Time Piece.* As he explains in his letter to Jefferson, he was arrested for sedition for allegedly libeling President John Adams, and was helped by Aaron Burr to move secretly to Virginia.

[Received 19 June 1801]
Amelia County [Virginia]

Thomas Jefferson President U.S.

SIR,

Strongly impressed by the belief that the first magistrate of the Republic is obliged not merely to administer what are termed its political concerns, but to give countenance also, and patronage to the exertions of Genius; I venture, not without reluctance, to enclose for your perusal, extracts from a poem of the epic kind, entitled the Columbiad. You will perceive from the title, that [it] is written to eternize the glory of your Revolution, which ought to be immortal; and your judgement will easily decide whether it is in its management and execution calculated to produce such an effect.

I am aware that considerable Objections will be against the poem whatever may be its execution, from the recency of the event it undertakes to celebrate. The critics to a man, contend that a subject drawn from a remote antiquity or from an era, whose history is sufficiently obscure to leave room for the display of the marvellous, where imagination may weave her fictions without a gross and palpable departure from popular belief, is the best subject for *epic.* Without combating this opinion, I hope you will agree with me that the recent discovery of America, her vast extent, her stupendous mountains, her lakes, rivers and natural curiosities; her diversified manner and political institutions, the battles by land and Sea, the distresses, perseverance and public spirit of her people during the revolution; the various Indian nations, who inhabit her frontiers, whose customs the poet has to delineate and in the representation of which he may exert his genius without the censure of extravagance; but above all, the grandeur of the effect alike interesting to liberty and philosophy, are advantages more than Sufficient to counterbalance any defects arising from the recency of the main plot: indeed; the agency of the Indians and the late discovery of a world imperfectly known give the poet all the advantages, which Kaim and Blair contemplated in an high antiquity.[9]

In all other respects, (save the execution, of which you must judge) the demands of the critics are more than satisfied. The Subject is in the highest degree magnificent. The Shock of a revolution, which has sounded through the universe announcing the destruction of thrones & the establishment of Human happiness is well calculated to fill the mind with lofty conceptions; with a Curiosity impatient and agonizing.

In materials for the descriptive part (wherein lies the chief embellishment of the Poem) no subject was ever more fertile: the materials for episode, to be drawn from facts alone are numerous and interesting. I send you as a specimen, the well known story of Miss MacRae, from the execution of which you will judge of my ability to paint the pathetic. Neither the Nysus and Eurialus of Virgil, nor Glover's Teribarus and Ariana in my mind, approach within many degrees of the tenderness of this pathetic story *if told* with Simplicity.*

In the opportunities afforded for the delineation of characters, (which critics call the manners of the Poem) my subject is equally happy. The Soldiers and Officers from allmost all countries, composing the British and American hosts furnish a stock for this department not to be exhausted.

The machinery is suited to the particular belief of all nations. A part of it is entirely new. You will discover it in the extract No. 1 where the Spirits of the just are represented leaning towards the earth from heaven, contemplating with pity the ravages of Tyranny and Superstition on the Several Countries. In this attitude and disposition they are found by the Messenger of the Allmighty, who summons them to repair to his presence for the purpose of pointing out to them, the Revolution in America and unfolding the prospect of human innocence, wisdom and happiness in the new age.

The moral of the Poem is obvious.

The operations of the Army under Montgomery & afterwards, under Gates are related in a tent by moonlight in the camp before York Town by an Officer of that Army.**

---

* In Book V of the *Aeneid,* during a running contest, Nisus stumbles just before the finish line, but manages to trip the second-place runner so his friend Euryalus can win. Aeneas awards prizes to all three runners. Teribarus and Ariana are characters from the blank-verse epics of Richard Glover (1712–85). *The Cambridge History of English Literature* (A.W. Ward and A.R. Waller, eds. [New York, 1907–17]) comments on Glover's works, *The Athenaid* (30 books, 1788), and *Leonidas* (9 books, 1737): "It is difficult to imagine, and would be hardly possible to find, even in the long list of mistaken 'long poem' writers of the past two centuries, more tedious stuff than his."

** Richard Montgomery (1736–75), American Revolutionary War general, killed at the Battle of Quebec; Horatio Gates (1728–1806), American Revolutionary War general, victorious at the battle of Saratoga, defeated at the battle of Camden.

I beg your patience a little longer Sir while I explain my motives for forwarding those extracts. Possibly you have heard how I have been compelled by the tyranny of the Irish Government to take refuge in this country; how soon after my arrival here I became subjected to new persecutions. Arrested on a charge of libel at the suit of Mr. Adams, knowing the moral certainty of fine and imprisonment from the violence of party spirit and the mode of packing juries, considering also that even in the improbable event of an acquital; as an alien I was still at the mercy of the President and being moreover anxious of removing to some place sufficiently near my country to permit me to assist by my zeal and exertions in any expedition that might be projected for her emancipation, I prevailed on Mr. [Aaron] Burr to procure if possible permission for me to depart by the release of my recognizance.[10]

This solicitation was successful. I was to leave America and to return to it no more. From an actual attempt to seize me whilst fulfilling the stipulations of this contract on board a cartel bound to Bordeaux and from well founded apprehensions that I was watched by the spies of the British minister I was induced by the advice of some of the best men in America to postpone my departure.* Want of means when I might perhaps have gone in safety has since compelled me to remain.

For more than two years have I by an indirect exercize of the alien law been in fact exiled from society passing under a feigned name, known only to a few confidential friends, rendered incapable of profiting by the exercise of my faculties, contracting debts the while dispirited allmost hopeless. Urged at length by the energies of a spirit, which had not yet lost its elasticity, by indignation against the authors of my distresses I made the Secretary of State [James Madison] acquainted with my place of residence and declared my readiness to take my trial.

After this I was induced to become Principal of a college

---

*A cartel is a ship used to exchange prisoners.

lately founded in this county and after seven years of agitation and calamity I began to enjoy the sweets of repose and independance.* But it seems as if I was destined to be the sport of fortune. A ridiculous man Suspects a criminal connection between me & his wife, and attempts to assassinate me. He has since borne public testimony to his wife's innocence, but the indignities I have suffered have sunk deep into my mind and I have determined to leave this county. I am now precisely as Milton represents our first parents—

"The world is all before me where to choose—"**

Should you estimate highly as I do the value of my Poem I ask for it your public patronage & exertions. Three of my dramatic performances have been repeatedly represented with applause. My compositions in prose and verse have carried off the largest premiums ever awarded in the university where I was educated: my political compositions & exertions (my friends imagine) have been of some use to the cause of liberty, and yet by some fatality the consequences to me from qualifications so imposing are *nothing.****

A small stipend arising from some office or employment where I might be of service (for I have no claim to a sinecure, nor would my idea of independance permit me to accept it) & where, I might be enabled to finish my compositions without being subject to those ridiculous embarassments, which have allready destroyed or abridged my usefullness, is the extent of my wishes during my exile. Mr. Burr who has been to me in the place of a friend & father will vouch for my honor & integrity. If I am not deceived, few circumstances of a private nature would afford him more pleasure than my establishment & independance. I pray you Sir, to return with as much dispatch as the important duties you have to dis-

---

*Jefferson College, Amelia, Virginia. Burk was president of the institution.
**Milton, *Paradise Lost* 12.646: "The World was all before them, where to choose."
***Burk was educated at Trinity College, Dublin.

charge will permit, an answer to this letter with the extracts enclosed. I have no copies of them. . . .

I am Sir, with the greatest respect,
JOHN D BURK

You will find the copy very inacurate, often pointed wrong sometimes scarce legible. It is my only one. It has not been touch'd for four years. I have neither time or spirit to write a fair copy. I have a prose Composition finished, a reply to Mr. Adams' defence and I am employ'd in writing lives of American public characters.*

You must not consider me as an applicant for a place. By employment or office I had nothing more in view than some private station such as private secretary to any departmental officer to which your patronage might recommend me. My Composition Such as it is [is] done with facility. I forebear to refer you to the ingenious criticisms on the extracts from my poem published, copied from the English into the American papers. Your Judgment wants not the Influence of *Authority*.

Burk was one of several poets who were inspired to write an epic poem on the Revolutionary War and call it *The Columbiad.* Joel Barlow wrote two such poems; it is his final version that lays claim to the *Columbiad* title in American literary history. There is no record that Burk ever finished his poem. He published excerpts from it, however, in *The Time Piece.* One forty-eight-line section was the same part of the poem he sent to Jefferson to show his ability to "paint the pathetic." As he explains and justifies in his letter, it is written in blank verse.

The lines relate how an Indian murdered a captive white

---

*John Adams, *A Defence of the Constitutions of Government of the United States of America,* 2 vols. (London, 1787). This work was attacked by Jeffersonian Republicans like Burk as an attempt to support monarchy.

woman, Mistress MacRae. The slaying occurs after two Indians quarrel over whose prize she will be. The head of the
tribe, Ontai,

> He fearing that the interests of the tribe
> Would suffer by this contest of the chiefs
> Snatches a Tomahawk, and with savage zeal,
> Seizes the lovely, trembling, guiltless cause
> Of this disunion; and inhuman strikes
> The iron deep into her panting breast:
> Her beauteous limbs relax'd, she falls along
> Like to a roe, whose comely side the spear
> Of Hunter pierces; wonder seized the tribe;
> And even the prudent ruffian felt his soul
> Assail'd by pity; on her i'vory breast
> The wound appears as if a stream of blood
> Had thawed a hole upon the virgin snow. . . .[11]

The following response to Burk from Jefferson has been
frequently quoted because of Jefferson's comment that he could
no longer appreciate poetry. Although the president offered
no patronage job, he did help Burk later with his history of
Virginia by lending him research materials from the Monticello library. Burk dedicated the book to Jefferson. Burk met
an untimely death at the age of thirty-six when he was killed
in a duel in 1808 by a stranger who took offense at a chance
remark made in a tavern.

To John Daly Burke esq.
Washington June 21, 1801

Sir,

I have safely received your favor from Amelia, with the
sheets of the Colombiad which it covered, and have given to
them the hasty perusal which my less agreeable but more
indispensable occupations have permitted. Rarely indeed do

they permit me one moment's reflection from the volumes of official papers which every day presents. The few minutes I now spare to this object, I will say, were agreeably employed and ⟨I read⟩ your sheets with much satisfaction. To my own mortification however I must add that of all men living I am the last who should undertake to decide upon the merits of poetry. In earlier life I was fond of it and easily pleased. But as years & cares advanced the powers of fancy have declined. Every year seems to have plucked a feather from her wing, till she can no longer elevate me to those sublime heights to which it is necessary to accompany the poet. So much has my relish for poetry deserted me that at present I cannot read Virgil with pleasure. I am consequently utterly incapacitated to decide on the merits of poetry. The very feelings to which it is addressed are among those I have lost. So that the blind man might as well undertake to ⟨understand⟩ a painting or the deaf a musical composition.

On the subject of office my principles & those constantly asserted by the republicans, that no one should be removed for mere difference of political opinion, has given little to do in this way. It is moreover only the offices of the first grade which are at my disposal; those of the 2d being subordinated to them; [. . .] the office of each grade being thus in the gift of the one next above. I will with pleasure ⟨mention⟩ you to the heads of departments: but not to do you an injury by nourishing expectations which might not be fulfilled, I am bound to observe that I know there has been a vast redundancy of applications, so that it is not likely that any vacancy exists. Indeed among ⟨officeholders⟩ there are many supernumerary who ⟨are⟩ to be dismissed, or the numbers are not ⟨to be⟩ recruited till reduced to a mere sufficiency by ordinary accidents. Accept my respectful salutations and good wishes.

P.S. the sheets are herein returned.

Th: Jefferson

Jefferson received a number of long poems in the mail, including part of the epic about General Horatio Gates's victory over Burgoyne at Saratoga titled the *Gatiade*.[12] He also received short pieces of verse, such as the note from Samuel Harrison announcing his desire to see the president:

> Philanthropist, Illustrious Sage;
> The Pride and Glory of our Age;
> An Audience grant I pray.
> Vermont Sam Harrison has come
> From Chittenden to Washington
> To Visit the Great Jefferson:
> A lengthy tedious way.[13]

One of the most ingenious poems was a 170-line acrostic from Jonathan Edmester of Malden, Mass.[14] In the first 131 lines, the first letter of each line spells out: TO THOMAS JEFFERSON PRESIDENT OF THE UNITED STATES OF AMERICA MAY GOD THEE BLESS FROM JONATHAN EDMESTER OF MALDEN COUNTY OF MIDDLESEX STATE OF MASSACHUSETTS. Edmester took pains that the president would notice the acrostic message by placing a comma after the initial letter of each line. The verse begins:

> T,hou art the Man, thy People have ordain'd,
> O,n all occations their rights to maintain
> T,hy precepts do shew forth Gods light within
> H,e into Thee has poured his holy Flame
> O,n thine Heart his kind rays of Light does dawn
> M,ounting their Splendor like the Rosy Morn
> A,rraying of thine Head with Knowledge bright
> S,o should thy Reason like the Sun Unite
> J,oining the Fountain which first give it Light
> E,very riseing thoughts God Spirit Makes
> F,or on the Heart it shines and life creates
> F,or of God's Son every one partakes
> E,ver expanding their hearts: To perform

R,arefaction their Minds for to adorn
S,o does mans thoughts arise that grace the head
O,ut of the heart begot; by Light: from Shade
N,othing but Infinite can guide aright. . . .

Jefferson apparently missed the acrostic message entirely, or at least failed to detect the author's name and address embedded in the poem, for he endorsed it "Anon."

THE following lines of patriotic verse were inspired by Jefferson's decision to decline to run for a third term as president. They are typical of the numerous pairs of heroic couplets sacrificed in his honor by young admirers.

New Hartford, Oneida County, New York
May 5th. 1808.

To His Excellency Thomas Jefferson,
On his resolution to retire from the Presidency.
"Grande decus columenque rerum."*

Illustrious Sage! while a whole Nation's voice
Hails Thee their fav'rite, marks Thee as their choice,
While eager Senates press to pay the due
Of grateful praise to wisdom and to You;
A humble *youth*, unknown among the great,†
Hard-struggling with the storms of wayward fate,
Presumes—audacious task—to tune the lyre
To such wild wood-notes as his thoughts inspire,
And pay that boon, which *patriot worth* demands,
A boon not mean, though from ignoble hands. . . .
   At that dark hour, when British Tyrants swore
To drench Columbia's soil with patriot gore,

---

*"Grande decus columenque rerum": the great glory and prop of existence. Horace, *Odes*, 2.17.4.

When e'en the wise scarce hop'd for skill to save
Their darling Freedom from a timeless grave;
The Goddess look'd with anxious glance around,
But none to shout her magic name was found,
All trembling stood, and silent ey'd the blow
That hung in air, to lay her glories low.
Then, a swift suppliant, to her chosen Son
The Goddess rode, and call'd her *Jefferson!*
The Patriot heard; to aid his Queen he sprung,
And *INDEPENDENCE* thunder'd from his tongue:
Britain abash'd, the dauntless deed survey'd,
Shrunk from such godlike worth, and stood dismey'd,
While Freedom's vot'ries hover'd round the land
And arms secur'd what patriot wisdom plann'd. . . .
    Illustrious Sage! of Man the gen'ral friend,
Sway'd by no party views, no private end;
Thee to thy wish'd retreat, a Nation's pray'r
Shall follow still; "That Heaven would bless Thee, there."
    Withdrawn, at length, from ev'ry public strife,
Happy, secluded, down thy vale of life
Long, long in peace may thou be left to stray,
Pleasure and health attendants of thy way,
While a blest People's thanks are daily shed
In grateful tribute, round thy honor'd head.
†—"jure perhorreo
Late conspicuum tollere verticem"*

SAMUEL B. BEACH.

Jefferson received a number of communications from writers with literary aspirations, but none quite so breathless with hope as the following letter from a young woman.

---

* *"Jure perhorrui late conspicuum tollere verticem"*: Rightly I shrank with dread from excessively high place. Horace, *Odes*, 3.16.18–19.

Bethlehem [Pa.] January [6,] 1806

To His Excellency the President of the United States . . .
Sir,

Hope, being the most powerful sentiment of the human breast has encouraged me thus to address the Ruler of this country humbly petitioning that he will listen to the prayer of an orphan girl upon whose exertions her own & a littler Sisters advancement depends.

I have Sir, already foreseen that you may possibly consider me either a maniac or an Ideot supposing that I could not otherwise have this assurance.

But when I went to those great characters who have listened to the tale of distress from their indigent subject and have like demigods assisted their laudable exertions I have confidence in the clemency, honor & benevolent condescendsion of your Excellency. And though I have already fancied my humble Address committed to the flames as soon as received, hope has influenced me to proceed.

The sum of my humble petition is Sir, beseeching you to speak a few kind words in behalf of a small volume, the production of my fancy, entitled The Sylph or Maniack. I have but one friend, a lady of distinction who has encouraged me to this proceeding & who assures me my manuscript is a composition of considerable merit & all that is requisite for its success is the approbating words of some great personage.

And if Sir, at some of your public entertainments & convivial meetings you will give an Item to your favorites in behalf of the Volume entitled The Sylph, to be printed in Philadelphia, the acquisition of three or four thousand subscribers would establish the happiness of two youthful individuals who, else have no means of support.

But if on the contrary you should feel no impressions in my favor I would rather permit me & my Sister to languish in indigence than humanely to imploy a few moments for the essential purpose of our happiness. If the latter suggestions should be the case I beg you will not expose my temerity, being both young, friendless, & poor. The odium of having thus infringed the prevailing rules of the age & proved intirely unsuccessful would be more than I could survive.

Therefore, I hope Sir that after having deliberately perused my petition if your decision is against me you will scorn to put it in the power of any persons to exhibit a burlesque upon your humble servant & petitioner.

But knowing my arrangements to be laudable I am so far from despairing in your benevolence that I have hopes you will generously devote some attention to this request & allow me to receive some kind of encouraging reply. The manuscript is now ready for the Press & I have but one friend & an eight Shilling piece in the world.

I am Sir, your very humble Servant

HARRIET E WICKHAM

There is no record that her manuscript was ever published.

7

Invention

"Nature has designed me for inventing"

NO United States president was more closely identified with science than Thomas Jefferson. He was president of the American Philosophical Society from 1797 to 1815, and was known to be familiar with all the scientific disciplines and to relentlessly encourage and promote "useful knowledge." His friendships and correspondences with scientists were frequently publicized, as was the part he took in the scientific controversies of his time. Challenging, in his *Notes on the State of Virginia*, the Count de Buffon's theories of the degeneracy of human and animal life in the Americas, for example, endeared him to his countrymen as a champion of the nation's claims of parity with all things European.

His scientific interests were so widely admired that his political enemies assailed them as unfitting for a statesman. His collection of mammoth bones was satirized in the Federalist press to the point where "mammoth" became a code word to attack any of his programs. A youthful William Cullen Bryant derided Jefferson's interest in natural history and paleontology with the lines:

Go search with curious eyes for horned frogs,
'Mid the Wild wastes of Louisiana bogs;
Or where the Ohio rolls his turbid stream
Dig for huge bones, thy glory and thy theme.[1]

Jefferson was not a professional in any of the sciences or technologies he investigated, but like an indefatigable tourist, he was so inquisitive that he learned more about the regions he explored than many who worked there all their lives. Because he was president of the American Philosophical Society, the latest discoveries in astronomy, archaeology, botany, agriculture, mathematics, and chemistry came across his desk. He was himself the inventor of an improved plough, and architect-builder of one of the nation's superb dwellings, Monticello. It is not surprising that Americans turned to their polymath president as one who would be sympathetic to their scientific inquiries, and might place at their disposal the resources of the United States government. In this they were to be sadly disappointed, for Jefferson's commitment to a "government rigorously frugal and simple" precluded the support of individual scientific or technical projects at federal expense.[2]

Jefferson made this clear in his reply to an entrepreneur who asked for government aid in setting up a steel plant. The only encouragement offered by the government, he noted, is the fourteen-year patent on inventions. Manufacturing carried on privately, he wrote, is "so much more economically conducted than by the public," that the government undertakes "no manufactures of any thing which can be got at market."[3]

Nevertheless, unsolicited schemes for all sorts of inventions and scientific enterprises were mailed to Jefferson throughout his presidency, their authors in search of a governmental subsidy. The most frequent project presented to him was one that became the siren lure of the age: perpetual motion. It seems that virtually every millwright, mechanic, student, or tinkerer in the United States was convinced that he possessed the secret of a machine that would run without any exterior source of power.

Perpetual motion was the philosopher's stone of the early republic, the hope of something for nothing. Given the universal optimism of the times, it was perhaps inevitable that Newton's laws of motion, which decreed, in effect, that energy could never be created, would throw down a challenge to every would-be inventor in the land.

So credulous had the public become to perpetual-motion devices of every kind that a newspaper story related, without a hint of ridicule, that two prisoners in a New York jail had carved a perpetual motion machine from cedar with a penknife. "The machine consists of about 30 cog and spar wheels of various dimensions," the story stated, "and is set in motion by weights. It can be adapted to a clock, saw mill, grist mill, or any other piece of machinery that moves by weights, water or wind, and will continue them in motion so long as the machinery will last."

"Every friend to the Arts and Sciences will lament," the story concluded, "that the public are deprived of the benefit of this discovery by the imprisonment of its authors." The two prisoners, who were jailed for counterfeiting dollar coins, were obviously as artful at self-publicity as they were with a penknife.[4]

The idea of perpetual motion was not new; it went back at least to the sixteenth century. Indeed, many of the perpetual-motion principles thought to have sprung newborn from their creator's fancy, had been first proposed more than a century before. The perpetually moving wheel was perpetually being reinvented.

Jefferson did not respond to letters on perpetual-motion devices. His opinion on the subject was expressed several years after he left the presidency in a comment on a celebrated perpetual-motion hoax by a Philadelphian, Charles Redheffer. The continuous motion seemingly produced by Redheffer's machine was found, by no less an inventive luminary than Robert Fulton, to be generated by an old man in an adjoining room turning a crank handle. Jefferson wrote to Dr. Robert Patterson, who informed him of the deceit, that Redheffer

> is the first of the inventors of perpetual motion within my knowledge, who has had the cunning to put his visitors on a false pursuit, by amusing them with a sham machinery whose loose and vibratory motion might impose on them the belief that it is the real source of the motion they see. . . . A poor Frenchman who called on me the other day, with another invention of perpetual motion, assured me that Dr. Franklin, many years ago, expressed his opinion to him that it was not impossible. Without entering into contest on this abuse of the Doctor's name, I gave him the answer I had given to others before, that the Almighty himself could not construct a machine of perpetual motion while the laws exist which he has prescribed for the government of the matter in our system; that the equilibrium established by him between cause and effect must be suspended to effect that purpose.[5]

He recognized that the problem was friction. "The diminution of friction is certainly one of the most desirable reformations in mechanics," he wrote. "Could we get rid of it altogether we should have perpetual motion."[6]

Typical of the enthusiasm of the unlettered mechanics who wrote Jefferson about perpetual motion was the following proposal from two brash inventors:

[Woolwich, N.J.]
May the 10th 1805

This is to inform the presedent of the United States that the invenshen of a wheel that Runs perpetedle with out wind or warter or Steam that never Runs down can be Represented in a Short time at the feet of Congress, the Greatest invention that ever has bin found out for the use of clocks and Mills of all cinds from Six inches to eighty feet diammeter the greatest addition to the none world. And if the Congress thinks proper to notice these lines in as much as to Send an answer to the same, further if they think well on our foreding Such wheel mussheen we will indever to com forward in Short time with the Same. We are now in the State of west New Jersy in the County of Glaucester in the township of Woolwedge at the Malligo Mills on the head of Prins Morrises River. These from your Friends

John Trimmel
Oddy B Skeldin

One reason why so many mechanics and millwrights set their minds to perpetual motion is expressed in the following letter from Heman Culver, who had heard one of those rumors that make the rounds in every era that a reward was being offered for some kind of fabulous accomplishment.* In this case the president himself was reputedly offering $30,000 for a perpetual-motion pump.

---

*The first name of Culver's signature is clearly spelled Heman. Jefferson, however, misread it and endorsed the name "Herman Culver," and it is so spelled in the Library of Congress *Index to the Thomas Jefferson Papers* (Washington, 1976).

March the 21—1808
Mounthbel [Mount Bethel] Township
And State of Pennsylvania

To the honrable President of the United States

SIR PLEAS YOUR HONOR

I have A Desire to know the Certingty from under your Honnors own hand if your honnor pleases to give it from Under your own hand for I have know Sertenty of it, and It is Concerning an offer that your honner offered as I have Understood by Individuals that your honnor has offered Thirty thousands Dollers to any man that will find out The Invention of a pump working it Self and I expect That your honnor will be perfectly willing to give That at least for I do amagine that it will be an Invention Of the greatest valieu to the United States that ever Has been found out as yet for I do think it will Be worth millions of Dollars to the United States for it Will not only answer that one point but it will answer For that point and for many others likewise and I Am a mecanick that follows the millright and Carpenters Bisness for to git my living and I Should be very glad to Obtain Sumthing in an honest way that I Could obtain A living Sumthing easier in my old age than to have To work So hard and So if your honnor will be pleasd to Send me answer in full as quick as this letter Comes to hand & Your honnor will obleag your humble Sarvent Sir for I would wish to have answer amediately So that I Can Amediately Commince to make the moddle for that Will be the main point that will Satisfy your Honnor and I have no doubt in my mind but I Can Satisfy your honnor in full by the motion of The moddle that it will be of great valieu to the United States in deede and So I desire your honnors Friendship in this Case in as Short a period of time As posible it Can be done in and your honnor will Be pleasd to Send a letter to the postoffice in East Town the County town of North Hampton County And by

your honnors So doing it will obleage your Humble Sarvent*

HEMAN CULVER

And as for my letter it is not very Correct but I hope your
honor will be pleasd to excuse me as I am but a poor Scollor.

The following letter is the last of several written to Jefferson over a three-year period by Chauncy Hall, whose perpetual-motion machine was based on a series of magnets
attached to two concentric wheels. So determined was Hall
to have his idea tested, that he traveled from Connecticut to
Washington, met with William Thornton, head of the Patent
Office, and even with the president himself. His letter captures the willingness of the scientific visionary to risk all for
his conviction, and the depth of his frustration at failing to
convert others to his faith.

Wallingford [Conn.] May 23 AD 1806

To Thomas Jefferson President of the United States
Mr. Jefferson

SIR

    Ever Delighted with Contemplating on the Works of Cre-
ation and the Order and Rectitude that Each pa[r]t of the
Materials of this World Consists But haveing no one to assist
me I am but a Little acquainted with those great advantages
that Art and Genius have gained. Therefore I hope that my
Integrity will be an Excuse for my troubling You with the
Ideas I have formed and Presented to You in the first Letter
and in this. Haveing had no Satisfactory objection from any
one I rest firm in the belief that upon the Plan which I Sent

---

*Culver's mailing address is Easton, in Northampton County, Pennsylvania.

to You there may be a time piece Made that will Continue in Regular Motion So Long as the hardest Matereal Substance will Endure. But at the time that I first went to the Pattent Office and asked the Secratary if a Perpetual Motion had been accomplished he Said it had not been done nor was it Possible. I told him that I had heard that it was done and that I believed it Could be Done and that I would Draw a plan and Show it to him. But he Exclaimed as though in a passion that he would not so mutch as Look upon it to gain any knowledge and advised me not to Draw a Plan for all would Laugh at me that Saw it.

Then Disappointed and almost Confounded I went to my Lodging and Drew the Plan that was Presented to You and then I Spent Some time in Seeing the City and Satisfying my Cureosity. Determining to Come home, I did wish to see Your Person, though with fear, not knowing what oppinion was formed of my Plan. I Came into your Presance Yet I Could not Speak my mind but I hope that if There is found an Objection against the whole or any Part of the Plan or Reasons that I Gave to You at that time or at this, may be attributed to my want of Learning. But Should this be an Objection that the fluids of the Magnetts will be Liable to Spred in the open Air and Subject to Vary on the account of other Magnetic Bodies this is the greatest impedament that I Could think of.

But after I had formed the Principle on whitch I Drew the Plan that was Presented to You then I took it [in] Mind to find if there was any Created Substance that those fluids would not pass through and in a Long and tedious Study I find that there is a Substance and by Compareing Nature with itself I firmly believe that these fluids Cannot pass through it and Yet it will not effect the fluids in any other form and in the Course of my Studying to find Some thing to Set Bounds to the fluids of Magnettism I formed an idea that there is a greater Invention than any that I have known of Being Discovered, Yet Unknown or Never Discovered to mankind. But Shall I,

who am not able to accomplish that which is the Least, pre-
pose a greate[r] one and more Compla[i]nt? I am now the
Subjeact of Derision among my acquaintance for preposeing
the first Plan but I am not able to get any Satisfaction at the
present nor do I think of any thing Short of the Experriment
and that will Decide it in my oppinion, for if this will not
begin to move of itself and Continue I know of no other Plan
or Principle that is worth Notice for to make a Motion that
will go Continuly.

But I have met with a Disappointment at home and have
now to pay two hundred Dollars for the House and which I
purchaced Last Autum and Now Live in but my Payments
are easy and I have two Years to pay it in and must be Prudent or I Shall not be able to make it. Theerefore if that the
Plan be worth the attention of any Genlemen and they find
any encouragement to try the Same I am willing to Give any
part or the whole, for Should I under take it and it Should
fail it would ruin me, altho if I am Prosperd and Can answer
to Demands that are against [me] and it is not done before,
or I find an Objection that I no not of at this time I Shall
persue it to the Experiment.

Sir I Should Receive a Letter from You with the Greatest
Satisfaction Informing me what may be the Objections if there
are any for I wish not to harber an Erroneous idea.

From Your Humble Servent

CHAUNCY HALL
Merriden Society in Wallingford New Haven County
Connecticut May 23d AD 1806

George Buchanan, a physician with whom Jefferson had
corresponded more than a decade before, conceived of a perpetual-motion machine using compressed air, and accompanied his letter with a sketch of his device. As a power source
for perpetual motion, compressed air was little different in

principle from water; all such devices assumed it was possible to use air or water to drive a wheel with enough energy left over to operate a compressor or to lift water back to the top of the wheel. Jefferson did not answer Buchanan's letter.

Wadesboro, Anson County N. Carlolina.
July 1st. 1807

Sir,

I beg leave to Submit to your consideration, as a member of the American Philosophical Society, the principle on which, I have conceived, the construction of a machine, capable of perpetuating its own motion, is practicable.

The following outline embraces the principles.

Let a wheel, of an adapted make to receive its revolution from a current of air, be enclosed in an airtight trunk, as snugly fitted as its requisite Strength & the unimpeded motion of the wheel will admit. Into the trunk, & a small distance through it, so as to give the most effectual direction to the current on the wheel, let a funnel-like pipe for admitting the necessary quantity of air, be inserted.

Let this admitted current of air find its outlet through a similar pipe leading from this into another trunk similarly constructed & fitted out with its wheel—& let this pipe extend through its second trunk the requisite distance to direct the continued current of air, as before. Let 1, 2, 3, or as many more trunks, with their wheels, as may be found necessary, be continued on by the same kind of tubular connection—& to the last pipe, at the termination of the series of trunks, let a large air pump, or pumps, be affixed.

The trunks are to be arranged circularly, with the axes of the wheels raised perpendicularly, their elevated ends extending through the trunks to receive cogwheels, so as to be brought to a common bearing on one large wheel prepared to receive their united force. This large wheel is to work the pump.

The idea is briefly sketched. It would be superfluous to go

into any detail of contrivances till the assured basis for the plan be tested. You will particularly oblige me by giving your opinion whether the application of the principle, under any modification, to machinery, can be productive of any real accession of force.

I am your very humble Sevt.

GEOR. BUCHANAN

Like many who wrote to Jefferson for small sums of money to alleviate a severe distress, one wonders why Jonathan Morgan, a law student, could not have scraped together the thirty dollars he needed to build his perpetual-motion machine. He apparently, like many other perpetual-motion addicts, carried his design with him "in silence to the Dust."

Brimfield (Mass.) August 3. 1804

His Excellency Th: Jefferson Esqr.

SIR,

Your Excellency will, I hope excuse me for intruding, in so unwarrantable a manner upon your leisure. . . .

The Last year of my Collegiate life, I concieved the rude plan of a machine, which should give and perpetuate motion to itself. The manner of perfecting this plan has occupied all my leisure, for two years past, untill about two months past, when, as I am fully convinced as far as theory can advance, I hit upon the true principle of motion, which has been overlooked by those, who are and have been far my superiors in Philosophy, only on account of its simplicity. I am dependent, at present, upon what little my industry can afford, the sufference of an Uncle with whom I am reading Law and such trifles as the low circumstances of my Father can afford. I have not the means wherewith to go into the experiment myself, tho' simple and cheap. It will cost one two or three weeks time, and I shall be under the necessity of removing to Cambridge on Boston, for materials, as they cannot be had in the Country. I have been trying to make the whole, at home, with my own hand, but cannot.

I have applied to such of my friends as I have judged worth my attention in the matter, for patronage, but have found none but frowns and contempt. . . .

I have rested my power of motion or primum Mobile upon the eternal Law, by which the God of nature has built, moved and preserves the system. The experiment may be fully tried for the sum of Thirty dollars. If your Excellency should feel disposed to hazard so small a sum upon the experiment, if it should succede I will not be backward in acknowledging you Sir, as a benefactor, or in remunerating, & shall hope, with an anxiety almost unknown to the human mind, that your Patronage and my long and werisome labor will be both amply rewarded. If it succedes, it will have, I expect, a power of motion to impart, so as to make it usful in many things. I have communicated as much of the real principles to you, Sir, as I have or ever shall to any person, and if I should still be so unfortunate as to find no friendly abettor, I am determined, if I should never be able to prosecute the design myself to carry it, with me in silence to the Dust.

I am Sir, with every sentiment of real & sincere esteme your friend and humble servent,

JONATHAN MORGAN JR.

P.S. If it should please your excellency to comport with my wishes, you will please to direct yours to Brookfield Post Office. I wish as a particular favor that you would [be] so kind to me as not to let this be seen as its publication might cost me some sneers and tonts, in case I should not succeed.

Matthew Wilson does not explain what he means by "pressure" as his perpetual-moton principle, but his chatty letter is full of the self-confidence of one who has not yet tried and failed.

Martch ye. 18th 1805
Mead.Ville Crawford County & State Pennsylvania

DEAR SIR

I hope you will pardon my asureance in Troubleing Your Excellancy with the Reeding these few lines, but as they come from the hand of a true Republican an old Soldier & Volintier & A Sincier friend to his Cuntery, You will be pleased to Reed them and Return me an answer as Soon As possable.

It has pleased the Almighty God to Gift me with a great portion of Natural Enginuity So that I Can Contrive & Compleet Anything I Undertake. The greatest Power & the wonderfullest branshes of ingenuity are yet to be found in My opinion. There is five powers namely Water—Wind—Steam or fire—Weights & Springs. By these All Mills & Machinery whatever Actuates. There Remains yet One to be found which I Cann See affar of[f] but I am not Able to reetch to it for the want of a bite of the Root of all Evill. But the Evill Lyes in Useing it to answer Evil purposes.

I Call it the Power of pressuar, By which A timepeise may be made Smaller than Common Watches to revolve as Long as the Works Will Last Without any thing but Regulating. Likewise Timepieses May be made for Sailing On Sea that Will Effectually Compleet Longsitude also Cariages May be made that the Loading of preshuar of its Load will be the means of its Valosity. Also A Boat May be Calculated that the preshuar of the Load will forse it against the Currant. Likewise be Usefull for Spinning ingines and All Sutch Matchinary. The World has Vulgarly Called it the Perpetual motion but I Call it the power of pressuar (I have already found it on water & by wind I have Calculated A boat to go against the Currant the Stronger the Currant the faster its motion against it by means of the Currant & its own action. Also a wheel cariage that will runn Against the Wind the Stronger the Wind blows the faster its motion Against it. On these Same principles will the power of pressuar Work when Rightly Constructed.

I will State it fair in the Rune of Three to those who Do not Credit the finding of the power.* If Water and Wind can be made to work against Each other—Why not Weights and Springs. The 2d. Day of February Last I was in Lanchaster with Mr. Elicut, Secretary of the Land office an Old Aquaintanc of mine.** I told him my Entention and asked him to assist me With A Little Money to Enable me to make an Experiment. He refered me to Our Assembly. I also Conversed with Severals of them but found they were not willing to venture Any thing Upon Unsertantyes Without they Could Reep immediate Benefit. So I advansed no further. I also told Mr. Elicut of a Discovery I made Last September On the Bank of Lake Erie in York State of a Large body of Iron Oar which is a Grand Object for Som Able Men to Come and Start Iron Works Where there is thousands of Tunns of oar Lying in Water mark washed out of the Slate Rocks Ready dug for mans Use. And the Best Seat for forges at the Rappids of the outlet of the Lake that is in the Union. I Could Wish that the United States Would Embark into that busness for Castings and Iron Could Be transported By Water Over All our Western Cuntery by Water Cariage.

I was 42 years Old When I maryed in 1797—has now five Smal Children in Eight years Next June. My Wife is then 25 year & I 50—but Very Stout for my Age. I am a Building a Grist Mill Upon A new Construction from the foundation. She is to go Without Cog—or round or wheel. Multiplication of Works Diprisuates Strenth is my Creed. That that

---

*What Wilson meant by "Rune of Three" is unclear. Rune: "A letter or character of the earliest Teutonic alphabet. . . . Also, a similar character or mark having mysterious magical powers attributed to it." *Oxford English Dictionary*.

**Andrew Ellicott, (1754–1820), secretary of the Land Office at Lancaster, Pennsylvania, is best known as surveyor of the city of Washington.

Costs the Least & Does the Most Execution is the best
Envented plann.

I look Up to Your house as A Son to A Father for a Littl
Assistance & I will bring you the power of pressuar Dedd or
Alive. If alive it Will be usefull to the World. I ad no more
but Remains Your Affectionat Wellwisher

MATTHEW WILSON

N.B. I send this Letter by post from MeadVille. Direct Your
Letter to care of Joseph Hackney MeadVille.

Jefferson's dentist, Thomas Bruff, who practiced his
profession in Georgetown and Washington for years, advertised in the Washington *National Intelligencer* as the "inventor
and patentee of the perpendicular extracting instruments."
He also sold toothbrushes and "genuine tooth-powder," the
latter noted for "its efficacy in polishing the teeth and hard-
ening the gums."[7] Bruff makes clear in his letter to Jefferson
that dentistry was merely an avocation with him, a living to
provide for his large family; his real talent was his inventive
imagination. With encouragement and some luck he might
have been another Watt or Fulton.

Among the inventions not mentioned in his letter was a
patented window-washing machine. He advertised it in the
Washington *National Intelligencer* as a "labor saving Machine"
that makes windows "perfectly clean, outside as well as in,
is so simple that any servant, male or female, may use it after
being once shown."[8]

George Town Decr. 16th 1801.

SIR,

A person unworthy your attention has taken upon him, to
address a few lines to you, in consequence of a promise last

winter to make and present to you, a machine for perpetual time. As you had not time properly to investigate the plan I considered your sentiments as rather unfavourable, but you gave me every assurance of patronage that I could wish, provided I brought the machine into operation. I should not have taken the liberty to address you had not unforeseen events, prevented the fulfilment of my promise. I beg you will excuse the detail of my misfortunes, as I cannot expect you, as a stranger to my character, to consider the bare assertion of misfortune as a proper apology.

I mentioned to you, that I had concieved a plan for a spoon manufacturing machine, which previous to my interview with you, I had engaged to George Riggs of this place, silversmith, for which he was to give me one thousand dollars, which sum would have put me in a situation to work on the time piece. Notwithstanding a fair bargain before evidence, he refused it when done, after causing me a great deal of expence and labour to bring to perfection, and I had to sue him for the money. I had it tried here and at Philadelphia, by different silversmiths, in the presence of a number of gentlemen; and have by me certificates to shew, that the product is more than 60 to one faster than with the hammer, and same number of hands. I then sold one for Charles Town S. Carrolina, but the purchaser hearing of my dispute with Riggs, followed his example, and by the two, I have missed 1300 dollars, which in my circumstances has been severely felt.

I was calld from this scene of disappointment, to my family 9 in number, out of which 5 were taken dangerously ill, 3 of whom died; and the expence aded to other losses, and being kept all the summer from my business, has brought me into such difficulties, that I am obliged to travel all the winter for support. My companion in life was one of those who were ill; her constitution is broken by the disease; she has every symptom of an approaching decline, and I am seriously apprehensive, that my absence at this time, will soon effect our final seperation. You will readily percieve, that amidst these difficulties, having on me the care of a helpless family, whose wants calld aloud for my exertion, I could not with a human heart, set down to such a piece of business as the machine, with the degree of composure necessary for so nice a performance. The only experiment I have had in my power to try, has proved beyond all controversy, in my opinion, the efficacy of the plan; and permit me to repeat that the first time I have it in my power to undertake it, free from other anxieties, it will be seen that I was not prepossessed in favour of my own production.

I have laid out, in improvements and patents, all the money I ever had, and there is little encouragement either publick or private, for the most useful inventions, and he that does most to lessen the enormous price of labour, unless he has the means of providing a capital, is like to be the poorest man. I now stand in need of publick patronage, and if I can find in the House, any gentlemen of the members, who are friends to genious, and can make any interest amoung them, I mean to apply. Nature has designed me for inventing; such things are almost as easy to me, as to eat or sleep; and if I could live by it, I would devote my life in that way, to the service of my country. Many useful things I have thought of, but for want of means to bear me out, I have let them pass.

Exclusive of the machine I am most anxious about, I have brought to perfection, the patent tooth instruments, and others; a coffee mill, that grinds a pound in 4 & ½ minutes; the spoon machine, that produces from a flat bar, a spoon, ready for the punch, in 12 seconds; fixings for bed steads, to superceed the necessity of screwing them and lacing the sacking. I have modeld here, a machine for treading wheat, cheap and simple, avoiding the fault of those lately patented, such as leaving in the straw, from 60, to 100 bushels of a thousand, and cuting off the heads where the straw is unsound. I have pland a grist mill, to be set up like a coffee mill, and turned by hand; and a sider mill, that is to be worked the same way, to grind, to press, to seperate the pummice, and conduct the liquor to the cask, all by the turn of one hand. These are not all, but sufficient to shew, that nature has formed me for such employment, and I hope you will say, I ought to have assistance. Hoping my promise, respecting the time piece, will be considered as my apology for calling your attention to the subject, I remain with all sentiments of respect,

Your Huml. Servt.
THOS. BRUFF.

Seven years later, Bruff again wrote Jefferson, this time with plans for a steam engine and a windmill. (The "fire engine" he mentions was a contemporary term for a steam engine—a machine that derives its power from combustion.)

March 21st 1808
Six buildings [Washington]

SIR.

I am persuaded that any attempt to call your attention, at this interesting period of our publick affairs, to any thing I could produce, needs an apology and the only one I am able to offer, arises out of the present situation of the country, and the necessity there will shortly be of exerting mechanical talents, which I hope will yet find encouragement in a land so favourable to their compleat success.

Since I took the liberty of addressing you on a former occasion, I have produced, besides some smaller maters, two things which I think of some moment to the public, a new fire engine, intirely different from anything I have seen or heard of, and a permanent horizontal wind mill, capable of moving machinery of any burden.

I have witness'd the deficiency of engines in several instances, ob⟨served⟩ with astonishment what labour was applied, and to what little pu⟨rpose⟩. At that time I had never seen or had a description of their inside works, but adjusted a plan in my mind, of such a machine as I supposed ought to be used, and if used, could not immagine how such a labour could be necessary.

After commiting the outlines of my plan to paper, I got an opportunity of examining one in this city, and to my surprize, found not only the principle entirely different from mine, but many more obstructions than I could have had an idea of. I look'd at it with amazement, and could not immagine how it was, that in so old an invention the defects had never been discovered. I then examined the Enciclopedia, but finding nothing in the cuts like mine, determined further to consider and mature my plan, till some fortunate circumstance (if such ever occur'd) should enable me to execute it to my mind.* The lever of the smallest I have seen, measures 40 inches from the pivet on which it turns, to the extremity; in such an one, I gain 9 inches, in the application of force, which is 2/9th of the whole, an advantage I think worthy of attention, but I have others that are more than equal to it Viz. applying the force in a right direction, removing obstructions to the course of the steam, condensing the water gradually, and preventing the danger of choaking.

I have made a windmill in miniature, on my plan, 21 inches diameter, which when placed in the wind, goes so fast, the sails could scarcely be seen, if they were not white. They are defended from the weather, there is no counteraction from the wind, as it can only act where it is wanted. It recieves the blast as well from one quarter as another, the force can be increased or diminish'd to almost any degree, and is so perfectly manageable without reefing, as to accommodate it in a few seconds to the rising and falling of the wind in variable weather. Being moved by the application of two levers or arms at the same time, its motion is so uniform and steady, as to fit it, in the opinion of the best judges, for the manufactory of flour, sawing lumber of any size, or for working

*Denis Diderot and Jean Le Rond d'Alembert, *Encyclopédie* (1751–80).

machinery of any kind. Ten or twelve feet squair of canvass, spread full to the wind, like the taught sail of a vessel, will give great force; and that force may be increased by enlarging the sails or lengthening the levers, as my calculation is only made to 24 feet diameter. I should take much pleasure in laying my plans before you, if an opportunity should present itself that would make it agreable to you.

I am very respectfully
Your Hl. Servt.
THOS. BRUFF

None of Bruff's inventions ever brought him the recognition and financial security he craved. He seemed on the brink of success with a new way of manufacturing shot, but when the British blew up the Washington Navy Yard during the War of 1812, he lost $10,000 worth of machinery, and failed to get compensation from Congress.

In 1816, Jefferson received a letter from Bruff's daughter Susan Maria. Her father had traveled to New York, "induced by the almost certain prospect of making a brilliant fortune," but had fallen ill and died. Instead of a fortune, he left behind five children and a few letters. Jefferson wrote her the following note.[9]

April 17. 16.

I sincerely condole with you Madam, on the loss of your worthy father, of which your letter gives me the first information. To the public he bade fair to be very useful by his inexhaustible ingenuity; and to his family he must have been inestimable. These afflictions are our common lot; and they come from a hand to which we must bow with resignation. The example of virtue and industry he exhibited will be useful to all; and honorable to his family. To them I know that no words can carry consolation. Time & silence are the only

medecines which can abate their sorrows: and under this persuasion, I think it a duty not to awaken painful recollections
by dwelling on them further than by assuring you of my
sympathy, and my high respect and best wishes for his family and for yourself.

TH: JEFFERSON

Where Bruff was only a theoretician of steam, Oliver Evans
was one of the American pioneers in the construction of steam
engines. He built a high-pressure engine in 1804 that could
"grind 300 bushels of plaster of Paris, or 12 tons in twenty-
four hours." He and George Clymer, the inventor of a patented water pump, reportedly "superior to any then available," produced a scheme for revolutionizing naval warfare
by aiming a steam-driven jet of water at an opposing ship to
disable its cannons.[10] Evans first described the idea to Jefferson, and Clymer followed up with a detailed explanation,
adding a suggestion that one of his own pumps be used to
power the water cannons.

Phila. May 8th. 1805.

Thos. Jefferson President of the U. States
SIR
    I have obtained liberty of Mr. Clymer to communicate his
project—he conceives that an enemy may be effectually prevented from firing a gun either cannon or small arms and be
thrown into the utmost confusion by such a shower of either
cold or hot water as could be thrown on them by a strong
fire engine or a strong steam boiler such as I use with the
power of 100 or 150 or 200 lbs to the inch at the distance of
40 or 60 Yards. Hot water however cannot be thrown to so
great a distance as cold, because the heat leaves it as quick
as lightning after it is exposed to the open atmosphere reduc-
ing it to the temperature of 212 degrees. The heat in leaving

it would disperse the column and thereby prevent it from being thrown so far. Any further communication as to the execution of the project Mr. Clymer is willing to give if required. Your most

Obdt Humb Servt
OLIVER EVANS

Philada. May 15 1805.

To Thomas Jefferson Pres. U. S.

SIR

As my favorite method of attacking the Tripolitans has been in part communicated to you by Mr. Evans, I think incumbent on me more, more fully, to explain my ideas on that subject.

To capture or destroy their Vessels is the thing we desire and I think an attack in the following way, if rightly ordered & well conducted would infallibly enable us to attain that end. Let suitable Vessels be furnished with good *fire Engines* which would enable us to throw the water in such torrents on them and into their Port-holes as to prevent them from firing a gun after we get from 60 to 30 yards of their Vessels. Precautions, however ought to be used to prevent them from boarding our Vessels; as that would be their only means of resisting us. The Engines must be placed *below,* to prevent their being injured by the Enemy's shot, before we get near enough to play them and stop their fire. The Engines may have a constant supply of water without any trouble; and as flight would be their only means of escaping, our Vessels ought to be such fast sailers as to enable us to prevent it. As the Vessels proper to put this theory into practice would be light, active and in continual motion I presume that not much danger is to be apprehended from the enemy's Forts, especialy, after vessels got intermixed with the enemy; as they would be as likely to injure their own Vessels as ours.

If this mode of attack should be adopted, I had contemplated to recommend my Patent Pumps for throwing water, in place of the common fire Engines: but although they have been so much applauded, after long and effectual tryal where all other Pumps on different constructions had failed, yet as I have not had leisure to try how far they would excel the common Engines in throwing water, (they would nevertheless have the advantage of not occupying above one fourth of the Space on board.) I should recommend those Engines that use has rendered more familiar; as the water can be thrown far enough with them to produce the desired effect....

> I am Sir yr. Obedt. Servt.
> GEO: CLYMER

Clymer wrote another letter recommending that hot water could be hosed onto opposing vessels, in spite of Evans's doubts about the feasibility of it. "The project is new and on that account may properly be turned to ridicule," he admitted, "but this does not appear to me a Sufficient reason for withholding a communication on the Subject."

Jefferson wrote back to each man thanking him for the suggestion, but in both cases avoided commenting on the plan itself with a plea of ignorance: ". . . Having no knolege of the subject myself, I am unable to give any opinion respecting it. But it shall be suggested to those who are in the way of making it useful to the public if it can be so."[11]

LIKE Evans and Clymer, Joseph Chambers hoped to revolutionize sea warfare with his invention of a diving suit.*

---

*This is one of a number of letters written over a fifteen-year period by the Pennsylvania farmer-inventor Joseph G. Chambers (1756?–1829). Besides the diving suit described in this letter, he also invented a phonetic alphabet and a repeating rifle. During the War of 1812, he received a contract to supply the Navy with his repeating firearm. Catanzariti, *The Papers of Thomas Jefferson*, 24:293n.

The description of his headgear sounds surprisingly like a modern snorkeling or diving mask; however, an air tank the size of a small boat, with two chambers, one for fresh and another for exhaled air, made the suit impractical. As his letter shows, Chambers learned from his experiments the importance of an uncontaminated air supply for any closed underwater system.

West Middleton, Penna.
Novr. 17. 1807.

To the President of the United States.

Sir

. . . I will . . . give a brief description of the idea & plan of operation contemplated by me. And first as to the operator himself. He is to be furnished with a dress made of Leather (or other flexible material) impervious to the water. The Body furnished with circular elastic Ribs which would give free room & convenience to respiration. This was devided into several parts: as the pantaloons which covering the lower extremeties were joined to the body piece by an insertion similar to the closing of lids upon snuff boxes &c. The arm pieces & head piece were united to it in the same manner. Suppose this Dress thus fixed on, impervious to the Air or water & other loose Clothing under, according to the temperature of the Season or Water. Suppose the head piece (which must set close, especially on the face, by means of an elastic lining) furnished with a Tube passing across the mouth from one ear to the other & so from the Ears to the top of the head where they open to the external Air for breathing, having a suitable stoppage or covering that can be opened or Shut at pleasure at this superior orifice.

The face piece must be of some thickness & solid; the eyes furnished with glasses to see withal. And for the practibility of breathing in this manner the Tube which crosses the mouth

(& there communicates) is furnished with two delicate valves with springs so that in respiration the air must enter at one side and pass out the other (that is, pass through the tube entering at one end & issueing out of the other in the same manner that Water passes through a pump, supposing the communication as of the mouth, between the two valves). There was also a precautionary apparatus against the effect of water accidentally falling into the Tubes which need not be particularized. Now it is obvious that a person furnished in this manner (the whole apparatus adopted in a small degree specifically lighter than Water) would have a great facility in enduring & swimming upon the Surface.

In the next place for the purpose of passing under the water we prepare a vessel as follows to carry a sufficient stock of air for the use & consumption of the operator. Suppose a vessel of an oblong form adapted to the best progressive motion through the fluid to contain from one or two Hundred gallons to any greater requisite quantity. I need not mention the mechanism for moving or rowing this vessel with a celerity nearly equal to that of any vessel of equal weight above water (by the operator who may be placed either before or behind it) as not comprising any novel principles. This vessel (being air tight) is furnished with a Curtain or separating membrane (of thin moist parchment skins or other thinest lightest flexible material) adapted to the shape of the internal cavity & attached to its sides horizontally (in a line dividing it equally) to stop all communication between the air which may be inflated on one side of this curtain with the air on the other side of the same. The curtain thus fitted to the cavity & attached to the sides may be understood to fill or line the lower half of the cavity & by its own weight will lie & rest in that position. But if air be inflated into the lower division under the curtain (the upper having vent) the membrane will be raised up till it shall fill or line the upper half of the Cavity (& vice versa) and thus is produced a compleat separation between the air which may be contained on the one & on the other side of this curtain; that is, above & below the same.

Into this vessel thus prepared is inserted two flexible tubes (which may be enclosed on one sheath) the one communicating with the lower division & the other with the upper) (of any most convenient length) which, at their other end, are inserted (by a convenient junction) into the Tube of the head piece of the operator, at the two sides of his mouth, beyond the valves, so that when the superior orifices are stopped (above his head) he will draw the air out of the upper cavity of the vessel & return it into the lower cavity, or division under the curtain. The returning Tube has also a communication (at the neck) with the room or space around his Thorax the better to support the free circulation & equilibrium of the Air *in* & *out* of the vessel.

This whole apparatus with the operator attached is somewhat specifically heavier than the water (for the greater security of concealment before an Enemy) And if any accident or difficulty should occur the operator can instantly detach himself stopping the lower & opening the upper orifice of breathing & seek safety by swimming &c. With this Machine he might glide along the surface of the water like a fish and raising the top of his head piece above might breath the superior air saving the Stock in his vessel for occasions of sinking. And also by the same avenue (or by other suitable Tubes) replenish his vessel with fresh air when requisite. I supposed it practicable for Machines of this sort to be carried & occasionally ushered out of a ship of war through some kind of Port hole adapted to the purpose perhaps in its steps under the surface of the water. And as persons might by practice become expert in their use & inured to that fortitude & endurance of Danger usual in Military attchievments it would be very difficult to defend a vessel (even apprized) against the efforts of a number of them which might be directed either in the Day or night as found most practicable. As to the exploding machine it (not depending upon novel principles) need not be here described. . . .

This description (if intelligible) may give some Idea of the plan & the principles contemplated. I had prepared an apparatus (or *Torpedo*) conformable to this idea & proceeded to make such experiment as practicable in a Pond formed for the purpose upon a small stream (no larger being in convenient vicinity). And in this first attempt I found my lungs offended (as I supposed) with certain noxious exhalations from the internal surfaces of the machinery, particularly by the effluvia of Linseed oil or paint applied in some parts for rendering the tubes impervious &c. On this account (as I supposed) I could not conveniently remain long enough under the water to obtain an experiment compleatly satisfactory & successful. I determined to remove these obstacles by renewed preparation of the internal surfaces &c. and in this conjuncture the sudden irruption of the British Army deranged & interrupted the whole project.

Thus, Sir, have I been induced to communicate the idea of this experiment, tho perhaps in too clumsy or indistinct description. If the President shall be at leisure to peruse it . . . I shall cheerfully embrace the opportunity of ferther explanation. And Remain

Sir, with the most profound Respect &c.

JOSEPH G. CHAMBERS

In May, 1815, the *Enterprise,* a stern wheeler, with a patented engine built by Daniel French, journeyed from New Orleans to Louisville, becoming the first steamboat to travel upstream from the lower Mississippi to the Ohio. Two years earlier, French had placed a steam engine of his own construction on an altered river barge, christened the *Comet,* and navigated the Mississippi between New Orleans and Natchez.[12] He wrote Jefferson in 1804, at a time when his dreams for a successful steamboat appeared destined for failure. His appeal went unanswered, but it reveals a man much like Thomas Bruff, driven by a creative vision that had seized him at an early age and dragged him through one business failure after another to his final success.

The life story French tells is very much like that of John Fitch, the pioneer of steam in the United States, who built a working steamboat, but never achieved Fulton's commercial success or fame. Both Fitch and French were button makers, steam engine builders, and poor businessmen.[13] They also shared the Yankee mechanic's inventive genius, that transfiguring passion which, as French explains in his letter, "excites the nervous power," strengthens "the muscular fibers," and gives new strength and life "to every function of the body." It is the heat of that creative flame that powered the industrial growth of nineteenth-century America.

The jet-propelled engine and its accompanying sketch (see page 165) that French describes in his letter is not what he ultimately succeeded with. The Mississippi steamboats were driven by rotary-wheel engines.

New York July 5—1804.

HONOUR'D SIR.

In Some of the moments when your mind is relaxt from the weighty matters of your situation, I crave your patience and favour So far to Read a few lines from an American Mechanic who has some share in Invention of usefull Machines and improvements but from a number of misfortunes in different ways is unable from his pinching sicumstances to do that good to mankind which otherwise he would gladly do, wishing only to have a comfortable support for him self and family, and to be able to execute those usefull inventions; as the inventing and puting in operations those Ingines and improvements constitutes his pride and ambition.

Viewing the matter in the light that the mechanick who
by some usefull invention, an improvement can save one
Dollar to each family per year, does more go[o]d to his
Country than millions of money, and that the only thing which
distinguishes the civillizd from the savage state is the culti-
vation of the arts, and syences which have all sprang from
the inventitive mind in different ages times and countrys, but
to the shame of our Country, the inventitive mechanick is
mostly look'd on with contempt rideculed, and abused by the
multitude, at which however he ought not to be in the passion of anger, as they are ignorant of what they despise, they
ought rather to have our pity and forgiveness. For my self I
have sufferd much from such people, and expect to more.

Sir if you can have patience I will give you a short account
of what my situation in life as a mechanick has been, and
what it is now and what was the situation of my Fathers
Family but on this suffice it to say that my Father was left
without any property when yong, ⟨was⟩ by Nature of a slender Constitution, serv'd an apprenticeship to the Coopers
Business, which he set up soon after married my Mother.
About one year after, one of the neighbouring houses being
on fire, in his indeavours to extinguish the flames, he over
heated him self and never after was in health, but only for
short intervals. His family increasing, the trouble and difficulty of supporting his family became at last insirmountable,
and he was under the necessity of asking aid of the town,
thus wreched were we and despised by People in better circumstances.

Our deplorable situation deprived me of a common chance
for scooling, as I was oblig'd to work with my Father as soon
as I could do anything to earn one penny per day. When I
was thirteen years of age my Father died and my Mother was
left a widow with five yong children. I being the oldest, soon
after my Fathers death I was bound an apprentice to a Cooper
in the town with whom I serv'd untill I was twenty years of
age; at which time he told me, my service to him was satis-

factory, and gave me one year of my time, but during my apprenticeship I did not have one day to scool, but being all ways inclined to learn allthough deprived of the common advantages I learned to write a tolerable hand and to Read as well as People in common.

Part of my one and twentyth year I worked with my Master as a journeyman, and that year as much as possible applyd my self to studdy. The next year I set up my trade, workd at it one year. At this time my mind was so strongly bent on new inventions that it was impossible for me to be reconsiled to work at my trade, and finding my hands were made to work in any other trade without serveing one day, which I could do to the astonishment of all who knew me, the operations of such things on my mind was irresistable and must break forth into action, but this as much as possible I ideavourd to restrain and keep under untill I had gaind one thing I thought absolutely necessary. This was to gain a knowledge of Natural Philosophy, and the science of Mechaneks for which I spared no pains night or day untill I had gaind. As I saw, it was so nessecerely and intimately joind or connected with mechineacall operations, that one would be lyable to mistake a thousand times in the constructions of new Machinery without its aid, and this point I gaind from Sir Isaac Newtons Principia, B. Martins Philosophy &c.*

But the study of those things as it intruded on my time to work, subjected me to great trouble as my relations were all against me, saying it would never do me any good. The eyes of the town were fixt on me immediately, with disgusting frowns, which soon arose to such hight that there was talk of puting an overseer over me. About this time I had Invented a steam Boat and found a rich man of the town who was much pleasd with the plan, with whom I made a bargain to

*Sir Isaac Newton, *Philosophiae Naturalis Principia Mathematica* (Cambridge, 1687); Benjamin Martin, *Philosophia Britannica, or A New and Comprehensive System of the Newtonian Philosophy, Astronomy and Geography* . . . (London, 1747).

be at the expence of building one, which was done to be equally ownd betwen us booth. This giting to the ears of the authority of the town, they appointed a meeting to put a master over me, to make me get work at my old trade again. Of this I heard and went to the meeting to plead my own cause, but to no purpose; they were set against the thing, and put a stop to it.

The agatation of my mind was so great and produced such debility that it had like to have been fatal; dejected and all most broken hearted (as I had not learned to support myself under such trouble) I went with anxious sorrow to work in the field at days work, and with the swet of my Brow to earn my Bread and almost gave up the hopes of ever being in better circumstances; after this went to work at one Dunhams a tinman by trade, with whom I workd at that Business for some time.

At this time the manufactorying of buttens of a composition of copper and tin was caried on with great spirit in Connecticut, where I livd in the town of Berlin. From working at tin I turned my attention to makeing all the tools for making Buttons, such as laiths to turn Buttons in, and makeing Brass moulds to cast the Buttons in, of all figures, while to work at this I invented a peice of machinery to turn eight Buttons at the same time. This was so contriv'd that one wheal in constant motion caused the machine to do all the work with out one hand about it. The Buttons were thrown promiscuously into a hopper like a parcel of grain, and from this in regular manner, and without failure, put in and taken out of the spindles on which they were turnd, and flowered. But just as this works were finishing, the Buttons got out of repute, and the Merchants would not buy them. This to me provd bad as I had spent a great deal of time in makeing this Machinery, which at once became useless.

I then invented some Machinery for makeing wrought and Cut Nails, the Moddles of which are now in the Office of the

Secretary of States.* One forth of this invention I sold to Asher Miller esq Mayor of the City of Middletown for two thousand pounds Connecticut Courancy to be paid in one year. This raisd my expectations, as Miller was thought to be a good man. Of this sum he paid me one thousand Dollars on which I bargain'd for a house and land to the amount of seven hundred pounds. Two hundred and fifty pounds I paid, but Miller being largely concerned in the land speculation of Georgia, faild.** With the failure of that business, on this everyone came on me for what I ow'd them. This reduced me to a state worse than nothing, as it left me some in debt.

After this I bargaind with a company of men in Middletown to set up a manyfactory of cut Nails one quarter of which works, built at their expense, was to be mine and one fourth of the net proceeds. In this work was expend five thousand Dollars, and from the operation of said machine, it appeard that it would be very profitable to the owners. Wee had built four machines, each of which would cut and head sixty nails per minute, and those nails were very nice and would bring a better price in marke[t] than others but about this time & having the charge of the Business, I was abused by the other owners in a most unheard of manner which ran to that hight that a could stay in the[re] [no] longer, chusing to live in peace without property—rather than have it and live in discord. From offers from one of my workmen to my partners they thought to git the work done in more advantageous terms then what I could acceed to. Affter my leaving the works, this man would not ingage with them to take charge of said works, which for thre years have lain still and useless.

*French refers to the U.S. Patent Office, which was placed in charge of William Thornton in 1802, but was officially a part of the State Department under Secretary of State James Madison. Noble E. Cunningham, Jr., *The Process of Government under Jefferson* (Princeton, N.J.: Princeton University Press, 1978), 92.

**He refers to the Yazoo land claim speculations which resulted in losses to many investors. See Dumas Malone, *Jefferson and his Time,* 6 vols. (New York: Little, Brown & Company, 1948–81), 4:248–50.

After quiting said works I came to New York and set up a Machine for Dressing Shingles. This shaves booth sides at one stroke and joints booth edgees at one time. This has been in operation almost thre years and is a very profitable machine and does the work with the greaitest niceness. This is work'd by a Horse and will shave and joint five hundred per hour. One of those machines I Built last summer for which I was to have had the money in August last past to the amount of one thousand Dollars the want of which has got me into great trouble and fear worse to come.

This last spring I invented and built a new contrived machine for braiding or weaveing the catgut onto the stocks of gentlemens silver mounted Whips. This will weave one Whip in one minute of time. Of money for this I am also disappointed. Many new and useful things I have Invented but find no incouragement at present to build them, but one thing of them is worth millions of money and which knowing it to be so vastly valueable and trying for several years to find incouragement, I have at almost given the mater up. And it fills my mind with such anxciety, and restless sensations that it seems if it would have ben better for me had I never had the thing come into my mind.

This of which I speak, and of inventions of mine seems most valueable, is an Invention for a Steam Boat. This is amazeing simple in its construction haveing no wheals, paddles, swe[e]ps, or oars or any other thing to project eighther from the sides bottom or stern in any way or from what ever and the power applyed acts with the same force when against the stream as it does when moveing with it which is impossible in any other way. This principle I demonstrated in the presence of many witnesses and all the power applyd is spent in this way to the best advantage possible, being in a direct line and wholly free from oblique pressure. . . .

The Steam Engine I have greatly improved, made it very simple in its structure, not requireing more than one seperate peice to fifty in the old ways, or (for the boat) the Ingine is on the principle of Wats and Bottons double headed Ingine though very different in its form, takeing up but little room.* An ingine whose power is equal to the weight of two tons built in this way will not take up more than four feet in hight and will all be under deck. A small Ingine of this form, I have made which is now complete and goes to admiration. Several other forms for other uses, I have constructed, thre of which move with out any friction of the piston, and not requiring the cylinder to be bored for the piston to play in.

The power of the Steam Ingine requires no ilustration as it must be well known to you; and the only reason why the Steam Boat has faild, is not from want of power in the ingine, but from a want of proper applycation of that power. But in the way I have contrived, I think every advantage is combind, which I submit to your examination, which I have no doubt you will find to be strictly Philosophycal and true, and I look forward from the midst of adversity to the time when this will double the value of our western acquisition by fre[e] navigation of those waters which Nature has denyd in the common way, and convey to the interior of our Country the commiditys of all the earth.

Shall I be instrumental of procureing so great a blessing to my Country, Nature and experiment join in the affirmative; O how inlivening the thought while on my mind, excites the nervous powr, threnghens the Muscular fibers, the blood circulates vigerously and every function of the body seem to acquire new strench and life. My greatest intrest is to do good to mankind—for in indeavours to increase the hapyness of others I devise the greatest happyness to my self and virtue gos hand in hand with hapyness.

And now sir if it would be pleasing to you I would come to Washington and prove by experiment before your eyes that what I have said in relation to the steam boat is true and

*James Watt (1736–1819) and Matthew Boulton (1728–1809), developers of a successful commercial steam engine in England.

correct; the Boat should be rig'd with sails that when the wind is favourable we may make use of it with out the ingenes operation. The form of the Bailer to make steam as I have constructed it is very cheap and simple. I have an Ingine of the power of 500 pounds weight partly done for a Boat, but am not able to finish it for want of money, which if I had I could soon finish, and put in operation. If it be your mind, this shall be set to work in Washington which will fully determine the mater but for convenience I had rather do it in New York or at least to finish the ingine, which I could send round to Elexandria by water. If I had a few hundred dolars say four I could acomplish what I had itend by an experiment with this ingine to move a Boat. This Ingine would allways be usefull and pay the expence, so that no money would be lost in the experiment or but very little, and if you Sir or you with any other gentelemen will be so kind as to help such a mechanick who cannot help him self, you will do me a great kindness, for which I shall ever remain your Servant and Friend and this I do not ask with out an intention of satisfaction for if you please one half of the right shall be yours with all the advantages ariseing therefrom by your being at the expenc[e] of building. . . .

Sir if you think my indeavours in this way to do good in my day and generation, aught to be incouraged pray Sir do not forgit one of your country men, but be so kind as to answer your petitioner as soon as your business will permit, in so doing you will much oblige your—

Servant and Friend
DANIEL FRENCH

NB forgive any thing a miss as it is not from intention, Mr. Thomas Jeffersons President of the States. Direct your Letter to Daniel French of New York corner of Montgomery and Bedlow Streets.

There is no record that Jefferson ever responded to French.

John Brightthought, a Baltimore mechanic, wished to encourage manufacturing in America; he had invented a machine for printing calico and asked the president to present it to Congress.

Baltimore March the 22nd 1803

(Sirs)

To you that are interested in the public Welfare of your Country whose greattest Ambition is to reas larning and genious to its greatest perfection and whose prinsiples is to reward merrit and incurage the Arts of Manufacturing our own Country produce in All its Various Branches, A Spechily this Branch of Business that is At A low ebb in our Country Namely Manufacturing of Cotton And printting Calligoe, which we have to pay Yourope Twenty five per Cent more than we can do it for. Therefore we can with equal Skill And ingenewity bring Calico printing to as great prefection her[e] as in Any part of Yourop And do it Cheepor for which purpose I have invented A New machine for printing Calico to go By Water, hand or Any other powar And Will print With more exactness And will proimpress the Collars on more even than Can be done by hand And will print At the rate of Seven hundred And twenty yeards in Twelve ours with the Assistance of one man.

Much more might be said on the principals of the Machine But suffis'd to say it will Ar Origenate [originate] every Mashion Necessary to A Execute the Business to profection. I have modled this Machine in Miniature And found it to Answer the purpose I intended it for. Thinking it would be a benifet to the public At Large, I thought it my Duty to let my intentions be known first to the honourable Gentlemen that is Apointed to Conduct the Affaires of our Country And on whose Conorduct Depends such. I Shall leave the hole of this business to the impartial Judgment of the members of this House of Congres. If this plan is worthy of Atenshion pleas to rite to Baltimore for farder information. Derect your Letter to your humble Servant

JOHN BRIGHTTHOUGHT

T.J. presidend of the U: S pleas to read this to the House of Representives.

Richard Harris, a Virginia millwright, offered his services as a builder of "Cotton Spinning works" and canals. Like many of the artisans who wrote to Jefferson, he chafed with a restless energy for "Some great mechanical business to conduct" which would "be usefull to the public." Such appeals demonstrate how the ideals, as well as the rhetoric, of Enlightenment humanitarianism had filtered down from intellectuals such as Jefferson to the laboring classes.

Providence Rhode Island July the 10th 1808

SIR

I hope you will excuse me for thus Taking this liberty with you. I am a native of *Virginia,* was *Born* in the County of Hanover—was Taught the millwrights business, have done a vast deal of business in that kind in that State. The last mill I built was for Mr. Bullock in the County of Louisa. For 2 or 3 years past I have been at that place ingaged in making Flour—but as the matter of manufacturing flour has not for the last Season been so much incouraged I concluded that I could by giting acquainted with the art of the Cotton Spinning be more usefull to the Public, to accomplis which I left home on the 1st Day of May last with a full determination to make myself acquainted with the art.

I have perhaps Seen all the manufacturers to the best of this in the States which I have come through. At this place the art is in perfection—& notwithstanding they have gave caution in the papers against admitting me; as I had come on to get acquainted that I might Carry it on at the Southerd, yet I have made myself acquainted with the process of making the machinery & Spinning.

To come to the point I want Some great mechanical business to conduct which I have been ingaged in for 12 or 14 years past. I wish to be usefull to the public & at this Time perhaps you can inform me of Something in the way. I think the thing I would wish would be the Building Cotton Spinning works. If you Know not of any thing of this kind which I could get I would undertake the business of managing or laying out the ground for Canals, having done a good deal in that way—or the Building of any Kind of water works.

I have no Famely & am active & healthy. Pleas write to me at Provedence Rhode Island—I can get letters of Recomendation as to the Skill I have in *machanism*—and as an honest man.

I am with Respect Yr Friend
RICHD. HARRIS

Jeremiah Brown, a Providence, Rhode Island, farmer, had an irrigation plan that he thought would solve the food problems of the world.

Providence March 8 1801

DEAR SIR,

Inclosed you have Information of the most Important Discovery for Culture. Should immediate attention be paid it will increase the crop this year Sufficient to Feed 2-1/2 Millions of People, and by next year may be increas'd to 10 millions, which would be a great relief to the nations in Europe now in war, and add greatly to Harmonifing this two much divided Country. I request you to see my Patent right secured at the patent Office Agreeable to my Letter to President Adams the 9th of 2nd month. I request you to immediately Acknowledge the Recp't of this Letter.

Private reports represent your circumstance and Mr. Burrs to be embarrassed. Should that be the case I can with great ease and the utmost pleasure Accommodate you with each an adva[n]ce of fifty or one Hundred Thousand Dollars, as may be to you the most Agreeable. A short description of your Lands and whether Improved by slaves or free People will enable me to make Such arrangements in Macheenary as will affectually water your Soil, the principal material to Effect which will be plank of different thicknesses and Logs Suitably bored to form Tubes to throw the water any height Which the Situation may require. I shall immediately Answer yours and give you information how soon I can be at the seat of Government.

> I am Dear sir your most Affectionably
> JEREM. BROWN

This angry letter from Louis DuPré was the result of Jefferson's calling him a "madman." It was possibly made to his face, but more likely the expression was repeated to him by someone else. It was a term Jefferson frequently used to describe his impatience with religious fanatics. DuPré speaks of addressing the president for the sixth time in this letter. Because there are no records of previous letters, he may have visited Jefferson a number of times, for he had traveled from Charleston to Washington to promote his invention and wrote this letter from the capital. Although he does not mention what invention was revealed to him by "the hand of Providence," he was issued a patent for a steelyard scale on May 12, 1802.[14]

Washington 7th Feby. 1802.

SIR.

My apology for troubling you a *sixth* time on an unpleasant subject is recorded in the 21 & 22 verses of the 18 Chapter of St. Matthews Gospel.*

I agree with you that I am a *Madman,* but not in supposing that I am the Instrument in the hand of Providence to produce important blessings to my fellow men, but in sacrificing so much to *common fame.* From an early period of my life I evinced an unshaken attachment to the cause of liberty, & love of my country. Her interest has been ever dear to me, in supporting which I deem'd it necessary to advocate your interests, & in the struggle of politic's in *Charleston* was induced to sacrifice valuable connexions to my political sentiments. The joy resulting from the important discovery which was revealed to me woud, in itself have produced but half the satisfaction I experienced, when I considered that the important discovery had been reserv'd for an *American,* for a *genuine republican* & that at a time when a *Jefferson* fill'd the presidential Chair. This, Sir, is the sense of my *madness.*

But I have done with these fine spun theories. I have already paid dearly for them. Had I gone directly to Europe I should have been not only noticed there, but *cherished.* The discovery would then have reflected honor on my country. Or had I depended on a *British consul* after I arrived in this City rather than on the President & Congress of the United States, my laurels would not have been eclipsed by a Canadian *woodsman* (who I am told is now on his way to Europe) whose success, I hope, will not be blasted by his reliance on his own government.**

All that remains *now,* in your power to undo the very unfavorable impression that this business is likely to make on the

---

*Matthew: 18.21–22: "Then Peter approaching asked him, 'Lord, if my brother sins against me, how often must I forgive him? As many as seven times?' Jesus answered, 'I say to you, not seven times but seventy-seven times.'"
**DuPré does not identify the "Canadian woodsman" with a rival steelyard scale.

minds of the American people, is to recommend to the legislature to extend the usual term of patents on this occasion. I do not feel disposed to reserve a patent for *only fourteen years,* as America will then be very far short of its ultimate population.*

I remain, Sir, Your friend (notwithstanding)
L. DuPré

I have not shewn this to any person neither do I keep a copy—L D

One of the shortest announcements of a discovery was a note from a young British seaman who had no sooner set foot on American soil than he picked up his pen to write to the nation's president.

New York May 12. 1801

SIR

Pardon the Intrusion of an Imigrant from England on Ship Mary from Bristol (first time of my being att Sea). I was Sitting Across the Helm, the Ship Labouring With a Contrary Wind, An Idea Imediately Struck me With A Plan to Steer A Ship Against the Winds Eye (O that I may Steer my Course through Life in thoughts Words & Actions his the Ardent Desire of A Sinfull Mortal in the midst of Strangers). Sir if this his Deserving of Your Notice I am

Personally G⟨rateful⟩
COMMAND BATE DYKE

at Allexander Hemptons No 105 Maiden Lane
PS Landed here on Lords Day Last.

---

*DuPré was one of several inventors who complained that the fourteen-year limit on patents was too short.

A young Maryland man with a plan for using a screw mechanism for "communicating motion" elicited a response and an offer of an interview from Jefferson by reminding the president that he had visited him before. Jefferson's answer is yet another case, not only of his accessibility, but also of his generosity in giving his time to men with questionable claims on it.

City of Washing. Sept. 26th. 1808.

Tho. Jefferson Esqr.

SIR,

In the winter of 1806, you may recollect of my visiting you at the Presidents palace, & that without a previous acquaintance, or letter of introduction. The reason was, that I thought the introduction would be Satisfactory on both parts, by the Subject alone as by letters. Mr Dufief particularly offered me a letter, but I considered it intirely unnessary for the reason before mentioned; he then told me that he, had no introduction & Sir I believe it made [no] kind of difference.* If you recollect my purpose was, to make an improvement on the mode of Communicating motion. At that time I thought I had Compleated it, but Since I have found that I only Commenced it, for, not untill lately have I brought the affair to a Close.

I now propose a revolution in the present System of Communicating motion; & if my principles be Correct it also will produce a revolution in the System of Mechanics. As far as I have experimented my principle is Correct; on the windmill particularly I have applied the principle to the Sails, & from that attention I find that Twenty yards less will answer in the hundred the same purpose. I have not applied it as running

---

*Nicolas Gouin Dufief (d. 1834), was a French-born Philadelphia author and bookseller who sold numerous books to Jefferson and conducted a lengthy correspondence with him.

gear to my windmill, but I have to a grindstone with equal effect. The screw is the power with which I produce motion to the most advantage in every Case, either by Water, wind, Steam, or in any other way that motion is to be produced. I will say no more on the Subject now, but hope & pray, that you will give me permission to lay the whole before you.

I have been on the Subject of Mechanics for more than Six years; your knowledge of general principles is So extensive, that I know I should receive more Satisfaction in communicating with you than any other person in the world. Should I be mistaken I wish to know it & if I am not, I wish to know it also. If through any motives whatever you Should decline answering me, I should never forgive myself for writing to you. Figure to your Self a young man Scarcely more than Twenty five years of age, who has been, & Continues [to] be anxious to benefit Philosophy, who has secluded himself from the world & devoted himself to its Study. Mr. Dufief told me that you were always ready to correspond with & See, a deep thinking man; I am Confident I am one of that Class. Whether my thoughts will turn to the advantage of Society or not be Assured that no man esteems your Excellency more than I do.

DAVID K. HOPKINS

NB. If you write, have the goodness to direct to the care Matthew Hopkins Esqr Snow Hill Maryland.

Mr. David K. Hopkins
Washington Oct. 19. 08.

SIR

Your letter of Sept. 26. came to my hands on the 5th inst. I have entirely forgotten the subject of your visit in 1806, and the mode you proposed of producing motion; and I am sure you greatly overrate any service I could render you even did my public duties allow me the time to consider your proposition carefully. But these duties so entirely engross the whole of my time & especially on the approach & during a session of Congress that I should be able to bestow but a very superficial attention on it. Still, so much am I sensible of the improvement of the condition of mankind by the introduction & improvement of machinery, that if your business should bring you to this place, I should very willingly take such a view of your propositions as my time would permit, & suggest to you any extempore ideas which might occur. I know that I wish a public good, in wishing you personally success in your pursuits, and I pray you to accept my salutations & best wishes.

TH: JEFFERSON

8

Health

"Some persons almost fainted to look at me"

TWO opposing schools of treatment dominated medical practice in late eighteenth and early nineteeth century America. One was a "heroic" therapy, pitting an aggressive physician against wily diseases in a vigorous wrestling match; the other was a more careful, skeptical approach, emphasizing prevention, a respect for nature as a healer, and mild medications. Jefferson's sympathies lay with the more cautious practitioners.[1] He believed the body was self-restorative, and if left to its own resources it would in time cure itself. This natural process might be accelerated with gentle nostrums, he thought, but he objected to the physician who concocts "some fanciful theory" which "lets him into all nature's secrets at short hand." This leads to such adventurous practices as blood-letting, emetics, and mercury purges, advocated in particular by Jefferson's friend Dr. Benjamin Rush.* Such treatments, Jefferson declared, destroyed more

---

*Dr. Benjamin Rush (1745–1813), signer of the Declaration of Independence and one of the most eminent physicians of the age.

life in a single year than do bandits and highwaymen in a century.

Jefferson believed that the physician should understand the limits of his art, and become merely a "quiet spectator of the operations of nature." He could be most helpful by setting "a well-regulated regimen" and by encouraging "good spirits and hope in the patient."[2]

Medical treatment was a serious social concern in the Jefferson era; numerous lives were lost from the yellow-fever epidemics that struck the cities of the eastern seaboard with devastating regularity during his presidency. One of the most destructive attacks of yellow fever in the history of the nation had occurred in Philadelphia in 1793. It killed at least one-tenth of the city's population and virtually suspended operation of the federal government. Each succeeding year saw the disease invade some of the nation's major cities—Philadelphia, New York, Baltimore, Alexandria, Charleston, and New Orleans. Many of the victims of the disease were hastened to their deaths by the well-intentioned but debilitating treatment of massive bleedings and purges. There was no cure, or any treatment based on a knowledge of the origins of the fever. Its cause would not be discovered for another century when a medical team led by Walter Reed determined with certainty that yellow fever was carried by the *Aedes aegypti* mosquito.[3]

Because the annual outbreaks of yellow fever occurred during the late-summer mosquito season and vanished after frost killed the insects, many thought that cold temperature could cure the disease. A woman writer offered a logical solution—refrigerate the victims. She was not confident enough of the cure, however, to sign her name to the letter.

New York 8th July 1804

Sir

Doctor Buchan says in the Introduction to his domestic Medicine that "Very few of the valuable discoveries in Medicine have been made by physicians."* It has for a long time run strongly in the mind of an old woman that freezing rooms might be constructed where persons might be introduced with good effect in the Malignant or Yellow fever. It is a known fact that nothing but frosty weather stops the raging of the disorder. It is also known that by the means of ice, frosty air to any degree may be obtained during the hottest weather.

You Sir have it in your power to cause the experiment to be tried. From having observed your humanity in the preservation of human lives is the reason of this being addressed to you.

A Boston physician, Edward Rowse, suggested to Jefferson that because the symptoms of smallpox, the plague, and yellow fever are similar, inoculation with kine pox might immunize against yellow fever. The danger involved in such an experiment prompted him to suggest that it be tried on condemned criminals.[4] This letter elicited an opinion from the president, along with a swipe at one of his favorite targets—newspapers.

Doctr. Edward Rowse
Monticello Aug. 4. 05.

Sir

Your favor of July 13. was recieved at this place. Not being myself a competent judge of the analogies between the Cowpox, the small pox, the plague, & yellow fever, I readily

---

*William Buchan, *Domestic Medicine, or, A Treatise on the Prevention and Cure of Diseases by Regimen and Simple Medicines* (New York, Boston, Philadelphia, 1799). This work, first published in London in 1769, went through nineteen editions in the author's lifetime, in America, England, and on the Continent.

acquiesce in the opinions of those who are the proper judges. That the Cowpox prevents the small pox is now I believe doubted by nobody. But I had not supposed it to be established that it is preventative against the plague. Some paragraphs in the newspapers indeed had stated such a doctrine. But their editors admit falsehood with so much levity that a fact is not the more to be believed for being found in them. It may however be true altho' it is in a newspaper. With respect to the experiment whether yellow fever can be communicated after the vaccine, which you propose should be tried on some malefactor, no means of trying that are likely to be within my power. During the term I have been in office, not a single conviction in any capital case has taken place under the laws of the general government. The Governors of the several states would have it more in their power to favor such an experiment. . . .

TH: JEFFERSON

The belief that yellow fever was a scourge of God was no doubt held by numerous Americans; the following writer attributes the disease to providential displeasure with slavery. This was one of a number of anti-slavery letters sent by deeply religious people who were appalled by the existence of slavery in a land of liberty.

New London 28 November 1803

SIR

   . . . As it is obviously evident that the United States of America are under a great Calamity as a nation, and more especially some of our Cities and Capitals, in many parts of the Union, by reason of the Epidemical disease generally called the yellow Fever. And as I put no confidence in chance as that any thing can take place, without the limits of true Philosophy; there must be a special or natural cause for every thing that does exist, and finding that no natural cause can be assigned by our most skillfull Physicians, and much less on Philosophical principles, of the origin, of the aforesaid calamity brought on us by the yellow Fever. From which my mind was lead to search for the special cause of the aforesaid calamity. . . .

But when I contemplate of the many Thousands of our fellow men within the limits of the United States captivated to perpetual slavery, from generation to generation; either by Law, or without Law; all having from the God of our existence an equal right to liberty and freedom with all the rest of mankind. I am not at a loss for the special cause of the aforesaid calamity; when so many Thousands of our fellow men are deprived of their natural rights, and the just protection of Law; this truth being obviously witnessed from attended Circumstances to the rational mind.

Firstly. As I have had personal knowledge of several of our Eastern States for more than Fifty years, and I never heard of the yellow Fevers being in this Country, untill since our Independence took place; tho' there is no doubt, but that the subjugation of the Negroes to slavery took place in the very early settlements of America; but the sin of ignorance we read is winked at. But since the founding of our present Constitution upon its true Republican principles constituting equal good to all its subjects, which has been almost universally approbated and acknowledged, and in many Instances sworn to protect. We can no longer plead ignorance in suffering so many of our fellow man to be Subjected in slavery. For he that knoweth his masters will, and commiteth things worthy of stripes, shall be beaten with many.

Secondly. It obviously appears that the righteous Judge of Heaven and Earth, has marked out our great capitals and marritime Towns, and Cities, as the greatest offenders, and the just victims of his displeasure, as the judge of all the

Earth will do right. Showing us that those maratime Towns and Cities were in the first transgression, in subjecting these unhappy People.

Thirdly. It is obviously witnessed before our eyes, that God, in his providence has made a discrimination, as in Egypt, between the oppresor, and the oppresed; for this Ethiopean Nation, by Gods power, in almost every Instance are protected from this destroying pestilence that wasteth at noon Day.* From which circumstantial evidence, I feel justified in myself, and from the love I feel for my fellow men, to Solicit our chief magistrate, with the advise of our National Council, to see if these People now in slavery within the United States, cannot be liberated. . . .**

> I have the honor to be
> Your most Obdt. & very Hbl. Servt.
> PARK WOODWARD

The economic effects of yellow fever on laboring-class families was communicated to Jefferson by a New York shoemaker who wrote about an epidemic that struck New York in 1802.

> New York 8th. March 1804

His Excellency Thos. Jefferson Esqr.
SIR,

I would not address your Excellency if I had not hopes of Your complying with the Petition of a Poor Mechanic in Distress as I am at Present. I will Just state to Your Excellency

---

*It was erroneously believed that slaves, because of their African heritage, were immune from contracting yellow fever.

**Woodward ended his letter by proposing that slaves be purchased from their owners with public money and emancipated. He suggested that former slaves would be well suited to work in the newly purchased Louisiana Territory. The letter was not written by Woodward; the text is clearly written, but his signature is palsied.

my Situation, Viz I Began Business in New York in the Shoe-making line, about the middle of July last, and was doing Tolerably Well, but the Epidemic Coming on the 1st. of August Put everything to a Stand in this City for Three Months During Which time I was one among the few that were Obliged to Remain in the City During which time my Wife & self were Reduced very long by the fever & Want of Business as we Both had it Very Severely, though not Both at one time. At the close of the sickness Was obliged To Run in debt f[or] Materials To Carry on my Business and as I have had to pay off 3 months Dead Rent & 3 doctors Bills I am Reduced to almost Nothing.

What I have To ask of your Excellency, is the loan of 500 Dolls. or as much as can be Convenient to spare for one or two Years as Your Excellency may think Proper. And if Your Excellency will be so Humane as to Oblige me I will Send Your Excellency A Bill of Sale of Every thing I have or may have at the Expiration of the time if Your Excellency is Disposed So To Do To any one you wish should Receive it at the Rate of 8 pr. cent. I should wish You To send me an answer as soon as Convt. To Your Excellency.

By doing which You will forever Oblige Your unknown friend and Petitioner

Israel B. Parshall

Please Direct to No. 75 Nassau St.
New York[5]

Several self-educated healers with treatments for illnesses wrote to Jefferson. One, an immigrant schoolmaster with a cure for scurvy, wanted to sell his secret to the government. Because the symptoms of scurvy sometimes respond dramatically to vitamin C, the results described may have been truthful.

Brookhaven Suffolk County Long Island
Augt. 17th 1802

Sir/

Encouraged by that Philanthropy of disposition for which
you are so eminently distinguished among the human race, I
presume to lay before you a few particulars, which tho' they
only relate to myself in the first place, yet you may possibly
think not beneath your serious attention, as the object to which
they are finally and ultimately directed, is the relieving the
Miseries and Distresses of a considerable part of our fellow
creatures. Sir, not to be too tedious, I am an English Republican, from Yorkshire, whom the Despotic disposition of Mr.
Pitts administration in the year 1797, inspired with a resolution to seek for Liberty in America: the greatest part of the
time since my arrival here, I have acted in the Capacity of a
Schoolmaster, tho' bred a Farmer and Mechanic; and having
for many years past been inclined to the study of Physic in
my liesure hours, I have at length happily discovered a remedy for every kind of Scorbutic disorders [scurvy], let the
degree of Inveteracy be ever so great, and the time of its
countinuance have been ever so long. That you may not think
I am wilfully violating the Truth in saying thus much, I will
give you a brief detail of some cases which I have had in
hand since I came into America, with the times of their being
undertaken, in which my Endeavours have been blest with
the happiest success.

Case 1st. January 1799. Christr. Dunn of Throgs Neck,
West Chester, a Yorkshire man, Neighbour to me, a scor-
butis disorder in his face, so inveterate that his face was nearly
all in one incrusted scab, cured in 5 or 6 Weeks.

Case 2d. April, 1799. James Dunn Junr. brother to the above;
a scorbutic Ulcer on his Leg, brought from England 7 or 8
years before, incurable by the faculty there; cured in one
Month.

Case 3d. May 17th. 1800. William Baker of Patihogue,
Brookhaven Township, Suffolk County, Long Island, a Scor-

butic Ulcer on his Leg, 4 Inches long by 3-1/2 broad, deep, malignant and fetid; discharged incurable from the Faculty at New York 18 or 19 years before, and given up by many of the Faculty upon L. Island since; cured in about 12 Months.

Case 4th. December 21st. 1801, Samuel Green Son of the Revd. Zachariah Green, Minister of the Presbyterian Church in Satauket, Suffolk County, aged 11 or 12 years, the most inveterate scorbutic Case I ever saw: full of running ulcers from the crown of his head to the soles of his feet; of 4 or 5 years continuance; [appeared like] Lazarus; given up by the Drs. Comstock and Punderson; not expected by his parents to live many days, yet perfectly cured in 10 or 12 weeks, and had the Meazles in the meantime.

Case 5th. March 19th. 1802, Samuel Satterly of Satauket, an inflamatory scorbutic humor in his face, now well.

Case 6th. March 31st. 1802, Henry Newton of Middle Island, a scorbutic ulcerated Leg of 8 or 9 years standing, cured in 3 Months.

Case 7th. May 14th. 1802, Isaac Newton, Middle Island, brother to the above, a scorbutic ulcerated Leg, having 12 or 14 Ulcers of 9 or 10 years standing, now well.

These Sir are the cases I have had in hand, and which are well known to every person in the respective neighbour-hoods where they occurred. Now Sir, not having studied, and been instructed in the College at Edinburgh under the great Cullen,* nor had a Licence therefrom, I am sensible that in all this business I have acted without any legal power or Commission, and possibly thereby incurred the displeasure of the laws of America; in which case, on being notified thereof, I am willing to stay my hand; or if you Sir, and the Government at the head of which you have the honor to preside, think fit to grant me a License to continue the exercise of my abilities for the benefit of the afflicted, I am ready to accept

---

*William Cullen (1710–90), a Scottish physician, one of the most esteemed medical lecturers of his age.

it with thankfullness, as it will not only gratify my own feelings, but likewise the ardent wishes of those to whom I have had the happiness of administering relief; and as this dreadful Malady the Scurvy, is a Disease which has hitherto genrally baffled the skill of the most eminent Physicians in every Country, should it be thought likely to be of more extensive advantage to the community at Large; I am willing to make a full and perfect discovery of the remedy, upon receiving a pecuniary Compensation adequate to the [importance] of such Discovery. . . . If you think my proposals deserving your serious Consideration, I shall think myself honoured by receiving your Commands, and giving you any further Communication on the subject that you may wish for.

Please Sir to direct to me, to the care of Major Jonas Hawkins, Stony Brook, Satauket, Long Island. I am Sir, with the most profound respect,

Your most Obedient Humble Servant
WILLIAM FIRBY

The following letter is an account of the virtues of a whiskey-laced Indian root medicine, for which the writer wanted $50,000. Jefferson endorsed it "quack."

[received 12 February 1809]

SIR/

I had been inflicted with the disentary, piles and sore legs for five years. In the year 1808 local business called me to Kentucky. I was rideing on Cumberland exploreing land; my legs pained to that degree that I was obliged to alight from my horse to see if it would not ease them for awhile. While I was setting on the roadside an Indian Trader came past and ask'd me what was the matter. I told him that my legs was very sore and had been so for five years past and that no

Docter that I had ever applied to, could cure them. He then told me that he could prescribe a root to me steep[ed] in whiskey that would cure me in one week. I then proceeded to Major Caldwells in Livingston [Ky.] which was my place of abode while I was in that neigh[bor]hood. I reached there on Sunday evening. On Monday I proceeded to try the experiment proscribed to me as aforesaid. I continued to take the medicine until the Sunday following, never yet looking at my legs as they had got perfectly easy and that day shifting my Cloathing and taking the rags from around them I found to my great satisfction that they were perfectly well and are so until this present date.

In November last I left Kentucky for my own abode in Culpeper City [Va.] Near Norman ford. On my way home I got my legs very much hurt, the two as many as four different times which was accidentially done. I applied nothing to them but continued to drink the medicine as aforesaid as I kept it constantly with me. When I reach'd home they were as well as ever they were in my life.

As to the Consumption I have never yet tryed with the medicine but have one patient who has got it very bad and I am about to begin with him. I have alowed my self 30 Days; if it takes no effect in that time it will not cure it at all but in the course of ten days from this time I will write to you and the honourable Congress as I think in that time there will be an alteration.

As to any other disorder incident to the human body I have every reason to believe it will cure, as I have made some few experiments and it has not yet failed. A few days after my arival at home my business Called me to Falmouth [Va.]. On my arrival there I enquired of some of my acquaintance if they new of any one there who had the Venerial. I was told that a Mr. George Towles an acquaintance of mine had it very bad and had been under Doctr. B H Hall for about Eighteen months and that he could get no releif. I immediately sent for him to come to me. He did so. I told him that I unders[t]ood he had the venerial very bad. He told me he had it and that very bad. I then told him I could give him some medicine that would cure him provided he would follow my direction. He told me he would. I then gave him a bottle of whiskey and told him that he must drink one pint every 24 hours but his stomack was so weak that he could not bear it. I was then taken down with the plurisy myself which kept me in Falmouth about 30 days and when I left there he sent me word that he believed he was perfectly well he thot but would take another bottle to scour him out well.

But in the time of my being in Falmouth a day or two before I was taken down I was sitting in a shop with some of my acquaintances there came in a man after some thing to give to a young man who was taken with a violent Cholack. I asked him who it was; he told me it was John Bell Jr. I told him to carry up what he had come for and then come to my quarters with a bottle and I would send John Bell something that would relieve him. In a few minutes the same man came to my quarters. I then sent up a bottle of whiskey for the sd. Bell; he drank of[f] a pint as quick as he could which soon gave him releif. The next morning I saw sd. Bell and he told me that he was perfectly well and that if he had not applied the medicine as soon as he did that he does believe that he could not have survived much longer.

It is my opinion that the Honourable Congress ought to alow me Fifty thousands as a premium for disclosing the aforsaid roots which I will, provided they will give me ten thousand Dollars in hand. I will make it known to any physician whom they shall think fit but if they think it not worth there whiles to do so I will as soon as the Imbargo is lifted proceed to Europe as I think is my opinion that it will be the saving of a million of mony to that country or to the sd. United States if its only for the Armies and Navy of the sd. United States.

The practiable business on the Consumption they shall

know in ten days from this date provided nevertheless that I receive an answer, and if you think proper to send the money it may be left at Martins Ferry and then I will send you an answer informing you of the roots. If not I shall make aplication to the honourable Congress for leave to send an agent with the first ship that may be going to Europe and by that time I shall know whether or [not] that I can make a case of the Consumption.

I am with the greatest respect Yours &c.
THOS. COLLINS

James Houston, a cancer victim, kept a journal of the progress and ultimate remission of his disease and sent it to Jefferson. Unlike many who wrote to the president, Houston's motivations are humanitarian and altruistic. He does not make clear in his letter exactly what he wishes Jefferson to do for him, but he wants to journey to Washington to appear before Congress as an example of one who was cured of cancer, with the hope of getting governmental support for the treatment. He was also interested in having his journal published.

Philadelphia 4 Febr. 1804

SIR
Altho I am unaquinted with you in person and being but a farmer and you in the first charector of Statesmen yet I hope you will not be offended at my freedom in presenting the inclosed for your consideration and my instruction whether to proceed or not. I am a stranger in this Citty and when I had wrote my jornal knew not whether to let it lay by or not, having little or none aqaintance in Congress to communicate my thoughts in writeing unto, for the Member from the Dis-

trict I belong unto, which is Maj. Lewis I never have seen to my knoledge but once.* I live in Rockbridge Cty. near to the line of Augusta Cnt. [Va.] By reading the within you will know what has brought and detains me here (afflicted with Cancer). Meditating what to do I thought of the time as mentioned in my Jornal when I took Mercury and had my Cancer eate out with arsenac. . . .

When confined at that time passed away time when pain admited in reading Doctor Franklins life and your Notes on Virginia.** Diverted my pains as I thought at times and was much pleased to think that men would spend so much labour for the good of others instruction and improvement but wished to see something wrote on Cancers. Could procure none but Buckan and he leaves it in doubt whether cureable or not.*** I thought if it was in the power of Medecan [medicine] to try experiments and have sufferd much and think my relations of things perhaps would be of service to some poor afflicted persons in like complaints. I know writers only plough the Soil for envy. You have felt that, by one paragraph in your Notes which I always esteemed one of the most beatifull parts of your book.**** But we should always try to be doing good when it is in our power, for weeds will always mix less or more amongst wheat.

If you think this worthy of Notice please to write me an answer by post directed to me Phl. No. 42 Market Street, for I expect to be in this place untill last of March then to return to Rockbridge. If any thing was don I could go in Stage if required and let Congress behold my face and I could obtain I supposed Docter [Benjamin] Rushes description of My

*Rep. Thomas Lewis served in the House for one year, 1803–4.
**Benjamin Franklin, *Autobiography* (Paris, 1791; London, 1817–18); Thomas Jefferson, *Notes on the State of Virginia* (London, 1787).
***Buchan, *Domestic Medicine* (London, 1769).
****The paragraph from Jefferson's *Notes on the State of Virginia* that Houston refers to is probably Query XVIII, "Manners," the much-quoted section which deals with the human damage suffered by both master and slave from the institution of slavery. This relates to Houston's desire to "be of service to some poor afflicted persons. . . ."

Cancer when I came to this place, as he viewed me, but have not conversed with him of late. . . .

My circumstances are but midling, having been now two full years a heavy expence to my family. Having no slaves they are working hard for money to supply me And I could not well go to the Federal Citty, for it is expensive but if thought best would try, if my expences was paid but would except of no other reward, for what I could do would be contributed to this institution in hopes it would relieve some in like distress, as I have had.*

What I have wrote is wholy my own inve[n]tion and all founded on truth. The words that others spoke are mostly put down in my jornal. When any other person is included my familys letters would show that in my relation of things I built on truth and a foundation for every line there put down. I often viewed my case almost like one cast upon an Island and having no hope unless by chance some Vessel would light my way and now I am in hopes the Vessel is come. And have an anxiety that thousands of my fellow creatures scattered over this American Island may have a passage as well as myself.

My poetry some may think has too many lines on religion mixed through it but they ware the natural reflections that flowed on my mind, for I composed most poetry when under the most pain which was for six or seven mnths and often was dredfull to bear, as per Jornal. Docter Tates pills are easy taken, outward application but seldom, not much to suffer and in the corse of some months the Cancer rots and generally falls out, then runs for some time and in six 'eight ten and twelve months the constitution is clear of the complaint.

D[octor] Tate says it is constitutional disorder, works like the Veneral disease that will kill if not cured at some time or other and he has found the means to purge it away if they are not too farr gon in the compl⟨aint⟩. Mine was in my head

* "This institution" apparently refers to the Pennsylvania Hospital.

to the bone round the corner of eye, 3/4th of Inch betwixt eye and nose. Part of both upper and under eye lids ware eate away when I came to Tate. Could for some months after my cancer fell out blow aire out of the wound at corner of eye and in one place the Docter said there wase hole thorugh scull bone but whether or not I cannot assert positively but I knew the hole was deep and some persons almost fainted to look at me.

All is healed now but a small hole between nose and corner of eye. Otherwise I am healthy, active and lively as almost any of my age could expect. From a Countryman of yours confined in this citty and humbly submit this for your consideration and if no more is to be don please to return [my] papers by post. If you pay any postage write to me and I will re⟨pay⟩ it. With confidence yours &c.

JAMES HOUSTON

Jefferson replied to Houston that he was returning his manuscript, and added that the only thing Congress could do for him was to grant a patent for any discoveries that may have been involved in his cure.

Washington Feb. 10. 04.

Th: Jefferson presents his salutations to Mr. Houston and in compliance with the desire expressed in his letter of the 4th. returns him his journal. He is happy that Mr. Houston has got into the hands of the person who is certainly the most able he could have found in the unfortunate complaint under which he suffers. With respect to any application to Congress, it would be inefficient, because the Constitution allows them to give no other reward for useful discoveries but the exclusive right for 14. years, and the care of the public health is not among those given to the general government, but remains exclusively with the legislature of the respective states. He congratulates Mr. Houston on his prospect of recovery and sincerely wishes it may be completed.

A Philadelphia entrepreneur who succeeded in manufacturing carbonated mineral water asked for Jefferson's testimonial of its medicinal benefits as an aid in raising up to $15,000 in capital. The president's reply demonstrates how nimbly he could refuse an attempt to exploit his name commercially without wounding the feelings of his correspondent.

Phil. Dec. 21. 1807.

His Excellency Tho. Jefferson

Honoured Sir

Regarding you as the Patron of Arts & Sciences in our Infant Country, I am Led to Take the Liberty of offering to your Notice an Institution which If favoured with your approbation will I flatter myself produce a Publick Good. As such am Confident it will Need no other Commendation to Merit your Patronage.

The Beneficial Effects derived from the Use of Mineral Water, which have become Celebrated by affording Relief in Cases where most other Remedies have failed—has Induced the most Celebrated Chemists to Asscertain by a Correct Annalysis those Beneficial properties & by Chemically combining those parts to produce by Art what Nature had so bountifully bestowed. And so far have they Succeeded as to Merit a decided preference of the Artificial to the Natural Water by Increasing their Active properties and Excluding foreign particles not Necessary but Rather detrimental to Health.

You Respected Sir who are so well Acquainted with the principles of philosophy, are aware of the difficulties atending this process, in order to Sufficiently Impregnate the Waters with the Gaseous & which is Indeed the most Active principle in most of the Celebrated Waters. How far I have Suceeded in this difficulty have Taken the Liberty of Submitting to your Inspection by forwarding you a Specimen of the Balls Town, Pyrmont Soda Water and also Refer you to the Hon. Lemuel Sawyer (to whom we had the Honour of forwarding an assortment,) for some of the Seltzer of which am at present out of Supply, this being the most highly Impregnated Water containing from 250 to 300 pts. of the Carbonic Acid Gas, a Quantity Seldom attained or Exceeded by any Attempt in Europe.*

The Happy Effects derived from their Use have been already Evinced by an approving Publick, & Testimonies of the most Celebrated & Eminent Chemists & Medical Characters in this City—yet in order to Give it all the Advantages that Might Result It Requires the aid of a Larger Capital than in my power to afford. To Render it of that Extensive Utility to prove a Public Benefit, the aid of a Capital from 10 to 15000 dols. would Accomplish the object of Erecting a Suitable Building (in which fountains would be Placed, as the Waters are now delivered) and would be Sufficient to furnish a Supply to the United States as also to furnish them Gratuituously to the Poor to whom the Physicians might deem it Necessary.

Under your Auspicious favour Respected Sir this Might be Amply Effected & the Name of a Jefferson Receive an additional Tie to the Debt of Gratitude from his fellow Citizens already so Largely Incurred. Those fountains of Health flowing through his Patronage would Claim the Benedictions of Relieved Sufferrers and thus afford an additional Solace to a Retirement where the Prayers & Gratitude of the Worthy & Good will always follow you.

---

*Lemuel Sawyer (1777–1852), congressman from North Carolina: 1807–13, 1817–23, 1825–29.

I now Submit an outline of the Plan for your Approval. The above Sum to be divided into Shares of 50 dol. each payable in Installments, the Subscribers to be Entitled to Exclusive privileges. Receive the amount to themselves or order in Mineral Waters at a deduction of 20 pct from the Selling price. Your approval & patronage joined to the Respectable characters in this City will fully Enable me to accomplish this object & dedicate an Institution to you Whose Virtues an applauding World will Never cease to Emulate and which the Voice of Envy cannot Tarnish. Nor shall any Exertions on my Part be Wanting to Tender the Establishment Worthy of this Honour & aprove the Gratitude of

> Yr Respectfull Obt. Ser.
> ABRAHAM COHEN
> No 81 So. 2d. Street

> Mr. Cohen
> Washington Feb. 10. 08.

SIR

I have not been able sooner to acknolege the reciept of your letter of Dec. 21. which did not come to hand till Jan. 27. nor to return you my thanks for the mineral waters which came with it. I am happy to learn that these productions of nature can be successfully imitated by art, and that something may thereby be added useful to mankind. Of the degree of that utility I acknolege myself not a judge, being little acquainted with the composition of these waters, and still less with their effects on the human body. A consciousness of this would make it too presumptuous in me to suppose that any connection of my name with an establishment for their preparation would be a recommendation of them to the public. They would be sensible that it is out of my line and would view it as neither favorable to myself or the medecine. The names of the celebrated Physicians of Philadelphia are those which would give a just reputation to these waters, and present them with authority to the notice of the public. Giving every just praise therefore to the efforts which may relieve the afflicted from some of their sufferings, I feel it a duty to leave it's fortunes & it's direction in the hands of those so much better qualified to promote it's success: and I pray you to accept my best wishes for that, & my respectful salutations.

Th: Jefferson

The following letter from a Boston shipmaster reports his invention of a nautical instrument, but in attempting to clear his name of a reputation for drinking excessively, Matthew Groves reveals the dilemma faced by those with serious emotional disorders at this period of American history. So horrible were the mental institutions, where patients were manacled in filthy dungeons like animals, often for years, that narcotic or alcohol abuse was far preferable to "bedlam."[6]

Boston August 2nd. 1802

Thomas Jefferson Esqr.
President of the United States of America—
Dr. Sir
    The purpest of this letter is to inform your excellency, that the Subscriber sails from this port in a day or two for Alexandria, for the purpose of taking out a patent for a machine for the purpose of discovering the longitude at Sea.* I wish I may be so happy as to see your excellency at the New City [Washington]. I rest assured that after a little Conversation your excellency would be perswaded of the great probabillity

---

*An accurate way of determining longitude at sea was one of the most bewitching scientific puzzles of the age. The difficulty arose from two technical problems: how to take readings with an astronomical instrument on a pitching ship's deck, and how to produce a precision nautical chronometer without a pendulum. David S. Landes, *Revolution in Time* (Cambridge: Harvard University Press, 1983), 105–13, 146–57.

of my succeeding in this business; and if I am right of which I rest positively assured, the next object Nearest my heart would be, to bring it forward under the auspicious of the president of the United States. To gain this favour would be Contrary to my own wishes, unless the principle was founded upon so broad a bottom as to Support itself while god is pleas'd to uphold the Course of Nature.

I shall not trouble your excellency Concerning my sufferings while engag'd in this pursuit, one Circumstance excepted, which I feel bound in duty to clear up.

Sir, when I was carried to the town of Andover the Massachusetts bedlam, in Eighty Nine, after some days, my scattered Ideas began Again to Collect to one Center. In stooping to wash my face, I cou'd not again raise myself erect, the prodigious weight in my head was such, that I was under Necessity of Supporting my head with both my hands in order to raise myself up again. From this Circumstance, I concluded that the brains of madmen were either hard or heavy. In three or four days this oppression went off. In other after attemps similar to the former in pursuit of this favourite object, when at any time without Sleep for five or six days and nights, whenever I found this Pitiouss oppression collect upon my head, my god Sir what must be done in so terrible a crisis. The terror of bedlam became so Visibly terrible to me, without any prospect if confined there again, of ever being liberated.

My situation I conceald upon those occasions, and of two evils I chose the least, by Counteracting an evil with another. I had recourse to laudlum.* Sometimes this would help me, and when it did not I had recourse without any particular choice, to every thing upon those temporary occasions which had any tendency to stupify, and what yet made me peculiarly unfortunate in this Situation, was the irritation upon my Nerves was such that I could not stop one moment in

---

*"Laudanum. In early use, a name for various preparations in which opium was the main ingredient." *Oxford English Dictionary*

one place. I had to walk while my limbs would perform their office—when I was oblidged to give up.

My long Services in the town for twenty four years cou'd not protect me from being thought intemperate, by such as were not acquainted with my painfull Situation. I presume Sir, Should I not be so happy as to see your excellency, that Mr. Maddison will meet a man, who wears but little marks of intemperance. No mere Dr. Sir but remain with Sincerity and Esteem your Excellency's Humble Servant

MATTHEW C. GROVES

P.S. The few here Sir, to whom my situation is known believe me to be engaged in fruitless pursuit; the people in this place have so little Idea of things of this nature, that seven out of eight of them woud never know, I really believe, that there ever was such a body as the sun, if they were not scorch'd with his rays. In Washington I flatter myself I shall be treated with some delicacy. I remain as above M. C. Groves.

Jefferson met with Groves in Washington, and forwarded his method for taking longitude at sea to Robert Patterson, a vice president of the American Philosophical Society. Patterson reported what had long been known to navigators, that Groves's attempt to measure accurately the eclipses of the moons of Saturn with an astronomical instrument on a rolling ship was virtually impossible. This did not deter the inventor, however; the following year a newspaper disclosed that he had obtained a patent for his instrument and was on his way to England to claim a prize offered there for a practical method for determining longitude at sea. He was obviously unaware that the £20,000 prize offered by the British government had been paid before the American Revolution to an English clock maker, John Harrison, for an accurate nautical chronometer.[7] Despite this setback, six years later Groves was still appealing to Jefferson for help in raising funds for his instrument. The president advised him that his efforts would be "better applied to the comfort of your family," but still gave him fifty dollars.[8]

THE following long, biographical letter shows that even a highly trained physician in the Jefferson era could not be assured of success. Richard Savin studied in Philadelphia with Benjamin Rush, one of the nation's foremost medical educators, yet he found himself financially bereft. In telling his family history, there is an undercurrent of hostility toward the older brothers who dissipated the capital of the family farm he had worked so hard to save. He looks to Jefferson as a surrogate for the father, and the patron, who had been his salvation in the past.

Baltimore Jany. 28th 1806

His Excellency Thomas Jefferson Esqr.

Sir,

It has been my intention for some time past to address a letter to you, but I have been deterred from it heretofore, least you should suppose I was acting a part highly presumptuous. In the conflict between fear & necessity, I have at length determined to submit the following observations to you, fully in hopes that you will take them into consideration, & relieve me from those embarrassments which have so much impeded my progress in life. I suppose the favor which I am about to request, has never been made to you before, particularly by a person of whom you have not the most distant Idea; but I do seriously assure you that urgent necessity has compelled me to it. Before I proceed to give you an account of myself, I must humbly beg pardon for the liberty I have taken, in giving you the trouble of looking over a life so far spent in the greatest difficulties.

I was born and raised in Cecil County on the E. Shore of Maryland. My father, who from his own industry had accumulated a small property, not two hundred acres of Land, found means to educate the four eldest of his children before his death, in a manner not customary in that part of the world. As I was the youngest of those four, I had not left the walls of college before his decease—being then sixteen years of age. At the time of his death he bequeathed his property to be equally divided between his six children, and appointed my eldest brother, who was then a practitioner of medicine, as his Executor.

In order to comply with the request of my father he continued on the farm for more than a year, that the two youngest brothers might be properly educated. Finding that the place did not suit him as a Physician, he left it taking with him my Sister, when the care of the property devolved on me—being at that time little more than seventeen years of age. My brother who was next in years to the Doctor, had previously went to sea, from the Idea that the whole property was not more than sufficient for the comfort of one. During the time of the administration of my eldest Brother, the property became very much involved—he being wholly unacquainted with farming, & unaccustomed to that kind of frugality which characterized his father.

The property being much involved at the time when I undertook the care of it, from the bad management of my eldest brother, I soon found myself placed in that disagreeable situation from which time & industry were the only means that I had to extricate myself. Altho I had before been wholly unaccustomed to the working of a farm, I saw too plainly that necessity called aloud for my manual labor. I continued to follow the plough from that time until I was in my twenty first year of age, having in the course of the four preceeding years settled up the estate to the satisfaction of the creditors & my brother.

On his return to the farm I delivered it up to him as property entirely free from debts, and continued to live with [him] for six months, when he fell a victim to a fever then prevalent in that place. The next eldest brother, who had been absent for a long time, having previously returned, conceived after the death of the Doctor who made no will, that he, as the eldest, ought to administer the Estate—which of course he did. At this time being entirely destitute of any opportunity of doing anything for myself, I was patronized by a Gentleman who had formerly been a member of Congress, and who had been very intimate with my father, and taken under his care as a Student of Medicine.

At this time I was nearly two and twenty years of age. After having spent some time under his & his Nephew's care, he gave me letters of recommendaton to Dr. [Benjamin] Rush in Philadelphia under whom I completed my medical education. During my Studentship I had very little time to look into the manner in which my then eldest brother was conducting himself. However, before I had completed my education he died, & left the property more involved than it had ever been before. The administration then falling into my hands, I soon perceived that his debts amounted to more than that part of the property to which he would have been entitled. I immediately gave my bonds & notes to the full amount of all his debts; requesting the holders of them at the same time not to distress me for their respective claims.

But notwithstanding that request, during the latter part of studentship in Ph[iladelphi]a some of my creditors threatened to see me in that place, and many of them did actually draw on me at sight in favor of some of the Citizens, for the amount of their accounts. Placed at a distance remote from my friends & relations who would have assisted me in such an extremity, believe me that my situation was extremely disagreeable; and I should have been compelled to abandon the pursuit of Medicine entirely had it not been for the timely interposition of one of my relations to whom I had applied, and in whose power it was very little to serve me. Thus did

I spend the last winter, thro' the whole of which my mind was constantly on the stretch in consequence of my embarrassed situation.

In the Spring, having previously set my name down as a candidate for medical honors, I was compelled to appear before the Professors in order to undergo an examination, which I passed so far with credit and honor to myself that I received the plaudits of my examiners. I published a thesis (tho short, from my want of money to defray the expences of a more lengthy one) and obtained a Diploma on the fifth day of last June. At that time I obtained letters recommendatory from Dr. Rush, & repaired directly to this City, where I entered into practice with a celebrated character Dr. John Coulter.

I had not been with him long ere I discover'd that my income would not be sufficient to defray my yearly expences; and in consequence of that, I proposed a plan, from the adoption of which I thought we would both be benefitted; but as he declined, I left him, thinking that I could get at first as much business to do as would support me & my family. But in this I have failed. I had always dreaded the attempt, knowing how difficult it is for a professional Character to get into Business in a city, particularly for a young man, & he, poor. . . .

The amount of claims against me at this time is between 6 and 700£. It is true that the farm is still in possession of those of us who have been left from the ravages of disease, but if it was sold for 1200£ there would be but a small, very small part coming to the heirs. I have, and am yet extremely anxious to preserve the property, and if it should please you to loan me a sum of money, I shall ever consider myself under the greatest obligation to you. From your assistance at this critical period, I shall preserve the property from a sacrifice, and if it is my ill fortune not to have it in my power to refund the money without, it shall be sold, and you paid the whole of your money with interest on it.

I sincerely hope you will not suppose that I wish to impose on your goodness, by stating to you occurrences which have never transpired. If it pleases your Excellency to assist me in any measure, I will obtain letters of recommendation from the most respectable Physicians in Philadelphia, in this place, & in the place in which I was raised, & lay them before you.

As I have stated to you fully my necessitous situation, I sincerely hope, if it is not convenient for your Excellency to loan me any money from your own purse, that you will never make this application Known, as I wish it to remain a secret.

I shall be extremely happy to hear from your Excellency upon the subject as soon as it is convenient.

With my best wishes for your health & happiness, I am with the profoundest respect

Your Excellency's most obt. unknown Humble Servant

RICHARD L SAVIN

Although the association with Dr. Benjamin Rush did not help Richard Savin procure a position in medicine, Rush's reputation as an astute medical practitioner was fully accepted by Jefferson. When Meriwether Lewis was making preparations for what was to become the famed Lewis and Clark expedition, Jefferson turned to Rush for health advice to pass on to Lewis. The president wrote the following memorandum, a compendium of some of the medical prejudices and practices of the age:

June 11. 1803.

Dr. Rush to Capt. Lewis for preserving his health.

1. When you feel the least indisposition, do not attempt to overcome it by labour or marching. *Rest* in a horizontal position. Also fasting and dilatory drinks for a day or two

will generally prevent an attack of fever. To these preventatives of disease may be added a gentle sweat obtained by warm drinks, or gently opening the bowels by means of one, two, or more of the purging pills.

2. Unusual costiveness [constipation] is often a sign of approaching disease. When you feel it take one or more of the purging pills.

3. Want of appetite is likewise a sign of approaching indisposition. It should be obviated by the same remedy.

4. In difficult & laborious enterprizes & marches, *eating sparingly* will enable you to bear them with less fatigue & less danger to your health.

5. Flannel should be worn constantly next to the skin, especially in wet weather.

6. The less spirit you use the better. After being *wetted* or *much* fatigued, or *long* exposed to the night air, it should be taken in an *undiluted* state. 3 tablespoonfuls taken in this way will be more useful in preventing sickness, than half a pint mixed with water.

7. Molasses or sugar & water with a few drops of acid of vitriol will make a pleasant & wholsome drink with your meals.

8. After having had your feet much chilled, it will be useful to wash them with a little spirit.

9. Washing the feet every morning in *cold* water, will conduce very much to fortify them against the action of cold.*

10. After long marches, or much fatigue from any cause, you will be more refreshed by *lying down* in a horizontal posture for two hours than by resting a much longer time in any other position of the body.

11. Shoes made without heels, by affording *equal* action to all the muscles of the legs will enable you to march with less fatigue, than shoes made in the ordinary way.

---

*Jefferson took cold foot baths throughout his life and attributed much of his good health to them.

In his correspondence with Jefferson and in notes made during the expedition, Lewis tells of illnesses he suffered, and of being accidentally shot in the thigh in a hunting accident, but he reported no recourse to Dr. Rush's medical advice.[9]

9

Lunatics and Lovers

1. "My mind is all over the world"

EVERY president of the United States has had to cope with eccentrics, cranks, and crackpots. Because of his accessibility and the free-franking privilege, however, Jefferson received more than his share of mail from people who were emotionally unstable. He was the nation's patriarch, and it was to him they turned to relieve a troubled mind. Many of these letters defy a comprehensible reading because they are the private meanderings of a vagrant consciousness. Some show a paranoid or depressed personality; others are a mix of religious rumination, biblical quotation, and ethical advice, so knotted as to be unintelligible.

Jefferson's attitudes toward insanity are not easily discovered because there are few mentions of it in his surviving papers. He writes frequently about health and medicine, but rarely discusses mental distress or its causes. One noteworthy exception is a letter to his youthful daughter Martha, written in 1787 when Jefferson was in France. He urges her to work constantly because of all the cankers of human happiness, none corrodes with so silent, yet so baneful a tooth, as indolence. Body and mind both unemployed, our being becomes a burthen, and every object about us loathsome, even the dearest. Idleness begets ennui, ennui the hypochondria, and that a diseased body. No laborious person was ever yet hysterical.*

This exhortation suggests that Jefferson believed that mental illness resulted from a moral lapse. In a rationalistic age, where the classical virtues of temperance and moderation were the accepted ethical standards, withdrawal on the one hand, or passion on the other, were seen as extremes that could lead to madness. Both of these excesses could be controlled by the will, hence insane persons were morally culpable because they failed to practice self-control.[1] Jefferson's friend, Dr. Benjamin Rush, an avid Republican, carried this speculation into the political realm by arguing that there had been more madness after 1790, a period of rampant Federalism, because "an increase in avarice and ambition" led to mental disorder. He also thought that some religions, presumably the evangelicals, "are more or less calculated to induce a predisposition to madness," a view Jefferson may have shared, for he showed extreme impatience with religious fervor.[2]

In the absence of direct comments on insanity, Jefferson's laconic, one-word endorsements on the letters of his correspondents—"insane" or "madman"—help define his attitudes toward mental disorders, for they indicate the kinds of

*John Catanzariti et al, eds., *The Papers of Thomas Jefferson* (Princeton, N. J.: Princeton University Press, 1950–   ), 11:250. Jefferson expressed the same belief during his presidency in a note that makes clear that what he meant by "ennui" was what we would today call depression: "The disease of the mind, ennui, for which the English have no name, tho' like others they know it's afflictions, and sometimes end them by the halter [suicide], finds it's true remedy in agitation or occupation & both the disease & the remedy have been wisely allied by nature, the one to idleness as it's punishment, the other to industry as it's reward." Jefferson to Thomas Law, 2 April 1806, DLC.

thought and behavior patterns he considered aberrational.

Although many of his correspondents were undoubtedly deranged, Jefferson was quick to term "mad" those writers with no talent for clear, logical thought, or those who lacked the ability to put abstract political or legal ideas on paper. Jefferson obviously did not have the time or inclination to read these letters closely, but by today's standards he was often hasty in labeling writers who were merely struggling to express themselves "insane." He was, after all, a product of the Enlightenment, a man with an incisive, analytical mind, quick to dismiss anything he perceived to be irrational.

One of the letters Jefferson endorsed "mad" was a request from a governmental worker.

City of Washington
Jany 11th 1806

The President of the United States is most humbly requested to order the Secretary of War, to furnish C William Esenbeck, (the messenger of the Secretary of the Treasury) *to furnish him* with 6 Six Indians for my assistance to hunt up all the Wild Beasts round the City of Washington. I have loged some in the Bank, and caution'd all the Gentlemen there to keep them, but they let them escape and now they will do all the Mischief against me; and especially a Young Scunk or Piss Cat. If I can not catch her I shall be undone for ever; but as she is an innocent young thing I shall soon have her and put her in the Bank. In hopes the President of the U. S. will be pleased to grant me this Simple request I have the honour to be with the greatest esteem

Sir! Your most humble & obed. Servant
WM. ESENBECK

Jefferson received no more letters from Esenbeck in the next two years. But then Esenbeck wrote the president on February 28, 1808, identifying himself as a former German mercenary who had fought against the Americans in the Revolutionary War. (His nationality may have accounted for his being hired as a messenger by Gallatin, who was Swiss.) Esenbeck related an impressive background. He had been a hunter—this explains his concern for the wild beasts of Washington—a glassmaker, a musician, and could read four languages.* He was also an inventor who had perfected a telegraph system for communicating over distances by firing four cannons of different pitch in sequences of one to five shots. By this means, he maintained, he could communicate all the letters of the alphabet and "reach from one end of the U.S. to the other in less than twenty-four hours."** He invited the president, his Cabinet, and both houses of Congress to a demonstration to prove that "every Cannon so fired off by my direction shall speake perfect Sense on any Subject whatever."

---

*On 28 June 1805, Esenbeck ran an advertisement in the Washington *National Intelligencer* stating that he planned to open a school to teach Latin, French, and German six days a week from eight in the morning to six at night for "ten dollars a quarter." Esenbeck claimed that "in the previous part of his life" he had taught these languages for ten years. His proposed school was unsuccessful, however, for six months later he was still working as a messenger for the Treasury Department.

**Esenbeck's system is imperfectly explained in a letter written 5 January 1808, DLC. In a margin, he jotted down the pitches of the cannons and the letters of the alphabet associated with each of the five firing sequences. Esenbeck was apparently unaware that a semaphore system similar to his had been published 140 years earlier. John Wilkins, one of the founders of the Royal Society, in *Mercury, or the Secret and Swift Messenger,* published in 1668, had described a method using only two pitches in a sequence of one to five, which could communicate the letters of the alphabet, using bells, "muskets, cannons, horns, drums, etc." Alfred Still, *Communication Through the Ages* (New York: Murray Hill Books, 1946), 12–18. An operational semaphore system had been established in Massachusetts in 1801. The Boston *Telegraph* reported: "A line of Telegraphs has been completed from the *Vineyard* to Cohasset. On Wednesday morning information of the arrival of the *Mercury* at the *Vineyard* from *Sumatra,* was very expeditiously and correctly communicated, passing through eleven different telegraphs. The line will soon be extended to Boston." Reprinted in the Washington *National Intelligencer,* 2 November 1801.

Nearly a year later, Jefferson received another letter from Esenbeck about animals, this time the president's own sheep. Jefferson bred, purchased, and traded sheep during his presidency, and near the end of his second term kept a herd of forty ewes and rams at the President's House.[3] He was preparing to have them driven home to Monticello when he received a letter from Esenbeck, now in the guise of a hunter rather than a cannoneer.

City of Washington
Dec. 2d. 1808.

The President of the United States, will be pleased to pardon one of his faithfull Subjects: If his Pointer Dogs should leap over the highest part of the Wall in search of their proper Game, If they should tresspass in killing any Sheep, or tame fowl I will answer for all damages by Peril of being put to Jail, but if the contrary, the sheep will follow them, the President will grant me this favor. I have the honour to be with the gretest devotion your faithfull Subject 'till Death.

WILLIAM ESENBECK*

A few weeks later, Esenbeck was again trying to interest Jefferson in his telegraph "language." By attempting to be clever and circumspect, however, he only convinced the

---

*Jefferson heard no more from Esenbeck about his sheep, but a month later he received a complaint about one of his rams from a Revolutionary war veteran, William Keough, who informed him "that in February 1808 in Passing through the President's Square he was attacked and severely wounded and bruised by your excellency's ram—of which he lay ill for five or six weeks under the hands of Doctor Elzey." Keough related this incident a year after it happened. The reason he was writing now, he explained, was that he was destitute, having failed to receive a pension as a war veteran, and was living in the Washington poor house. At the time of the incident, Jefferson had given Keough five dollars "charity," but there is no record that Jefferson responded to his letter. (From William Keough, 15 February 1809, DLC; William A. Bear and Lucia Stanton, eds., *Jefferson's Memorandum Books, Accounts, with Legal Records and Miscellany 1767–1826*, 2 vols. [Princeton, N. J.: Princeton University Press, forthcoming], 3 March 1808.)

president that he was indeed crazy; like his other letters, this too was endorsed "insane."

City of Washington
Jan. the 13th. 1809

To the President of the United States,

THOMAS JEFFERSON ESQR.

The Petition of William O———most humbly sheweth: that your Orator asks nothing what is unreasonable, only what is justly in his claim due to him, from the U.S. for his extra services as messenger to Albert Gallatin Esquire Secretary of the Treasury whom he thinks the most skillful Financier in the World; but his ofspring and Son Albert Gallatin junior Esqr. can beat him, for the Gentleman his Father after all what was acquired & paid, only left 14,000,000 in the Treasury; but his Son a Youth 10, or eleven Years of Age, after only 1/2 an hours instruction will prove by way of Telegraph (with me the Inventor of a Language which is not known in the World) that three times that Sum might flow in the Treasury and all matters in an hon'ble way be setled in favor of the United States By a German Sportsman William Esenbeck in the way of Sport in different ways, that there would be no cause to complain by the Belligerent Powers; if your Orator who is now a mere Cypher in politics, but he would be athorized by the Government to prove what he knows and is certain of it, may make a Figure at this present time; if this favor is granted your Orator will ever pray.

Jefferson also endorsed "insane" the following letter, which was delivered to his doorstep at Monticello by the troublesome author himself.

[24 May 1808]

HONOURED SIR

With the Divine blessings of heaven I now Attempt to write a few Lines to Inform You that we Shall Soon See happier times.

Your friendship and love is all I ask. No man of Reason Can Dispute Your honour. Please Sir to Receive these Lines from a friend that you never Expected to See, pleas your honour. Dear Sir to you I am a Stranger. I must obey the Commands of Almighty God Who Reins King on heavens high Throne and hominum Salvator Who burst the bars of Death and Rose triumphant from Grave.

May heavens blessings you each hour attend and may you never Loose or Want a friend.

I am with esteem your Sincere friend.

WILLIAM MEECH.

How much of a nuisance Meech made of himself at Monticello is captured in the urgency of a letter Jefferson wrote to the son of the miller, Jonathan Shoemaker, who leased Jefferson's Shadwell mill. The president was anxious to send young Meech back to his family in Philadelphia and was more than willing to pay his fare to get rid of him.

Mr. [Isaac] Shoemaker
Monticello June 5. 08.

SIR

Your father mentioned that as you were shortly to go on to Philadelphia, you would take on with you the young man, Meech, who is with you, to his father if you were certain of recieving from him his expences. I told him that if the father did not repay them, I would. In order to place the proposition on definite ground I will say precisely that I will in that case repay the expences of his journey, not exceeding twenty dollars, if the father does not. I tender you my salutations.

TH: JEFFERSON

Jefferson received several letters from men and women who were clearly paranoid. John Young, a Baltimore sail maker, relates a long history of emotional problems in a much-blotted letter.[4]

Baltimore August 30th 1808

Mr. Thomas Jefferson
President of the United States of America
    Sir, the uncommon and astonishing Circumstance emboldens me to inform you of myself and Peculiar Situation in wich I am placed. My Name is John Young. I was born in Philadelphia in the 5th day of August 1745—was brought up and Served my apprenticeship to learn the art Trade or mistery of a Sail Maker in Philadelphia. . . .
    Some time in September 1788 I went up to Philadelphia and married Miss Margaret Allison, Eldest daughter of Colo. Robert Allison and had by her two Sons and Seven daughters. Five of the daughters are now living, the rest are dead, my wife allso with her last daughter. I carried on my business to some extent in Baltimore. In the latter part of the time I have been visited with sever diseases and frequent spells of Hypercondrik nature as most of the Phisichans in Balt. can testify, insomuch so that I have not been able to follow or carry on said Business there three years past and am reduced to the disagreeable necessity of liveing on my friends who are wore out of patience, and attempts have been made to take my body and keep it in Confinement not agreeable to law. And as I now do solemnly declare that I believe my Life

as well as my liberty is in Contemplation I therefore as a Citizen of the United States and a firm wellwisher to the present administration Humbly implore their aid and Support for the following reasons:

First that I dearly believe my life in danger.

Second Not.

Third I am in want of your assistance.

Your attention to the foregoing will Confer a lasting Obligation on Sir

Your Most Obedient Humble Servant

JOHN YOUNG

The following note shows the effect of the new science of electricity on a mind disturbed by paranoia.

Philadelphia, July 12th 1806.

SIR/

With respect I take this method of communicating to You, the disagreeable information, that an enemy at present appears to prevail mystically in an endeavorment of killing me mystically by electricity or magnetism and it has prevail'd on the Soldiers on the 4th of July; there has also been contempt spoken against you of persons in my presence. I expect the[re] is a general endeavor against your Government.

I am your most obedient Servant,
GEORGE ODENHEIMER.*

It is not surprising that an emotionally unstable man could equate the president with God, a father who could command

---

*Odenheimer wrote another letter, 2 December 1808, DLC, warning that a British fleet was about to launch an attack on Philadelphia.

him to action and salvation. The writer of the following letter
was seemingly bent on a course of self-destruction.

MarysVille [Tenn.]
August 18th 1803

SIR

I am inspired by God Almighty; I am now at Mr. William
Burks in MarysVille; I am taking a large quantity of Arsneck
daily. It is in your power to releve me from my Situation.
The United States will be all ruined, if they do not desist
from such wicked practices. It is in your power to Order me
to the General Government; when that takes place I am ready
to obey your Commands. Should you Hang me that will close
the scene of my unfortunate life. I shall apply to Esquire
McGee for a Horse, Saddle and Bridle and he will not refuse
me if you give him the directions.

I am Sir your Humble Servt.
SAM HENLEY

The following letter is from an eighteen-year-old apprentice who admits that he has been sick, and that it has "decayed"
his mind. He is obsessed with the militia and his role in it,
but it is impossible to tell how much of his story is true.

Casenovia [N.Y.]
Feb 13th AD 1806

Thommas Jefferson President of U.S.A.

SIR MR. JEFFERSON PRES.

I now set down to let you know of my mind. My mind is
all over the world. I am thinking of the Laws of the states;
my mind is holy aggertated. I am but a poor apprentis boy
about 18th yers old, bound to Parson Williams, Cabbenet-
maker. Fro[m] the traid, I belong to the tro[o]p of horse.

In the yer of our lord 1805 I was chose 1st Lieu. of the company but I did not take my post that yer for I was yong but I like such busness very well.

Sir I wish you would wright to mea wher it is best for me to walk badly [boldly] befour man and take my office as it is given to mea. In my younger days this last fall I went into the field befor Gov. Morgan Lewis with my company of about 100 Soldiers to doe my duty befoure him.

It coms into my mind about [the] cruel and unsufferble retch of this world *Arnold,* the man that has whipped the child to deth. I have understood [from] last weaks [Hudson, N.Y.] *Balance* . . . that tha war for to save him from the gallo[w]s. If that is the case whi maint [why mayn't] I take my Sword and murder and kill as fast as I am a mind for to doe? But I hope you will turn thir minds if it is so. But I hope it is not so.

I am but a poor writer to what I ust to be befour. I have been sik and it has decade my mind in som mesur but I get beter very fast. I begin to think more of the world than ever. . . .

I wish you to write to me the particulers of your uniform. In your County in all comppanys, if you pleas. My company is about to sel thir uniform and get new next fall. I mean to march my company to sea the pesident of the United States of Ammeraca. And I wish you to send to mea this spring if posable so I can rig my self to yours humb[l]e servent.

I should be very glad if you could asist me with som powder. The company thinks if tha com to sea the[e] tha think if tha have thar powder found them tha can comb with grate splender.* I sppose I could find powder but it would be a hard for mea but I should be glad if your humble servent would asist mea for I am but a boy. You will find I am in my glory when I am marchin throw the wilderness woods. I am

---

*The writer refers here to hair powder.

determin to fite for liberty. I alwers have fout for liberty. I sa[y] rejoice Columbia sons rejoice to tirents never bend thir nea but join in hart and sole and voice for Jefferson and leberty.*

You must overlock theas fue scrabblous lines, for my pen is por my inck is pail

My love from you shal never fail.

So must I retire till anoter opportunity.

NEHEMIAH W. BADGER
of State New York town of Casenovia

2. *"The blessings and regrets of millions"*

Although young Nehemiah Badger's mind may have been "aggertated," his esteem for the president was communicated unambiguously in his letter. This admiration was shared by numerous writers, with and without wits, who were simply happy that Jefferson was president and wished to tell him so. One of the most charming letters of this kind was a single sentence from a man who was later to become governor of Tennessee.**

---

*These lines are from "Jefferson and Liberty," a Republican campaign song.
**When Willie Blount (1768–1835) wrote Jefferson, he had served one year as a judge of the Tennessee Superior Court of Law and Equity but was not then in public office. During Jefferson's presidency he was elected to the state legislature, and later became a three-time governor of Tennessee, from 1809 to 1815.

Knoxville November 14th 1801

Thomas Jefferson Esquire
President of the United States
Sir,

Being disengaged this evening from such pursuits as generally engage my attention, and it occuring to me that I might not be considered an intruder, since I am one of those who admire your doings and quite willing and desirous that you should continue to preside as President of the United States so long as you may feel disposed to act in that way, and feeling desirous you should know merely for my own gratification that there does exist within the limits of the United States a man of my name, have written you this letter, to which I in language of the purest sincerity subscribe it, as

Your unfeigned and
unalterable friend
WILLIE BLOUNT

When Jefferson was first elected to the presidency, letters from well-wishers arrived on his desk daily. Most of this mail was from political friends or acquaintances, but there were also letters from earnest strangers such as this one from a Pennsylvania Quaker:

State of Pensilvania Dalewar County
Birmingham township
Near Chads Ford on Brandewine hedquarters
March the 8th 1801

For Thomas Jefferson President

Most noble Jefferson at the hearing of thy Being Appoynted President was Caus of great goy to Mee wich I inwardly felt. I Love a tru & faithfull American who is tru to his Country, Not Valuing his private intrust Eaquel to that of his Cuntry['s] prosperytyes & growth. I thought it Must be Caus of greate Comfort & great goy to Say I hath bee[n] faithfull & Just in that trust Reposd in Mee. At the Close I may inform thee at thy being Appoynted President is Caus of greate goy in oure part of the Cuntry for thier is greate Confidence Reposed in thee wich I hath no Doubt will be Answarred According to Exspektatishon. From they Assured Friend Unknown but Yet Real

BENJAM. RING

NB I Wish to be Remembered to our tru Friend Curnell Bur[r], A tru Ameraken in whome thier is No gile. From

B. R.

I wish to be Excused for my freedom.

Another Quaker, a descendant of William Penn, wished to honor Jefferson by naming a town in Virginia after him.

Philada. 3 mo. 8th. 1802

To Thomas Jefferson
President of the U.S.

ESTEEMED FRIEND.

Not having any personal acquaintance with thee, it is with extreme Reluctance I thus address the Man whose eminent abilities has Raised him to be head of the Amarican Republic.

But having lately purchased a tract of Land in Randolph County Virginia on which as I am inform'd is an elegant Scite for a town, which I propose laying out the ensuing Summer—I so far Request thy patronage as to be permitted to call it "Jefferson," conscious at the same time that posterity will duly appreciate the merits of a Washington and a Jefferson without the feeble aid of Cities and towns to commemorate their illustrious names.

Being one of the descendants of Penn I am unused to the

Courtly style of sycophants, and which (if I am not deceiv'd in thy Character) is more dissonant in thy ear than unadorned truth—Accept this as an apology.

With every sentiment of Respect

I am thy well wisher
JAS. WALTER

If thee should condescend to favour me with an answer, please direct to No. 41 Almond St.

The president replied that there was already a town named Jefferson in that state, but he had little faith in its survival. He was right; it vanished, and was never replaced. It is something of an irony that, although there are populous counties and towns named after Jefferson in most of the states of the nation, in his own native Virginia there is now only a Jefferson Village and Jeffersonton, both small communities.

Mr. James Walter.
Washington Mar. 19. 1802.

SIR

Your favor of the 8th. inst. was recieved on the 12th. I am duly sensible of the mark of respect to me which you are pleased to testify by the name you propose to give to the town you are about to establish. It is the more grateful to me as it comes from a person, uninfluenced by personal acquaintance, and who has been able to judge me by my actions, unblinded by the mists of unprincipled slander under which public prints endeavor to cover me from the view of my constituants. With respect to the name proposed I have only to observe that it has already been given by an act of the Virginia legislature to a small town laid out on [the] James river, the situation of which however does not seem to promise success to it's establishment.

Accept my best wishes and assurances of respect & consideration.

[TH: JEFFERSON]

Many of the letters of praise received by Jefferson soon after his election were in the form of the memorial address, often with numerous signatures. Typical of these adulatory addresses was one from Pendleton, South Carolina, mailed by Capt. E. Browne of the 16th Regiment of the South Carolina militia. Browne could not have chosen a topic more sympathetic to the president—the difficulty of sifting truth from the distorted dispatches of the Federalist press, and the question of what action to take against opposition newspaper editors.

South Carolina Pendleton District
4th May 1801

To Thomas Jefferson President of the United States
SIR,
... That you may long continue in protecting, and preserving our Liberties and Constitution well understood, is the prayer of many.
The only acquaintance we have with you is through the medium of the public papers, Wherein truth, Merit and Justice have suffered so much, and have been so distorted, disguised and perverted that it often remained difficult and sometimes impossible for us to judge with precision between the great questions of right and wrong. Had we not steadily in view too such men as appeared to stick nearest to our rights and natural Independence we should have been lost with out hope. Among the many things that will fall under your province, we consider this as one of the greatest importance—to dispel the clouds that so frequently obscure [the] road to freedom—That we may no longer have to view the

sum of our Liberties through a mirror muffled and shrouded.

That we shall ever have a personal interview with you, is what few, or any of us dare expect, situate as we are remote from the seat of Government over which you have the honor to preside, but nevertheless you are the object of our choise, into whose hands we chearfully submit all the powers by the constitution.

Signed on behalf of Reg 16,

E. Browne

Jefferson attempted to coin addresses such as Browne's into political capital by including in his response the party line on issues raised by the writer. He explained this policy to his attorney general, Levi Lincoln: "I have generally endeavored to turn them to some account, by making them the occasion, by way of an answer, of sowing useful truths and principles among the people, which might germinate and become rooted among their political tenets."[5] Jefferson's response to James Walter, the Quaker who wished to name a town after him, shows, however, that he needed no prompting to attack the Federalist press. In this letter he gratuitously mentions the "unprincipled slander" of the opposition newspapers.

In his reply to Browne, Jefferson suggests he is a martyr to press freedom in standing up to the scurrilous attacks of the Federalist press. He will neither respond to them nor attempt to repress them. This view, however, was to shift a few years later when he urged state libel prosecutions against Federalist editors.[6]

E. Browne Capn.
[7 June 1801]

The very affectionate address which you have been pleased to present me, on behalf of the 16th regiment of South Carolina, demands & receives my warmest thanks. The interest you feel in my appointment to the Presidency, your confidence in my serious dispositions to oppose the exercise of all arbitrary power, & to preserve inviolable our liberties and constitution, and your promises of support in these pursuits are new incentives to the performance of my duty.

I am sensible, with you, of the distortions and perversions of truth and justice practiced in the public papers, and how difficult to decypher character through that medium. But these abuses of the press are perhaps inseparable from it's freedom; and it's freedom must be protected or liberty civil & religious be relinquished. It is a part of our duty therefore to submit to the lacerations of it's slanders, as less injurious to our country than the trammals which would suppress them.

I pray you to assure the officers & soldiers of the 16th regiment of my sincere wishes for their prosperity & happiness, & of my high consideration and respect.

TH: JEFFERSON

Several Americans showed their affection for the president by sending him gifts. Jefferson had just arrived in Washington to assume the presidency when he received the following letter.

March 2, 1801

SIR,

As tribute of respect to your merits as a Friend of the People, & a promoter of the useful arts, I beg your acceptance of a Patent Saddle the construction of which I hope you will be pleased with. It is sent by the stage this day directed to the care of Mr. Barnes.*

From Sir

> Respectfully yours,
> STEPHEN BURROWES
> Philadelphia 2d March 1801

The letter was accompanied by the following advertisement:

PATENT ELASTIC SADDLES
BY STEPHEN BURROWES,

At his Manufactory, No. 52, North Second Street, adjoining the George Tavern.

HAVING obtained an exclusive patent for the application of Silk, Hair, and spiral Wire Springs to Saddles, and constructed a number of them, several of which have been sold, and, on trial, have been highly approved of, I am ready to supply them for Ladies and Gentlemen, on the most reasonable terms. I warrant the saddles not to lose their elasticity; to be equally durable with those of any other construction, without being more liable to injure the horse, and to be of the best workmanship and materials. This valuable improvement affords great ease in riding, and will enable the weakly and infirm to enjoy the benefits of that healthful exercise.

I have also on hand as usual, and for sale, by wholesale and retail, a general assortment of *Saddles, Bridles, Portmanteaus, Trunks, Whips, &c. &c.*

Horses measured for saddles to fit in the neatest manner.

STEPHEN BURROWES.

---

*John Barnes was the Washington agent who handled Jefferson's business arrangements during his presidency.

The patented spring-supported saddle apparently suited the presidential seat very well, for Jefferson responded with an offer to purchase it. He refused to accept it as a gift, an ethical position he took with all items of any value offered him. He stated the specific kinds of gifts he was willing to accept and those he insisted on refusing when he returned an "elegant ivory staff" that was offered him. He would accept "no present of any sensible pecuniary value," he wrote. "A pamphlet, a new book, or an article of mere curiosity, have produced no hesitations, because below suspicion. But things of sensible value, however innocently offered in the first examples, may grow at length into abuse, for which I wish not to furnish a precedent."[7]

> Mr. Stephen Burrowes
> 52. N 2d street
> [Philadelphia]
> Washington March 12. 1801.

Sir, I received . . . your favor of Mar. 3 and the saddle also is come safely to hand. I am well pleased with it, and take it willingly, but on the single condition that you permit me to pay for it. I have ever laid it down as an unalterable law to myself to accept of no payment while I am in a public office. I assume that your own reflections on the tendency of the contrary practice will justify in your eye my adherence to this principle. I am sensible to your friendly intentions as if my situation had permitted me to accept of them and I shall consider your conforming to my wish as evidence the more of your favor to me. I take the liberty therefore of requesting you to call on Mr. Richard, whose address will be noted below, and who will pay you the price of the saddle.* Accept, I pray you, my salutations & friendly wishes.

[TH: JEFFERSON]

---

*This may be John Richard, a Philadelphia agent, who purchased some of Jefferson's tobacco the following year. See Betts, *Thomas Jefferson's Farm Book,* 283. Burrowes sent

The kind of gift that Jefferson accepted with pleasure was that offered by General James Wilkinson, who was later to be implicated in the Aaron Burr conspiracy. Wilkinson sent the president samples from the Mississippi and Arkansas rivers, waters that supposedly had curative powers. Sen. William Plumer of New Hampshire reported that Jefferson proudly served Mississippi water at a dinner party at the President's House, although it is doubtful whether it was the same water Wilkinson had sent almost three years earlier.[8] Along with the bottled water, Wilkinson sent several "petrifactions," fossils which Jefferson would have been pleased to add to his natural-history collection in the entry hall at Monticello.

Mississippi Territory
January 18th. 1802

Thomas Jefferson President of the U.S.

Sɪʀ

Presuming that a sample of the Waters of the Mississippi & Arkansaw Rivers, remarkable for their difference to each other & to the Waters of all other Rivers within my Knowledge, may not be unacceptable to you, I avail myself of a conveyance by Doctor Carmichael of the Army, who will have the Honor to deliver this, to send you a Bottle of each, taken from those Rivers in their lowest & least disturbed State—that from the Arkansaw being not full—& may not be uninteresting to remark, that the "voyageurs" of the Mississippi, who drink constantly of, & prefer, its Water, are never afflicted by the Graval, and that they ascribe curative properties to its external application in cutaneous affections.*

---

his bill for thirty-five dollars to Richard, "who immediately paid the money." From Stephen Burrowes, 21 March 1801, DLC.

* "Gravel. A term applied to aggregations of urinary crystals which can be recognized as masses by the naked eye (as distinguished from *sand*) also the disease of which these are characteristic." *Oxford English Dictionary*

In the same Box I have deposited a few distinct petrefactions, collected in the State of Tenessee during the late Season.

With the most respectful attachment I have the Honor to be, Sir

Your obliged, Obedient, & ready Servant

JA: WILKINSON

As Jefferson approached the end of his second term in office, Joshua Meigs, a Georgia educator, voiced the hope of many citizens that the president would run again.* Jefferson was adamant, however, in his decision to retire after eight years. He expressed the intensity of his determination to James Monroe: "My longings for retirement are so strong, that I with difficulty encounter the daily drudgeries of my duty."[9]

Athens, Georgia, Jan. 24. 1807

SIR,

I have no right to occupy a moment of your time, but I cannot resist the desire which I feel to express to you for myself & my Children our gratitude for your virtuous conduct of the great family of the United States.

It is a pleasing circumstance to me that I live in the midst of a people who are sincerely attached to the principles of the Constitution of the United States, and to your administration.

In this part of the Country every thing is prosperous. The people are rapidly advancing in wealth and in the sentiment of Independence.

---

*Joshua Meigs (1757–1822), had a varied career as a newspaper editor, college professor, and public official. When he wrote to Jefferson in 1807 he was president of the University of Georgia. In 1812, he was appointed surveyor-general of the United States, and two years later became commissioner of the General Land Office. After his presidential retirement, Jefferson carried on a correspondence with Meigs for a number of years.

We have had general health; and I believe that this part of the United States is as healthy as any part of the world.

I cordially join with the wishes of my fellow Citizens of Georgia that you will not decline from occupying the Post of our Chief Magistrate for another constitutional Period.

I am with high Esteem, and very respectfully Yours.

J. Meigs

Even Jefferson's most ardent admirerers, however, approved of the precedent, first set by Washington and now confirmed by Jefferson, of voluntarily limiting the presidency to two terms. On the day Jefferson left office, 3 March 1809, Samuel Harrison Smith, editor of the Washington *National Intelligencer,* expressed the mixed feelings of appreciation and loss experienced by many Americans at the president's decision to step down from office. "Never will it be forgotten as long as liberty is dear to man," Smith wrote, "that it was on this day that Thomas Jefferson retired from the supreme magistracy amidst the blessings and regrets of millions."[10]

John MacGowty, a Connecticut seaman, stated the same sentiment in a letter received by Jefferson after he had moved home to Monticello.

Windham Con. March 26th 1809

Thomas Jefferson Esqr.

Sir

I take the liberty of Writing to you as a seafaring man who has been to Sea for 22 years. . . .

Sir, I have been about the world considerably and have red some but I do not recollect to have ever read or seen the instance of a man having Honour and riches enough as it seems Sir, you have convinced the world that you have, which appears so by your Choice of becoming a private Citizen once more. I have seen and heard a good deal of this bad party talk against your measures and in particular against your Person, but at the same time I have not heard or seen any measures which you have taken to gard yourself, but by returning good for Evil, and at the same time Sir, you have said to them as the greatest king that ever was on Earth said, Father forgive them for they know not what they do.

As to your being President Sir, I coud have wished that you would have kept that office for four years longer, but as you have prefered a private life my sincere Prayers are that you may live to enjoy that Private Life with as much hapness, as your public life has been usefull to your Country. Sir, I beg that you will excuse my freedom I have herein taken, but Sir, as am American and Born in the Republican state of Virginia, but have lived in this state 20 years has made me here take the Liberty I have. Sir with the greatest pleasure—I am your most obedant and most Humble Servant

John MacGowty

The steady march of unsolicited mail across Jefferson's desk did not halt when he left the presidency, but it did diminish. The same kinds of letters continued to arrive, but more were praise and fewer threats—although he did receive a warning about a conspiracy to kill him and blow up Monticello six months after leaving office.[11]

Jefferson's correspondence continued to be burdensome to him after his retirement from office. He did not feel the urgency to respond to correspondents immediately, but the volume of his mail still kept him at his writing desk longer than he wished. In 1817, he complained to John Adams that he was beset by strangers "who oppress me with their concerns, their pursuits, their projects, inventions and speculations, political, moral, religious, mechanical, mathematical, historical, etc. etc. etc."

From sun-rise to one or two aclock, and often from dinner to dark, I am drudging at the writing table. And all this to answer letters into which neither interest nor inclination on my part enters; and often for persons whose names I have never before heard. Yet, writing civilly, it is hard to refuse them civil answers. This is the burthen of my life, a very grievous one indeed, and one which I must get rid of.

He did not get rid of it, however; in 1822, four years before his death, he wrote Adams that he had counted the number of letters he received in 1820 and they totaled 1267,

> many of them requiring answers of elaborate research, and all to be answered with due attention and consideration. Take an average of this number for a week or a day, and I will repeat the question suggested by other considerations. . . . Is this life? At best it is but the life of a mill-horse who sees no end to his circle but in death. To such a life that of a cabbage is paradise.[12]

He was no cabbage, but he *was* a mill horse, attached to the rites of his desk as rigidly as the rest of us are bound to the rituals of dining. Weeks before his death on the Fourth of July, 1826, his wrist stiff from an old injury and his fingers crippled by arthritis, he was still answering letters from correspondents who wrote civilly and expected a civil response.* His need to write letters may indeed have been compulsive, but, just as it is ungracious for a benefactor to question the motives of the altruist, neither should we, who share the largess of Thomas Jefferson's vast correspondence, question the generosity of this civil man.

---

*His final letters were written June 25, 1826, nine days before his death. They are recorded in a firm hand in his Summary Journal of Letters.

Sources

DLC: The Library of Congress, Washington, D.C.
DNA: National Archives, Washington, D.C.
MHi: Massachusetts Historical Society, Boston
MoSHi: Missouri Historical Society, St. Louis

Chapter 1

From Anon. 1 December 1805, 5 December 1805, DLC. From Henry Weaver, Sr., 11 February 1807, DLC. From Albert Gallatin, 21 February 1807, DLC. From Charles Geirs, 24 February 1807, DLC. From Alexander Ogle, 28 April 1805, DLC. From Anon. ("Mortuus"), 26 January 1808, DLC. From Anon. ("A Merchant"), 30 June 1808, 14 July 1808, DLC. From Anon. ("A Lover of his Country"), July, 1808, DLC. From Jonathan Hall, 12 August 1808, DLC. From Anon. ("A sitizen suffering"), 29 August 1808, DLC. From Charles Connell, 29 September 1808, DLC. From Anon. ("Friend of the Constitution"), 6 December 1804, DLC. From Anon., 19 September 1808, DLC. From George Hunter, 4 October 1808; to George Hunter, 14 October 1808, DLC. From Elijah Hayward, 12 October 1808, DLC. From Thomas Freeman, 14 November 1808, DLC. From Anon., 3 January 1809, DLC. From Mary Underwood, 21 January 1809, DLC. From Anon.

("Filo Liburtus"), 17 January 1809, DLC. From Anon. ("Prophesy"), 18 January 1809, DLC. From Edward Page, 19 January 1809, DLC. From T. Selby, 4 June 1808, MoSHi. From John L. Jones, 8 August 1808, MoSHi.

Chapter 2

From David Austin: 11 January 1802, 29 January 1802, 4 May 1802, 24 January 1804, DLC; 9 March 1801, 15 March 1801, 21 March 1801, 30 March 1801, 15 May 1801, 26 May 1801, 31 May 1801, 9 June 1801, 16 June 1801, 17 July 1801, 14 September 1801, 28 November 1801, 20 March 1802, 26 April 1802, 5 October 1804, DNA. To David Austin: 18 July 1801, DNA; 21 January 1802, DLC. From Larkin Smith 10 November 1804, MoSHi. To Larkin Smith: 26 November 1804, DLC. From Sarah Mease: 20 March 1801, DLC. To Sarah Mease: 26 March 1801, DLC. From W. W. Howard: 20 March 1807, MHi. From John O'Neill, 30 October 1805, DLC. From James Law, 9 November 1803, DNA. From B. W. Stuart, 12 April 1801, DLC. From T. J. Gassaway, 4 March 1805, DLC; to T. J. Gassaway, 12 March 1805, DLC. From Asa Gage, 14 February 1806, DLC. From Charles Steele, 1 October 1806, DNA.

Chapter 3

From Lewis Mayer, 21 February 1802, DLC. From Samuel Holmes, 17 May 1803, MHi. From Eben French, 29 October 1804, MHi. From Levi Hurt, 18 May 1801, DLC. From Thomas Skidmore, 6 June 1808, MHi. From Samuel Demaree, 6 January 1802; to Samuel Demaree, 6 May 1805, 4 October 1809, 12 January 1813, DLC. From John Norvell, 9 May 1807, MoSHi; to John Norvell, 11 June 1807, DLC. From Lacosta Harris, 14 July 1806, MHi. From Lover of Country, 9 May 1802, DLC. From W. F. Harle, 5 April 1803, MHi. From Anon. (A. U.), 21 March 1809, MHi. From True American Youth, 31 July 1806, DLC.

Chapter 4

From Jane Savary, 21 February 1807, MHi. From Anna McKnight, 29 October 1802, DLC. From Susana P. Roboson, 29 December 1803; from Mary Osborne, 12 October 1808, MHi. From Betsy Beauchamp, 11 March 1806, MHi. From Maria Digges, 25 October 1801, DLC. From Susannah Febvrier, 8 January 1805; 16 April 1806, MHi. From Mary Minor, 8 March 1808, MHi. From Mary Bond, 9 March 1805, MHi. From Mary Heater, 6 July 1803, MHi. From Affinity McGeath, 4 December 1802, DLC. From Elizabeth Chester, 15 March 1801, DLC. From Agnes Jackson, 22 January 1802, DLC. From Anna Young, 24 January 1802; to Anna Young, 4 February 1802, DLC. From Pricilla Kemble, 18 February 1808, DLC. From the widow Noland, 15 November 1804, MoHSi. From Sally Palmer, 30 January 1804, MHi (misfiled at 30 January 1809). From Eliza Penny, 8 April 1808, MHi. From Mary Underwood, 21 January 1809, DLC. From Lydia Broadnax, 9 April 1807. MHi. From Emilia Jervis, 4 November 1804, MHi. From Harriet Wickham, January 1806, DLC. From Louisa Keets, 16 July 1806, MHi. From Maria Rivardi, 6 January 1807, DLC. From Susannah Santoran, 14 March 1802, MHi. From Eliza Winn, 20 February 1803: to Eliza Winn, 21 March 1803, DLC.

Chapter 5

To Drs. Rogers & Slaughter, 2 March 1806, DLC. From Paul Brown, 24 January 1806; 22 June 1807, MHi. From William Dunn, 27 May 1807, DLC; 25 August 1809, MHi. From Cephas Carpenter, 24 June 1803, DLC. From Samuel Quarrier, 2 February 1802, 10 February 1802, 13 February 1802, 3 April 1802, 8 April 1802, DLC. From John T. Mason, 29 March 1802, DLC. From William Cranch, 19 December 1801, DLC. From Jesse Carpenter, 27 March 1808, MHi. From Richard Fenwick, 30 March 1802, DLC. From Philip Mayer, 19 March 1802, DLC. To George Blake, 12 March 1805, MHi. From Joseph Parsons, 10 October 1802, 12 October 1802, 18 October 1802, DLC. From Jonathan Faw, 22 October 1803; to Jonathan Faw, 25 October 1803, DLC. From George Todd, 8 November 1805, MHi. From Thomas Ferrall, 12 March 1807, DLC. From Edon Marchant, 23 March 1808, DLC. From James Carroll, 10 July 1802, DLC. From Richard Hoskins, 15 August 1808, DLC. From Nathaniel Ingraham, 10 April 1802, 21 June 1802, 28 April 1803, DLC. From Mary Ingraham, 30 October 1802, DLC. To Christopher Ellery, 4 May 1803, DLC. From Henry Brinkerhoff, 18 April 1801, MHi.

Chapter 6

From John W. Butler, 13 April 1801, DLC. From Christian Becker, 18 April 1807, MHi. From John Chamberlin, 12 August 1805, DLC. From Francis Green, 5 November 1805; to Francis Green, 15 December 1805, DLC. From John Davis, 28 November 1808; to John Davis, 3 December 1808, DLC. From M. W. Weems, 1 February 1809, DLC. From John D. Burk, 19 June 1801; to John Daly Burk, 21 June 1801, DLC. From Samuel Harrison, 12 February 1806, DLC. From Jonathan Edmester, 18 February 1808, DLC. From Samuel Beach, 5 May 1808, DLC.

Chapter 7

From Skeldin and Trimmel, 10 May 1805, MHi. From Heman Culver, 21 March 1808, DLC. From Chauncy Hall, 23 May 1806, MHi. From George Buchanan, 1 July 1807, DLC. From Jonathan Morgan, 3 August 1804, DLC. From Matthew Wilson, 18 March 1805, DLC. From Thomas Bruff, 16 December 1801, 21 March 1808; from Susan Maria Bruff, 31 March 1816, to Susan Maria Bruff, 17 April 1816, DLC. From Oliver Evans, 8 May 1805, DLC. From George Clymer, 15 May 1805, 18 May 1805; to George Clymer, 23 May 1805, DLC. From Joseph Chambers, 17 November 1807, DLC. From Daniel French, 5 July 1804, DLC. From John Brightthought, 22 March 1803, DLC. From Richard Harris, 10 July 1808, MHi. From Jeremiah Brown, 8 March 1801, DLC. From L. DuPré, 7 February 1802, DLC. From G. C. B. Dyke, 12 May 1801, DLC. From David Hopkins, 26 September 1808; to David Hopkins, 19 October 1808, DLC.

Chapter 8

From Anon, 8 July 1804, DLC. To Edward Rowse, 4 August 1805, DLC. From Park Woodward, 28 November 1803, MoSHi. From Israel Parshall, 8 March 1804, MHi. From William Firby, 17 August 1802, DNA. From Thomas Collins, 12 February 1809, DLC. From James Houston, 4 February 1804 MHi; to James Houston, 10 February 1804, DLC. From Abraham Cohen, 21 December 1807; to Abraham Cohen 10 February 1808, DLC. From Matthew Groves, 2 August 1802, 11 October 1808; to Matthew Groves, 7 November 1802, 19 October 1808, DLC. From Richard Savin, 28 January 1806, DLC. Note from Benjamin Rush, 11 June 1803, DLC.

Chapter 9

From William Esenback, 11 January 1806, 2 December 1808, 13 January 1809, DLC. From William Meech, 24 May 1808; to Isaac Shoemaker, 5 June 1808, MHi. From John Young, 30 August 1808, DLC. From George Odenheimer, 12 July 1806, DLC. From Sam Henley, 18 August 1803, DLC. From Nehemiah Badger, 13 February 1806, MHi. From Willie Blount, 14 November 1801, DLC. From Benjamin Ring, 8 March 1801, DLC. From James Walter, 8 March 1802; to James Walter, 19 March 1802, MoSHi. From E. Browne, 4 May 1801; to E. Browne, 7 June 1801, DLC. From Stephen Burrowes, 2 March 1801; to Stephen Burrowes, 12 March 1801, DLC. From James Wilkinson, 18 January 1802, DLC. From J. Meigs, 24 January 1807, DLC. From John MacGowty, 26 March 1809, MHi.

All illustrations are from the Papers of Thomas Jefferson in The Library of Congress.

Notes

Introduction

1. The literature on the historiography of the underclasses is extensive, but an overview can be found in Lawrence Stone, *The Past and Present* (Boston: Routledge & Kegan Paul, 1981), 22–23; chaps. 1, 3. For a more recent debate on new trends in historiography see *"AHR* Forum: The Old History and the New," *The American Historical Review* 94 (June 1989): 654–98.
2. Preface to the second edition of *Lyrical Ballads,* E. de Selencourt, ed., *The Poetical Works of William Wordsworth,* 5 vols. (Oxford: Oxford University Press, 1940), 2:386.
3. John Melish, author of *Travels in the United States of America, in the Years 1806 & 1807, and 1809, 1810, & 1811,* 2 vols. (Philadelphia, 1812); in Millicent Sowerby, *Catalogue of the Library of Thomas Jefferson,* 5 vols. (Washington, D.C.: The Library of Congress, 1952–59), 4:215.
4. Noble E. Cunningham, Jr., *The Process of Government under Jefferson* (Princeton, N.J.: Princeton University Press, 1978), 27–28.
5. The tape that binds the letter to the letter books frequently covers the endorsement on the margin and makes it unreadable.
6. Jefferson to Thomas Mann Randolph, 16 November 1801, DLC.
7. Jefferson to Benjamin Clagett, 7 October 1808, DLC.
8. Jefferson to Thomas Cooper, 1 September 1807, DLC.

Chapter 1

1. Jefferson to David Gelston, 12 November 1802, DLC.
2. 6 July 1802, DLC. This letter from a Republican woman demonstrates the increasing interest and involvement of women in politics in the Jefferson era. See Mary Beth Norton, *Liberty's Daughters* (New York: Little, Brown and Company, 1980), 188–94.
3. This was stated in a letter to his son-in-law Thomas Mann Randolph, 3 November 1806. Dumas Malone, *Jefferson and His Time*, 6 vols. (Boston: Little, Brown and Company, 1948–81), 5:245.
4. He refers to the Bill of Rights, Amendment 6, Criminal Court Procedures; 7, Trial by Jury in Common Cases; 8, Bail, Cruel and Unusual Punishment.
5. Thomas P. Abernethy, *The Burr Conspiracy* (New York: Oxford University Press, 1954), 15.
6. Malone, *Jefferson and His Time*, 5:218; 286–87.
7. The text of this letter is mutilated in several places.
8. Noble E. Cunningham, Jr., *In Pursuit of Reason: The Life of Thomas Jefferson* (Baton Rouge: Louisiana State University Press, 1987), 316. This work contains a concise review of Jefferson's difficulties with, and loss of popularity from, the embargo. Jefferson to James Madison, 5 August 1808, DLC.
9. *The Merchant of Venice* 4.1.
10. *Julius Caesar* 3.2.
11. Jefferson received a complimentary address from the New Hampshire legislature, supporting the embargo, and he replied 2 August 1808, DLC. See Malone, Jr., *Jefferson and His Time*, 5:607.
12. Robert N. Johnstone, Jr., *Jefferson and the Presidency: Leadership in the Young Republic* (Ithaca: Cornell University Press, 1978), 278.
13. See 14 February 1802; 26 February 1802; 22 August 1803; and 21 October 1803, DLC, for other anonymous threats.
14. Johnstone, Jr., *Jefferson and the Presidency*, 295.

Chapter 2

1. Jefferson to Abigail Adams, 13 June 1804, Lester J. Cappon, ed., *The Adams-Jefferson Letters* (Chapel Hill: The University of North Carolina Press, published for The Institute of Early American His-

tory and Culture at Williamsburg, Virginia, 1959; reprint 1988), 270. "Mr. A's Indecent conduct": Noble E. Cunningham, Jr., *The Jeffersonian Republicans in Power* (Chapel Hill: University of North Carolina Press, published for the Institute of Early American History and Culture at Williamsburg Virginia, 1963), 14. This work is the most complete account of Jefferson's appointment policies.

2. Page Smith, *John Adams,* 2 vols. (New York: Doubleday, 1963), 2:922.

3. 8 December 1808, DLC.

4. Jefferson to Dr. Benjamin Rush, 3 January 1808, MHi.

5. This is revealed in his letter of 20 August 1803, DNA.

6. The biographical details of Austin's life are from William B. Sprague, *Annals of the American Pulpit,* 8 vols. (New York, 1859–65), 2:195–206; Alan Heimert, *Religion and the American Mind* (Cambridge, Mass.: Harvard University Press, 1966), 81, 536–37.

7. To William Short, 13 April 1820.

8. Letters from Austin dated 11 January 1802, 29 January 1802, 4 May 1802, 24 January 1804 are in the Library of Congress, Jefferson Papers. All others are in the National Archives, *Applications and Recommendations for Office 1797–1801,* (12 vols. microfilm). Jefferson to Austin, 14 July 1801, is in the National Archives; 21 January 1802 in the Library of Congress.

9. Jefferson signed the appointment papers 11 November 1793, DLC. The senior Austin died four weeks before Jefferson took office and was replaced by Jefferson with a controversial Republican, Samuel Bishop. Noah Webster to James Madison, 10 July 1801, Robert J. Brugger et al, eds., *The Papers of James Madison,* Secretary of State Series (Charlottesville: University Press of Virginia, 1986–   ), 1:437–39.

10. "Second Great Awakening": Sydney E. Ahlstrom, *A Religious History of the American People* (New Haven: Yale University Press, 1972), 415–17; Austin to Jefferson, 17 June 1801, DLC.

11. Jefferson also apparently paid for the ceremony, for he recorded in his pocket account book that he "gave Mr. Austin (charity) ord. on J. Barnes for 25. D." He had previously given Austin twenty-five dollars as a contribution toward the minister's plan to create a "Lady Washington Chapel" at the Great Hotel in Washington. The room was dedicated 14 July 1801. James A. Bear, Jr., and Lucia C. Stanton, eds., *Jefferson's Memorandum Books, Accounts, with*

Legal Records and Miscellany, 1767–1826, 2 vols. (Princeton, N.J.: Princeton University Press, forthcoming), 5 November 1801; 25 June 1801.

12. On 1 February 1802 Austin advertised "The National 'Barley Cake'" in the Washington *National Intelligencer,* and in the same newspaper on 7 April he advertised another tract, "Republicanism Spiritualised, or the Great Salvation Rising upon the National Flood." These were not the first of Austin's publications. In 1791 he had published a collection of sermons, *The American Preacher,* 4 vols. (New Haven, Conn., and Elizabeth Town, N.J., 1791–93), and three years later he republished Jonathan Edwards's *Humble Attempt* and Joseph Bellamy's *The Millennium,* both in a single volume (Elizabeth Town, N.J., 1794). He also published a number of broadsides, sermons, and newspaper articles. See, for example, *The Connecticut Gazette,* 16 November 1803; 15 February 1804.

13. At that time, Jefferson gave Austin another twenty dollars in charity, possibly to pay his way back to New England. James A. Bear and Lucia Stanton, eds., *Jefferson's Memorandum Books,* 1 May 1802.

14. *Connecticut Gazette,* 30 June 1802, "republished by desire, from the *Norwich Centinel.*"

15. Jefferson wrote in a similar vein to Dr. George Logan, on 8 March 1806, DLC. He requested Logan to tell an office seeker who received no response from Jefferson that "a moment's reflection should convince any one that I can never answer a letter concerning offices, because no answer can be written to any such letter, either affirmative or negative which, may not commit one in some way. With me therefore the answer is always to be read in what is done or not done."

16. "I cannot pass through your neighbourhood": Smith to Jefferson, 3 September 1805, MoSHi; offered post to "Col. Larkin Smith": Jefferson to Smith, 24 September 1807, MHi; Senate confirmation, 9 November 1807, DLC.

17. Jefferson conducted an extended correspondence with Mease from 1801 to 1825.

18. Hall was replaced by John Smith, who campaigned rigorously for the job. Cunningham, *The Jefferson Republicans in Power,* 30–31; list of appointments, 1801–9, 22 February 1809, DLC: "Mar. 28. 1801. John Smith. Marsh. E. distr. Pensva. vice Hall removed for misconduct, to wit packing juries & severity in office."

19. Michel-Guillaume-Jean de Crevecoeur, *Letters to an American Farmer* (London, 1782), Letter III.
20. Cunningham, *The Process of Government under Jefferson,* 121.

Chapter 3

1. Thomas Jefferson, *Notes on the State of Virginia,* William Peden, ed. (Chapel Hill, N.C.: University of North Carolina Press for the Institute of Early American History and Culture at Williamsburg, Virginia, 1955), 148.
2. Jedidiah Morse, *The American Geography,* (Elizabeth Town, N.J., 1789). Many reprints and abridgments of this work were published. Noah Webster, *A Grammatical Institute of the English Language* (Hartford, Conn., 1783). This is the first edition of the speller; a grammar and reader were published in separate volumes.
3. W. J. Rorabaugh, *The Craft Apprentice from Franklin to the Machine Age in America* (New York: Oxford University Press, 1986), 32–36.
4. The Missionary Society movement is discussed in Sydney E. Ahlstrom, *A Religious History of the American People* (New Haven, Conn.: Yale University Press, 1972), 423–24.
5. David F. Allmendinger, Jr., "New England Students and the Revolution in Higher Education, 1800–1900," in B. Edward McClellan and William J. Reese, eds., *The Social History of American Education* (Urbana: University of Illinois Press, 1988) 65–71.
6. Frank L. Mott, *Jefferson and the Press* (Baton Rouge: Louisiana State University Press, 1943), 58–59.

Chapter 4

1. Herbert Ross Brown, *The Sentimental Novel in America 1789–1860* (Durham, N.C.: Duke University Press, 1940), 51–59.
2. On women's traditional role as caretaker, see Jean Baker Miller, *Toward a New Psychology of Women* (Boston: Beacon Press, 1976), 32, 60–61.
3. Jefferson to Samuel Henley, 3 March 1785, John Catanzariti et al,

eds., *The Papers of Thomas Jefferson* (Princeton, N.J.: Princeton University Press, 1950–   ), 8:12.

4. Mary Beth Norton, *Liberty's Daughters* (New York: Little, Brown and Company, 1980), 132–33.

5. Norton, *Liberty's Daughters,* 138, 142.

6. Wilhemus Bogart Bryan, *A History of the National Capital,* 2 vols. (New York: Macmillan Company, 1914), 1:384. See also the Washington *National Intelligencer,* 10 and 12 November 1800.

7. Jefferson to William Green Mumford, 18 June 1799, Merrill D. Peterson, ed., *Thomas Jefferson Writings* (The Library of America, 1984), 1065.

8. Julian P. Boyd, "The Murder of George Wythe," *William and Mary Quarterly,* 3rd ser., vol. 12, no. 4 (October 1955), 539.

9. Jefferson to George Jefferson, 18 April 1807, MHi.

10. Advertisement in the Annapolis *Maryland Gazette,* 14 February 1805. See also Norton, *Liberty's Daughters,* 281–87.

11. See her advertisement for a *Pension Française* in New Orleans in Thomas Woody, *A History of Women's Education in the United States* (New York: The Science Press, 1929), 298.

12. Jefferson to Albert Gallatin, 7 April 1807, DLC.

Chapter 5

1. Jefferson to Doctors Rogers and Slaughter, 2 March 1806, DLC.

2. Jay Fliegelman, "Soft Compulsion: Jefferson and the Problem of Oratory"; paper read before the Modern Language Association, December 1988. John Ward, *A System of Oratory* (London, 1759); Hugh Blair, *Lectures on Rhetoric and Belles Lettres* (Basel, 1783).

3. From William Dunn to Jefferson, 25 August 1809, MHi.

4. "Analysis of expenditures from Mar. 4. 1801. to Mar. 4. 1802. . . . charities 978.20." "Analysis of expenditures from 1802 Mar. 4. to 1803. Mar. 4. . . . charities 1585.60." James A. Bear, Jr., and Lucia Stanton, eds., *Jefferson's Memorandum Books, Accounts, with Legal Records and Miscellany 1767–1826,* 2 vols. (Princeton, N.J.: Princeton University Press, forthcoming).

5. 7 February 1809, DLC.

6. "Pistol into his own foot": James Thomson Callender to Jefferson, 15 February 1800, DLC; Millicent Sowerby, *Catalogue of the Library*

of *Thomas Jefferson,* 5 vols. (Washington, D.C.: The Library of Congress, 1952–59), 3:423. "Gave order . . . in favor Saml. Quarrier 25. D. charity," Bear and Stanton, *Jefferson's Memorandum Books,* 2 February 1802.

7. "A list of Debtors in Washington Jail," DLC, # 20988.

8. 3 April 1802, DLC; 8 April 1802, DLC.

9. William E. Nelson, *Americanization of the Common Law* (Cambridge, Mass.: Harvard University Press, 1975), 147–48.

10. 29 March 1802, "Dementions of Jail in Washington City," DLC, # 20988.

11. Daniel C. Brent to Jefferson, 30 March 1802, DLC.

12. 29 March 1802, "A List of Debtors in Washington Jail," DLC.

13. 27 March 1808, MHi.

14. *Washington, City and Capital,* Federal Writers' Project, American Guide Series (Washington, D.C.: Government Printing Office, 1937), 745–46; Edwin M. Betts, ed., *Thomas Jefferson's Garden Book* (Philadelphia: The American Philosophical Society, 1944), 344–45, 353, 409.

15. List of appointments sent to the Senate, 9 November 1807, DLC.

16. From George Blake to Jefferson, 19 June 1805, DLC.

17. William Cranch is the same judge who wrote Jefferson on behalf of Charles Houseman, who escaped from the Washington jail. In 1806, Jefferson appointed him chief judge of the Circuit Court of the District of Columbia, even though he was a Federalist. (List of appointments, 22 February 1809, DLC.)

18. 10 April 1802, DLC; 21 June 1802, DLC; undated petition, 1803, DLC.

19. Jefferson to Christopher Ellery, 4 May 1803, DLC.

20. 24 February 1804, DLC.

Chapter 6

1. "I read Greek, Latin, French, Italian, Spanish, and English of course, with something of it's radix the Anglo-Saxon." Jefferson to Joseph Delaplaine, 12 April 1817, DLC.

2. 8 May 1801, DLC. This press copy is only partly legible.

3. Sent Jefferson a prospectus: 24 June, 1809, DLC. Butler's publishing history is in Clarence S. Brigham, *History and Bibliography of*

American Newspapers 1670–1820, 2 vols. (Worcester, Mass.: American Antiquarian Society), 1:223, 251.

4. Jefferson endorsed Becker's letter "Wash. Apr. 18. 07. recd. Apr. 23." and it is so catalogued by the Massachusetts Historical Society. The book Becker is asking Jefferson to subscribe to, however, was published at Easton, Pennsylvania, dated 1806. It is possible that the publication date is inaccurate, or that the book was already in print and Becker contemplated subscriptions for another edition. An expanded edition was published in 1813.

5. Jefferson to Green, 15 December 1805; to Joseph C. Cabell, 24 January 1816, in Millicent Sowerby, *Catalogue of the Library of Thomas Jefferson,* 5 vols. (Washington, D.C.: The Library of Congress, 1952–59), 1:511.

6. See Kathleen L. Leonard, "Notes on the Text and Provenance of the Byrd Manuscripts," Appendix to Louis B. Wright, ed., *The Prose Works of William Byrd of Westover* (Cambridge, Mass.: Harvard University Press, 1966), 417–23.

7. Mason Locke Weems, *The Life of George Washington* (Philadelphia, 1808).

8. John Daly Burk, *The History of Virginia, from its First Settlement to the Present Day,* 3 vols. (Petersburg, Va., 1805); vol. 4 completed by Shelton Jones and Louis H. Giradin, (Petersburg, Va., 1816).

9. Henry Home, Lord Kames, *Elements of Criticism,* 2 vols. (Edinburgh, 1762); Hugh Blair, *Letters on Rhetoric and Belles Lettres,* 3 vols. (Basel, 1783).

10. Burk's arrest is announced in *The Time Piece,* 9 July 1798.

11. *The Time Piece.* 20 July 1798.

12. To Jefferson from John F. Vacher, 30 April 1803, DLC.

13. To Jefferson from Samuel Harrison, 12 February 1806, DLC.

14. To Jefferson from Jonathan Edmester, 19 February 1808, DLC.

Chapter 7

1. Bryant is quoted in John C. Greene, *American Science in the Age of Jefferson* (Ames: The Iowa State University Press, 1984), 34; and Dumas Malone, *Jefferson and His Time,* 6 vols. (New York: Little, Brown & Company, 1948–81), 5:606.

2. Jefferson to Elbridge Gerry, 26 January 1799; Merrill Peterson, ed., *Thomas Jefferson Writings* (The Library of America, 1984), 1056.

3. Jefferson to Jay Marsh, 4 March 1806, DLC.

4. *The Connecticut Journal,* 13 February 1800.

5. Jefferson to Robert Patterson, 27 December 1812, DLC.

6. Jefferson to Robert R. Livingston, 4 February 1791, DLC; John Catanzariti et al, eds., *The Papers of Thomas Jefferson* (Princeton, N.J.: Princeton University Press, 1950–   ), 19:240.

7. Washington *National Intelligencer,* 28 December 1801.

8. Washington *National Intelligencer,* 4 November 1807.

9. Susan Maria Bruff to Jefferson, 31 March 1816; Jefferson to Susan Maria Bruff, 17 April 1816, DLC.

10. H. W. Dickinson, *A Short History of the Steam Engine* (New York: Macmillan, 1939), 94–95.

11. Clymer to Jefferson, 18 May 1805, DLC; Jefferson to Clymer, 23 May 1805, DLC.

12. John H. Morrison, *History of American Steam Navigation* (New York, 1903; reprint, New York: Stephen Daye Press, 1958), 202–3.

13. James T. Flexner, *Steamboats Come True, American Inventors in Action* (New York: Viking, 1944), 26.

14. U.S. Patent Office, *Digest of Patents Issued by the United States from 1790 to January 1, 1839* (Washington, D.C., 1840).

Chapter 8

1. Paul Starr, *The Social Transformation of American Medicine* (New York: Basic Books, 1982), 32–35, 42; Richard Harrison Shryock, *Medicine and Society in America 1660–1860* (Ithaca, N.Y.: Cornell University Press, 1962), 44–76.

2. Jefferson to Dr. Caspar Wistar, 21 June 1807, Merrill D. Peterson, ed., *Thomas Jefferson Writings* (New York: The Library of America), 1182–84.

3. M. Foster Farley, *An Account of the History of Stranger's Fever in Charleston, 1699–1876* (Washington, D.C.: University Press of America, 1978), 41, 170–75.

4. Edward Rowse to Jefferson, 13 July 1805, DLC.

5. When he received no reply, Parshall wrote a follow-up letter on 23 March 1803, DLC, giving the same information.

6. Carl Binger, *Revolutionary Doctor, Benjamin Rush, 1746–1813* (New York: W. W. Norton, 1966), 255.

7. Landes, *Revolution in Time,* 156–57, 428n.

8. Robert Patterson to Jefferson, 1 November 1802, DLC; Jefferson to Capt. Matthew C. Groves, 7 November 1802, 19 October 1808; from Groves 11 October 1808, DLC; the *Connecticut Gazette,* 28 September 1803; Silvio A. Bedini, *Thomas Jefferson Statesman of Science* (New York: Macmillan, 1990), 324–25.

9. Donald Jackson, ed., *Letters of the Lewis and Clark Expedition with Related Documents, 1783–1854* (Urbana: University of Illinois Press, 1962) 329, 342, 515. Jackson believed that Rush may have personally given Lewis a copy of his "Rules for Health," and that Jefferson's copy was made for his own use. (55n.)

Chapter 9

1. Mary Ann Jimenez, *Changing Faces of Madness: Early American Attitudes and Treatment of the Insane* (Hanover, N.H.: University Press of New England for Brandeis University Press, 1987), 68–69.

2. Jimenez, *Changing Faces of Madness,* 73.

3. Edwin M. Betts, ed. *Thomas Jefferson's Farm Book* (Princeton N.J.: Princeton University Press for the American Philosophical Society, 1953), 112, 116.

4. This letter is misfiled in the Library of Congress Jefferson Papers under 5 September 1805. Jefferson's endorsement, "Young John. Balt. Aug. 30. 08. recd. Sep. 5" gives the correct year.

5. To Levi Lincoln, 1 January 1802, quoted in Robert M. Johnstone, Jr., *Jefferson and the Presidency, Leadership in the Young Republic* (Ithaca, N.Y.: Cornell University Press, 1978), 239.

6. Johnstone, Jr., *Jefferson and the Presidency,* 245.

7. To Samuel Hawkins, 30 November 1808, DLC.

8. On 3 December 1804, Plumer attended a dinner at the President's House where "there were also exposed on the table two bottles of water brought from the river Mississippi. . . ." Everett S. Brown, ed., *William Plumer's Memorandum of Proceedings in the United States Senate 1803–07* (New York: The Macmillan Company, 1923), 212.

9. To James Monroe, 18 February 1808. Paul Leicester Ford, ed., *The Works of Thomas Jefferson,* 12 vols., Federal edition (New York: G. P. Putnam's Sons, 1905), 11:11.

10. Quoted in Dumas Malone, *Jefferson and His Time,* 6 vols. (Boston: Little, Brown and Company, 1948–81), 5:666.

11. From William Smith, 10 August 1809, MoSHi. This letter may have been motivated by extortion.

12. Jefferson to John Adams, 11 January 1817, 27 June 1822, Lester J. Cappon, ed., *The Adams-Jefferson Letters* (Chapel Hill, N.C.: The University of North Carolina Press for the Institute of Early American History and Culture at Williamsburg, Va., 1959; reprint 1988), 505, 581. The 1267 letters for one year was an exaggeration; this was actually the number received in three years. (John Catanzariti, "Thomas Jefferson, Correspondent," *Proceedings of the Massachusetts Historical Society,* forthcoming.)

Index

Abernethy, Thomas P., 6*n*
Ackerman, Abraham, 188–89
acrostics, 212–13
Adams, Abigail, 39
Adams, John, 4, 39, 41, 94, 204, 207, 209*n*, 313, 314
address, forms of, 112–13, 118
adulation for Jefferson, 301–3
  gifts, 307–11
  Jefferson's responses to, 304–5, 306–7, 309
  naming of towns after Jefferson, 303–5
  from poets, 213–14
  press critics, attacks on, 305–6
  third term issue, 311–13
  from women, 135–37
  from young men, 97–99
Alexandria, Va., 173–75
  letters from, 32, 109
Allison, Robert, 297
Amelia County, Va., letter from, 204
American Philosophical Society, 217, 218

Andover, Mass., 281
Annapolis, Md., letters from, 64, 131, 191
anonymous letters, 4, 14–19, 27, 35–36
apprenticeship system, 77–80, 117, 119
Arkansas, letter from, 57
assassination threats and warnings, 26, 156
  embargo of 1807 and, 26–27, 35, 36
Athens, Ga., letter from, 311
Aurora and Franklin Gazette, 92
Austin, David, 40–41
  background, 41–42
  ecumenical project, 46, 48
  family of, 49
  final years, 50*n*
  governmental office, campaign for, 42–50
  Jefferson's replies to, 46–48
  oratorical skills, 46
  pamphleteering, 48
  poetic nature, 42